THE
GOLD
OF
CARRE-SHINOB

THE GOLD
OF
CARRE-SHINOB

The Final Chapter
in the Mystery of the Lost Rhoades Mines
Seven Lost Cities and Montezuma's Treasure
—Including Maps—

Kerry Ross Boren & Lisa Lee Boren

ISBN: 1-55517-411-6

v.3

A	B	C	D	E	F	G	H	I	J	K	L
1	2	3	4	5	6	7	8	9	10	11	12	13	14	15	16
17	18	19	20	21	22	23	24	25	26	27	28	29	30	31
A	B	C	D	E	F	G	H	I	J	K	L	M	N	O	P	Q	R	S	T

Published by: **Bonneville Books**

Distributed by:

925 North Main, Springville, UT 84663 • 801/489-4084

CFI
Cedar Fort, Incorporated

| Publishing and Distribution Since 1986 |

CFI Distribution • CFI Books • Council Press • Bonneville Books

Edited by Lee Nelson
Cover Design by Corinne A. Bischoff & Sheila Mortimer
Printed in the United States of America

To the Ute People who have respected and protected with their lives the sacred artifacts of their Ancestors.

Table of Contents

Foreword

SINCE THE PUBLICATION OF *FOOTPRINTS in the Wilderness: A History of the Lost Rhoades Mines* in 1971, I have been deluged with requests to publish an up-dated version of the popular book. The original edition sold out in a short period of time, and in 1980 a paperback edition did the same, and today the book is extremely rare. Most libraries have had their circulation copies stolen, and the few editions which can be found for sale by dealers command as much as $200 per copy.

Footprints in the Wilderness was a landmark book. It was the first history written about the now famous lost gold mines. While several other accounts have appeared during the nearly thirty years since the debut of *Footprints,* none have been as popular nor have they elaborated much on the original.

Footprints was co-authored with my cousin, Gale R. "Dusty" Rhoades. Gale's grandfather, Walter Boren, was my uncle, a brother of my father, Edward Boren. As boys, Gale and I used to romp the hills together, stripped to the waist and armed with home-made bows and arrows, emulating Indians. Both of us lived in the shadow of the Uintah Mountains—Gale on the south slope and myself on the north slope—and we grew up steeped in the history and the legends of the region.

During the early sixties I went away for a few years to study the motion picture business in Hollywood. When I returned, I began writing a history of the Uintah Mountain region which included a section on the Lost Rhoades Mines. I encountered Gale again in 1965 and when we realized that we had been researching the story of the mines independently, we decided to collaborate on a book, resulting ultimately in *Footprints in the Wilderness.* It took us six years to complete the work. Much of that time was spent in the high Uintahs, following old trails, pursuing clues, locating and photographing Spanish markings,

interviewing Indians and whites, and dusting off moldy archives.

It was an interesting period in our lives. We trekked across the 13,000-foot-glacier-packed crest between Spirit Lake on the north slope to Whiterocks Lake on the south slope, carrying dynamite and blasting caps in our backpacks during a ferocious electrical storm, and pursued on the trail by a stalking mountain lion. There were fun times, filled with comraderie and adventure, and there were also occasions of dread and intrigue. We were followed incessantly by a certain group of mercenary gold-seekers and opportunists, threatened frequently and even shot at once while prospecting the upper Rock Creek drainage.

During this time secrecy became our by-word. It became necessary to correspond in code and to alter maps in our possession to prevent their use in case of theft. Indeed, several maps were stolen from us, or surreptitiously copied, but due to our precautions they did little good to the plagiarists. I have since seen several of these maps published and identified as "authentic."

Following the publication of *Footprints* in 1971, Gale and I went separate directions, though we kept in close touch. If we wanted to meet we had to do so secretly, for it seemed that whenever we got together our pursuers believed we were going to the mines and watched our every move. Our reasons for going separate ways stemmed from a difference of opinion: I was primarily interested in the history while Gale became increasingly more involved in mining and prospecting ventures with some rather unsavory characters. I refused to associate with these men and so I agreed with Gale, amicably, that we should continue our research efforts independent of one another.

There was yet another reason for the separate courses which Gale and I endeavored to take, and it centered around a difference in our basic philosophies. Gale firmly believed that the mines belonged to the Rhoades family, of which he was a direct descendant, because it had been to Thomas Rhoades that the mines were first revealed. He adamantly opposed the popular belief that the mines belonged to the Mormon Church (Gale was Seventh Day Adventist). Neither did he believe that the mines belonged to the Indians, a belief he was willing to set aside whenever he negotiated with them about mining rights on reservation land.

I, too, did not believe that the Mormon Church had any valid claim on the mines, but at that point our philosophies had divergent angles. In spite of the fact that Chief Walker had given the secret of the mines to Isaac Morley even prior to the advent of Thomas Rhoades, I firmly believed then, as I do now, that the mines belonged exclusively to the Ute Indians and that no white man had any claim to them whatsoever. Because I maintained this stand, and because I expressed no interest in the gold itself, *I was persona non grata* in mining circles. I was not exactly welcomed into Gale's confidence at that particular time.

For more than a decade we pursued our separate courses. Gale, totally obsessed with finding the mines, spent all of his time, effort, and fortune in search of them. I, conversely, became involved in the Governor's Commission on Historic Sites and Preservation, the establishment of the National Association for Outlaw/Lawman History at Utah State University, and the production of several film documentaries with actor Robert Redford. In the interim I spent considerable time in Central America, exploring the Mayan ruins and getting married in Honduras.

That is not to say I had no involvement with the mines. Indeed, it was probably my most productive period. I became privy to information that I could never have imagined or supposed, information which was to change the course of my life and involve me in a web of intrigue. I would be privileged to view what others only dare dream of, and ultimately it would cost me everything. But I saw Carre-Shinob!

In 1978 or 1979 I was approached by a man who professed to be a friend, but whom I would soon come to realize was the most unscrupulous con-man I ever had the great misfortune of knowing. This alleged friend proposed a business transaction, wherein I would incorporate all of my material—including that pertaining to the Rhoades mines– into the holdings of a production company. This included my royalties on the book, *Footprints in the Wilderness*.

During my absence in Central America, this scoundrel utilized my power-of-attorney to rob me of all of my company stock and personal possessions, and began to levy legal blackmail against me to pressure me into turning over certain maps and documents pertaining to the mines—specifically the Happy Jack journals and maps. Refusing to be intimidated into violating my oath to the Ute people, I walked away from the company, losing a lifetime of work and research in the process.

Subsequently, I learned that my cousin Gale had been lured into this scoundrel's web of intrigue, and cooperated with him long enough to produce a second expanded edition of *Footprints*. In this edition was incorporated much of the material he had confiscated from me, notably the journal information and maps of Aaron Daniels, interviews with Mary Reed Harris, and much more. Inasmuch as I had lost my royalty rights to the book with the company, there was little, legally, I could do about the plagiarism.

In 1985 Gale Rhoades came to see me on what he described over the telephone as "urgent business." It had been nearly a decade since I last saw him and I hardly recognized him. The robust, hardy outdoorsman I once knew was pale and drawn, with greying hair and several days' growth of beard. He explained that he was in a state of declining health. That much was obvious.

Gale brought me up to date on what had happened to him during the interim of our separation. His association with the scoundrel, he said, had ended predictably with the man robbing him of much of his documented material on the mines. Afterwards, he had formed a partnership with a few others on prospects on Rock Creek, together with some other leads in Arizona, but these associations, too, had fallen through. He was facing possible charges of stock manipulation in the company, had suffered the loss of his wife and daughter, as well as his home and even his Jeep. He was then living with friends in Salt Lake City where he was indulging their generosity while trying to rebuild a used car for transportation.

Gale wanted me to collaborate with him on a third edition of *Footprints*, incorporating our combined up-dated information, but I knew to do so would mean renewed involvement with our unscrupulous ex-associate, and so I declined. He seemed genuinely disappointed by my decision, saying that in that case he had no recourse but to write an account of his own based solely upon his own information. He had been in hopes that I would contribute some journals and original maps I had come into possession of, because during his years of hunting for the mines, he had neglected the history; all he had were accounts of his own searches. I regretfully assured him I would not be able to comply. He had no idea that I had been to Carre-Shinob more than a decade earlier, nor did I dare impart this information to him, being still uncertain of his connections with my former shyster business partner.

Gale then disclosed some personal information, just between cousins—cousins who had also been good friends during a lifetime. He revealed that he was writing two accounts of the Lost Rhoades Mines: the first account would be an up-dated version of *Footprints*, from the proceeds of which he hoped to recoup his financial losses; the second account, he stated, would be the "complete and true story of the mines, with the original maps and everything I know about the mines." He already had a draft of both accounts nearly completed, and, after publishing the first book, he intended to retire to Arizona and complete the second version. His last words to me were these:

"I have wasted my life searching for the mines, and in the process I lost everything I owned. I'm firmly convinced there is a curse on the mines, and whoever hunts for them will fall under it. I'm never going back into those mountains again. I intend to write the true story before I die, because the only two people still alive who know the truth is you and me. I hope someday you will write your story, because when we are gone, the secret of the Rhoades Mines will never be known."

I never saw Gale Rhoades again. Several years later I received a sad letter from my aunt, Lucy Boren, of Price, Utah—Gale's grandmother, who raised him—saying that Gale had gone back into the mountains to search for the mines, and had suffered two massive consecutive heart attacks. My beloved cousin and good friend was dead at the age of 48. I couldn't help but think that perhaps he had been right about the curse. Nevertheless, I knew my cousin better than anyone else could, and I realized that this is the way he would have wanted it. Now he was part of the legend.

The story doesn't quite end there, however. Gale Rhoades died in the vicinity of Hoyt Peak in the Uintah Mountains on 27 September 1988. Because of the isolation involved, his body was not immediately retrieved. He had left his vehicle parked at the foot of the mountain. My late friend and author George Thompson informed me that my unscrupulous former business partner was seen burglarizing Gale's vehicle. He removed Gale's attaché case containing his personal papers, and they have not been seen since.

There can be no doubt whatsoever as to the existence of the so-called Rhoades Mines. They are verified by numerous existing records and artifacts, not the least of which are several maps and considerable ore samples in possession of the Church of Jesus Christ of Latter-day Saints (Mormon). Don't bother to ask them about it—their policy is to deny any knowledge of the mines. However, for some years I worked in the Church History Department, with a great deal of latitude to examine documents, journals and artifacts, before Church policy changed and forbade access. I have seen enough to be assured of the Church's knowledge of the existence of the mines.

For example, there exists in the Church's vault several document boxes, marked "TOA#5" and "TOA#6," containing several sheets of copper leaf and several sheets of gold leaf. Each of these sheets are approximately 4" x 6" and are worked with a floral design and cross-pattern in bas relief. Enclosed with one of the gold leaf sheets (which is rolled and tied by a ribbon) is a piece of paper, on Church letterhead, which describes the contents as follows:

Copper and gold leaf strips used in the original design of the angel Moroni. Copper obtained from Dyer smelter. Gold from Caleb B. Rhoades storage tithe. Moroni plate from same source over copper and brass framework. Samples for storage. Likenesses were placed in time capsule, foundation stone of Eagle Gate. I attest to the Authenticity of my craftsmanship.

—(signed) TRUMAN O. ANGELL

Truman O. Angell was a craftsman and architect who supervised much of the construction of the Salt Lake Temple, including the statue of the Angel Moroni (a Book of Mormon character) which crowns its tallest spire. The statue, which rises 12 1/2 feet from head to foot, is gold plated, and, as Gale and I related in our book, that gold came from the Sacred Mines. Truman O. Angell's document certainly verifies the source of the gold.

Other documents also verify the existence of maps in the Church archives, but when I spoke to Presiding Bishop Joseph Anderson in 1970, he stated emphatically: "The Church will neither confirm nor deny the existence of the so-called Lost Brigham Young Mine [which the Rhoades Mines are sometimes called], and will not either confirm or deny that it has any evidence or artifacts in its possession pertaining to the mine." And so it remains to the present day.

This account, which is a supplemental history of the Lost Rhoades Mines, contains all new information from the unpublished journals of Isaac Morley, Aaron Daniels, and Happy Jack, as well as from interviews with such pertinent characters as Jimmie Reed and others intimate with the topic.

I obtained the journals of Aaron Daniels from his great-granddaughter, who obtained them from her dying father, together with five maps drawn by Daniels on buckskin, three on parchment, and one burned into a pine slab.

I came across the Jimmie Reed interviews, maps and information through my relationship to that family. Bill Reed, three-quarters Indian by blood, was my uncle, married to my father's sister, whose niece married a grandson of John Joseph Rhoades, a brother of Caleb Rhoades. These relationships may be complicated, but they are tremendously important. They have opened doors totally inaccessible to others.

Herein for the first time is told the story of my third great-grandfather, Isaac Morley, and his association with the mines, which occurred even prior to the Thomas Rhoades participation. Morley's close friendship with Chief Walker of the Utes became the basis of the revelation of the existence of the mines and the primary reason for Walker's gift of the gold to Brigham Young.

The journals and maps of Happy Jack, Caleb Rhoades' longtime Indian companion, reveal numerous new clues to many of the gold sources on the reservation, though much of the journal information has been withheld to protect an oath I made to the Ute Indians many years ago.

Therefore, while this narrative breaks new ground in the history of the mines, the reader should not expect to be given directions to Carre-Shinob; the primary purpose of this book is to verify the existence of the world's largest gold source, to reveal the secret of Carre-Shinob, and to supplement the history of the famous lost mines.

Nevertheless, the wise treasure hunter should be aware that the best clues to lost mines and treasure are not to be found in other people's claims, but in the history. There are sound clues in this book, if one knows where to look. But it is not our intent to guide the reader to Carre-Shinob. The authors have no intention of contributing to the discovery and exploitation of this sacred treasure of the Indians, and would discourage rather than encourage a search for it.

Keep in mind that thousands have lost everything in their quest for the fabulous wealth of the Rhoades mines, and hundreds more have lost their very lives. It should be kept in mind that even if one is fortunate enough to find the treasure of Carre-Shinob, there would be little opportunity to capitalize on the discovery. Under the Antiquities Act, all of the ancient artifacts must by law be turned over to the federal government. Indeed, the unauthorized removal of even one item could result in a lengthy jail term and a sizeable fine. Even if one retains a portion of the artifacts, taxes and restrictions eat up profits quickly, as can be attested to by Mel Fisher, discoverer of the sunken treasure aboard the Spanish galleon *Atocha*.

Fisher spent more time in court, fighting for his rights to the discovery, than he spent in the search for the wealthy cargo.

Well, perhaps you will have better luck finding one of the Sacred Mines. Certainly you would be wealthy beyond your wildest dreams — if you lived long enough to enjoy it. If the site is on the reservation, you are out of luck. The Utes will not relinquish it. If it is on Forest Service land, your fight for ownership has only just begun. Much of this region is wilderness area, protected by law against mining.

Most of all, the gold does not belong to you — it belongs to the Ute people. The Uintah Mountains are their home and the treasure is their legacy. Let us suppose you own a home and in your house you have a secret safe, and inside the safe you have gold jewelry handed down through your family for many generations. If some stranger obtains a map to your home, showing where your safe is located, does he have the right to enter your house and take your legacy from you?

The Utes are not simply protecting a treasure: they are protecting their sacred heritage and preserving their history and identity as a people. And they are a great people, with a great history. Carre-Shinob is their last stronghold against white encroachment.

This book, then, is written not to encourage the relentless search for the Lost Rhoades Mines, but to demonstrate the moral need to respect the sacred secret of Carre-Shinob.

Perhaps such a plea is an exercise in futility: treasure hunters are a relentless breed who will invariably search in spite of all pleas to the contrary. But it doesn't really matter. I am convinced, as was Caleb Rhoades, that no amount of searching is going to uncover the treasure of the Old Ones. Search if you must, and best of luck to you. I have seen what you will never find. And it is fabulous!

—KERRY ROSS BOREN
20 February 1998

Chapter One

The Sierra Madre de Oro

IN 1519 MONTEZUMA REIGNED AS emperor of the magnificent Aztec Empire of central and southern Mexico; but in that very year he was destined to fall, and the greatness of the Aztecs would pass to Spain. Teuhtlitl, chief of a neighboring territory, sent a runner to the great capital city of Tenochtitlan to inform Montezuma of the arrival in his territory of a strange convoy coming from the east. The caravan consisted of some 400 soldiers dressed in metal armor, 15 men riding strange beasts which the Aztecs had never before seen, and seven cannons drawn by these same beasts (horses). These strange men had conquered villages en route, and had impressed into service 1,300 Indian warriors and another 1,000 porters.

The procession was led by a bearded man of exceedingly white skin and wearing shining armor, whom the Aztecs believed must be Quetzalcoatl, a white-skinned and bearded god who had arrived long ago from "across the eastern sea." Quetzalcoatl had taught the Aztecs great things, then departed, promising that at some future time he would return. This strange bearded invader riding an even stranger beast appeared to fit the description of this god, and so they offered little or no resistance.

This man was not Quetzalcoatl—a mistake that Montezuma was to learn all too late—but the Spanish *conquistador* Hernán Cortes. Hernán Fernando Cortes had been born in the year 1485 in Medellin, a small village of Extremadura, Spain, son of Martin Cortes de Monroy and Doña Catalina Pizarro Altamirano. In 1504, at the age of nineteen, Cortes landed at Santo Domingo; by age twenty-six he became Governor Velazquez' secretary and the King's treasurer in the island. In 1519 this ruthless conquistador had been sent by the governor of Hispaniola to explore the coast of Mexico and Central America. Disembarking from their ships at Vera Cruz, Cortes and his men marched inland to conquer and seize the land in the name of Spain. Fray Bernal Diaz del Castillo, chronicler of the expedition, recorded that "We came here to serve God and the King, and also to get rich."

Within a week after entering the territory of Chief Teuhtlitl, the Spaniards were met by a procession of Indians headed by several Aztec noblemen and more than 100 porters bearing gifts from Montezuma. The gifts were fabulous beyond description: boxes of enormous pearls and precious gems of every description, jewel-encrusted gold vases, silver vessels and plaques imbedded with gems, richly adorned capes made from the sacred and colorful plumes of the sacred Quetzal bird, and two huge disks the size of cartwheels, one of gold and the other of pure silver, engraved with glyphs and sacred writing. Montezuma had hoped the gifts would appease the "god," whose powers he feared, and induce him to go away; instead the treasure only whetted his appetite for more, and he marched on towards the capital.

Tenochtitlan was a great city encompassing some five square miles and comprising more than 140,000 inhabitants. Cortes marched boldly into the city, his eye ever on its wealth and riches, and Montezuma greeted him royally and furnished his guests with great luxury in his palace.

In time, Cortes secretly placed Montezuma under "house arrest," and under threat of death commanded that the great emperor issue his orders. The first order was that all gold, silver and other treasure be collected and turned over to the Spaniards. Much of the city's treasure was brought to Cortes as ordered, but the bulk of it was secretly gathered by the Aztecs and concealed within the rooms of several great palaces.

Cortes was not to be denied, however; he had set spies everywhere, and they soon reported the existence of the hidden treasure. One of these spies, Bernal Diaz del Castillo, described

Montezuma's treasury in the "Sunken Gardens" (vaults) beneath the palace as being a massive room piled to the ceiling with gold and silver, much of it in ingots and much of it worked into fine jewelry, statues, masks, and other items, while boxes of precious gems lined the walls. Cortes, upon seeing it for himself, wrote: "It seems incredible that any worldly ruler should possess such riches."

In the midst of seeking out the hidden treasure, a courier arrived to warn Cortes that the governor of Cuba had dispatched a large force to Mexico, commanded by Panfilo de Narvaez, to oust Cortes and seize the treasure from him. Cortes was compelled to assemble his troops and march to meet the Cuban force, leaving one of his lieutenants, Pedro de Alvarado, in charge of Tenochtitlan.

While Cortes was away from the city, a group of Aztec noblemen petitioned Alvarado for permission to hold a festival, the annual May celebration called the "Incensing of Huitzilopotchli," their patron god of war. The festival normally consisted of chanting and dancing, brandishing weapons, culminating in human sacrifices. Alvarado granted permission on the condition that they would not brandish weapons, dispense with human sacrifices, and the Spaniards should be in attendance.

The Aztec leaders reluctantly agreed to the restrictions and more than 600 performers assembled in the streets, magnificently attired in costumes of Quetzal feathers. But Alvarado noted something else: the dancers were wearing jewelry, with collars of gold imbedded with emeralds around their necks, and bracelets of gold and silver on their wrists and ankles. Enraged that the Aztecs had not brought all of their treasure to the Spaniards as ordered, Alvarado directed his soldiers to attack the performers. The massacre of the unarmed Aztecs was complete and brutal, and as hundreds of Indians lay grotesquely murdered in the streets, Bernardino de Sahagun, in his *Historia de Nuevo España*, wrote: "The pavement ran with streams of blood, like water in a heavy shower."

News of the bloody massacre soon spread throughout the territory. Incensed by the merciless slaughter, the Aztecs mobilized forces to retaliate against the invaders, whom they now knew could not be gods as they had supposed.

While the Spaniards were busily engaged in battle, Montezuma summoned his noblemen and issued instructions for the secret removal of the treasure. More than 1500 royal bearers were assembled and loaded down with as much treasure as they could carry and led quietly out of the city and towards the north. For weeks they trekked along the route which the northern tribes called the "Trail of the Old Ones." At last they arrived at their destination, seven sacred caves, and there deposited the treasure out of reach of the avaricious Spaniards.

In the meantime, Cortes had overcome the Cuban force during a severe thunderstorm in the dead of night, and wounded and captured Narvaez, whose remaining forces surrendered. Within days of this victory, a courier arrived with news of the Aztec siege at Tenochtitlan, and Cortes made a forced march to go to the aid of Alvarado.

Cortes found Alvarado and his men fortified behind stone walls, barely able to maintain against the vastly superior force of Aztecs. Cortes induced Montezuma to intercede with his people, saying "We will willingly depart if the way is opened." Montezuma reluctantly agreed and appeared before his people, calling upon them to lay down their weapons and allow the Spaniards to pass unmolested. But the Aztecs remembered the massacre of the dancers who had put aside their arms, and became enraged that Montezuma should require it of them again. They turned their anger at him and stoned him, striking him several times in the head, and when he fell they became frightened and ran. Montezuma, badly injured, was carried to his quarters where he was treated for his injuries, but on 30 June 1520 he succumbed to his wounds and died.

In the confusion of Montezuma's death, the Spaniards were able to collect as much treasure as they could carry and slip out of Tenochtitlan, taking less than half of what they had accumulated. Montezuma's successor was a great war chief, Cuitlahuac, who led a pursuit against the retreating invaders. The Spaniards were unduly burdened by the gold they carried, even though Bernal Diaz del Castillo lamented that "Much gold remained, piled up in heaps." The greedy soldiers refused to abandon their gold, and as they fell behind the retreating column they were captured and killed, and their plunder returned to Tenochtitlan. More than a third of Cortes' army perished during this flight from the Aztecs.

Cortes rallied a new army and returned in 1521, fighting his way back to Tenochtitlan and conquering the Aztec nation completely. For his services, fifteen years after the conquest of Montezuma's empire, Cortes was by royal patent created Marquis of the Valley of Oaxaca and Captain General of New Spain and the Coasts of the South Sea. He was now absolute ruler of the land from the Caribbean to the Pacific, but his vast coveted treasure was gone, and remained his one most nagging defeat.

Cortes only managed to learn that Montezuma's treasure had been removed from the "Sunken Gardens" beneath the great palace and carried north from Tenochtitlan and concealed within several large caves. This became the foundation of the legend of the famous "Seven Cities of Cibola," and would constitute the basis of a frenetic search by the Spaniards for the next three centuries.

The Aztecs, Toltecs, Incas and Mayan Indians, as well as numerous sub-tribes living in the Central American land-neck, have traditions of sacred caves in the land of the north, from which caves their cultures originated. The Mayans, for example, describe their ancestors as seven tribes which emerged from seven sacred caves. Aztec traditions are similar, describing a sacred cave with seven mouths through which seven tribes, one of which being the Aztecs, emerged from the underworld. The Aztecs referred to their place of origin as *Chicomoztoc*, which means literally "Seven Caves."

The Aztecs also have recorded traditions of their origins in which they claim to have once lived far north of Mexico, near an inland sea with many marshes, and on an island in that sea; the very name *Aztec* is derived from *Aztlan*, a word meaning both "Island of Herons" and "White Land." This description aptly fits the region of the Great Salt Lake, not only to its islands' population of herons and other birds, but the "White Land" would seem to indicate the surrounding Salt Flats. The Aztec dialect was Nahuatl, a language belonging to the Uto-Aztecan linguistic stock which exists in the Western United States, and from which was derived the Shoshonean languages, which includes the Ute dialect.

The recorded history of the Aztecs indicates that they left their northern home in about 1168 A.D., and migrated into what is now northern Mexico during the 13th century. They vanquished other tribes in the path of their migration, and moved into the Valley of Mexico near the beginning of the 14th century where they founded the cities of Tenochtitlan and Tlateloco on islands of Lake Texcoco in 1825. Paleontologists have debated why the Aztecs would choose to build an island city with immense effort when more choice locations were readily available to them. The answer seems to be that they were creating an island community much like the one they had once possessed in the north.

The legends also confirm the fact that to the east of their ancient northern island home, the Aztecs revered a range of mountains as being sacred to their race. While this might accurately describe either the Wasatch or the Uintah Mountains in present-day Utah, only the high Uintahs continued to be sacred to the lingering tribes such as the Utes. To return Montezuma's treasure to the protection of the sacred caves from which it derived was, to the Aztecs, the only plausible resolution, as long as the Spaniards ruled in Mexico.

Recent discoveries have shed new light on the origin of the Aztec gold. In the year 1170 A.D.—roughly coincidental with the Aztec's arrival in Mexico—Madoc ap Owain Gwynedd, a prince of Wales, landed at Mobile Bay, Alabama, on the Gulf of Mexico, where he established a colony. He returned to Wales to outfit a second expedition, but on the second voyage to the New World in 1171 his ships were blown off course in the Gulf of Mexico and he landed instead on the Yucatan Peninsula. Welsh legends are replete with mentions that Madoc became King of the Aztecs and the ancestor of a long line of kings down to and including Montezuma. Powel's *Historie of Cambria*, published not long after the conquest of Mexico, stated:

> A common report of the inhabitants of that countrie (Mexico), which affirme that theyr rulers descended from a strange nation that

came thither from a farre countrie: which thing is confessed by Montezuma, king of that countrie, in an oration made for quieting his people, as his submission to the king of Castille, Hernando Curteis (Cortes) being present, which is laid downe in the Spanish chronicles of the conquest of the West Indies. *[The Historie of Cambria, Now Called Wales,* David Powel, D.D., 1584]

In 1805 the renowned poet Robert Southy (1774-1803) had published posthumously his famous poem *Madoc*. In commenting on this epic poem, author Richard Deacon has said:

> …much (of Southey's material) would seem to have come from Aztec legend and the writings of Francisco Lopez de Gomara. He works himself into a melodramatic menopause as, with a middle-aged woman's delight, he tells of Madoc returning from America and visiting his brother's court of "Aberffraw in Gwynedd," how he went back again to the country of the Aztecs, being captured by them and chained to the stone of human sacrifice. Then, to make a happy ending, Cadwallon rescues Madoc and the Aztecs are driven out of Aztlan. [*Madoc and the Discovery of America,* Richard Deacon, George Braziller pub., New York, 1966, p.58]

The sources placing Madoc among the Aztecs are too numerous to quote here (for a full discussion of this topic, see: *The Widow's Son: The Esoteric History of the Prophet Joseph Smith and The Origin of Mormonism,* by Kerry Ross O'Boran with Lisa Lee O'Boran, privately printed, Salt Lake City, 1997), but it is important to once more quote Richard Deacon:

> There are extravagant accounts that Madoc and his companions reached Mexico and established the Aztec Empire, and then traveled on their all-conquering way to found the Mayan civilization and the Empire of the Incas in Peru. It has been suggested that because there are red-haired people in the Galapagos group that they eventually sailed on there. For good measure there is the legend that one of them named Mormon lived to write their story which was duly handed down to Joseph Smith, who founded

the Mormon religion…Brigham Young told Captain (Daniel) Jones, one of his lieutenants, of a Welsh settlement on the Rio Colorado and that he believed that the Moquis were descendants of Madoc. [Deacon, Ibid., pp.151-152]

Not only is Madoc equated with Mormon, but also with Quetzalcoatl, benevolent god of the Aztecs. Author John P. Brown has stated:

> The god was white and he had a beard. He was certainly no Indian. How would the Indians have known of such a person unless he existed? The legend contributed largely to the comparative ease with which Cortez conquered Mexico…The god really existed and he may have been Madoc, who arrived in Mexico on the second of his voyages, earned the affection of the Indians, taught them, and eventually left them, but promising to return…The Indians thought that the Fair God, Quetzalcoatl, had returned to them when Cortez came. [*Old Frontiers,* John P. Brown, as cited in Deacon, p.197]

The significance of these connections will be made clear in subsequent chapters. For now suffice it that Madoc, the Aztecs, and Mormonism all played a significant role in the history of the lost mines.

To the Spaniards, the loss of Montezuma's treasure was the spark which ignited a three-century search, the most concentrated effort having been made during the first two centuries. While they never found Montezuma's horde, their searches did uncover vast wealth from numerous other sources. The Spaniards plundered the wealth not only of the Aztecs, but of the Maya and Inca empires.

Of all the riches shipped from the New World to Europe during this era, more than 85 percent was that of Spanish coins and bullion. In the year 1543 alone, more than half a million ducats worth was shipped to Spain, and this amount doubled each year thereafter until eventually some five billion ducats worth had been plundered for the greater glory of Spain. By today's standards this amount would exceed $60 billion and perhaps surpass $100 billion, considering the hundreds of ill-fated galleons which were lost at sea to storms and piracy. As much as one tenth of all Spanish treasure secured in the New World is estimated to have ended up in "Neptune's Treasury"—the bottom of the ocean.

The Spaniards wasted no time in mounting expeditions to the north in search of Montezuma's treasure and the legendary "Seven Cities of Cibola." Only about fifty percent of these expeditions were preserved on record, although many accounts may yet lie in the musty archives of Mexico City, Seville and Madrid. The best known of those expeditions are as follows: Marcos de Nizza, 1539; Francisco Vasques de Coronado and Garcia Lopez de Cardenas, 1540; Hernando de Alarcon, 1540; Frays Agonstin Rodriquez, Francisco Lopes and Juan de Santa Maria, commanded by Francisco Sanchez Chamuscado, 1581; Antonio de Espejo, 1582; Gaspar Castano de Sosa, 1590; and Juan de Onate, 1597-1608.

Don Antonio de Mendoza, the first Viceroy of New Spain, entered Mexico in 1535, accompanied by Francisco Vasquez de Coronado, whom he had met in Spain. Coronado was born about 1510 in Salamanca, Spain, son of Juan Vasquez de Coronado, Lord of Coquilla, and Isabel de Luxan. Francisco married Beatriz de Estrada, daughter of Alonso de Estrada, who was the Royal Treasurer of New Spain and a displaced son of King Ferdinand. Her mother was Doña Maria Gutierrez Flores de la Calsatteria.

The interest in the lands to the north of Mexico began in 1539 with an expedition led by Fray Marcos de Nizza (or Niza), which included Francisco Coronado as captain. Upon their return in July, bringing back stories of Indian towns extending many leagues to the north, a new expedition was commissioned to penetrate even farther into the north country.

Antonio de Mendoza chose Coronado to head the new expedition as Captain General. Mendoza contributed 60,000 ducats and Coronado added 50,000 more. Pedro de Tovan, younger son of the Lord High Steward and guardian of the demented Spanish Queen "Mad" Juana, was appointed Ensign General. Captains of the expedition were: Tristán de Luna y Arellano, Diego de Guevara, Garcia Lopez de Cardenas, Rodrigo Maldonado, Diego Lopez, Diego Gutierrez (commanding artillery), Melchor Diaz, Juan de Zaldivar,

Francisco de Barrionuero, Francisco de Orando, and Juan Galiego. Other members of the expedition included: Alonso Manrique de Lara, Lopez de Urrea, Juan de Cespedes, Juan Jaramillo (who wrote a valuable description of Coronado's exploits), Juan Paniagua, Andrés de Campo, Francisco de Santillana, Cristobal de Quesada, Antonio de Rivero de Espinosa, Fray Marcos de Nizza (guide, having led the previous expedition), Fray Daniel, Fray Juan de la Cruz, Fray Luis de Escalona, Fray Juan de Padilla, and a number of horse and foot soldiers.

On Monday, 23 February 1540, the northern quest began. Cattle, sheep and swine were driven before them, as well as 600 head of horses. They crossed the Rio Grande de Santiago to the coastal plain between the Pacific and the Sierra Madre to San Pedro, crossing the rivers Acaponeta, the Canas, to Baluarte. They arrived at the Indian village of Aztatlan, on the lower Acaponeta River. In mid-March, Coronado's army reached Chahmetla on the Rio Presidio, a town named by Guzman, a contemporary, as Espiritu Santo.

On 22 April, Coronado set out with 70 horsemen, including his personal friends Alvarado, Diaz, Tovar, Pablo de Melgosa, and Garcia Lopez de Cardenas, together with 25-30 foot soldiers, as an advance party. They first came to the Indian village of Petatian, and three days later crossed the Rio Cinaloa. On 36 May they came to the Valley of Corozones ("hearts") where they rested, out of food and hungry.

They next crossed the Rio Senora to Saya— now into Arizona—and stopped at Chichilticalli, and on 23 June marched onto the Colorado Plateau. Their route took them through the White Mountains and through the upper drainage of the Colorado Chiquito ("Little Colorado"), by way of the present town of St. Johns, to the Zuni River. They came at last to the "River of Cibola"—they named it the Rio Vermejo or Red River. They had traveled from Mexico City to the outskirts of Zuni on the east-central border of Arizona, a distance of 500 leagues (2.52 leagues equal a mile).

Having reached the Indian village of Zuni, the Spaniards believed they were now in the country of Cibola. The chronicler Baltazar de Obregon wrote, circa 1584:

The principal reason why the discovery of, and expedition to, the provinces of Cibola and the original home of the Mexicans was desired was that the marquis (Cortes) had found, among the tribute, possessions, and treasures of the powerful King Montezuma, some chronicles, drawings, and paintings which revealed the origin, spread, and arrival from those regions of the Culguas and the ancient Mexicans.

At the Gila River in Arizona in July 1540, the Zuni Indians told Coronado of a place far to the north where the natives lives on the shores of a great body of water they called Laguna del Norte—the Lake of the North. These Indians were reported to wear trinkets of gold and to know the location of gold sources in the mountains called, in Spanish, the *Sierra Madre de Oro*—the "Mother of Gold" mountains (the Uintah Mountains). Inasmuch as the source of this gold was the primary quest of the expedition, Coronado determined to send some of his men to the north in search of it.

Coronado dispatched his friend Don Garcia Lopez de Cordenas and twelve men towards the north from Zuni in search of a route to the Laguna del Norte. The Cardenas party traveled across the desert for twenty-days, at first going westward, until they arrived at the rim of a colossal canyon (Grand Canyon). They spent another three days trying to locate a path to the river below, with no success.

Unfortunately, no account of the Cardenas expedition exists which describes their route and activities from this point, but other accounts have been preserved, both oral and written, which inform us of what transpired.

While Cardenas and a small party attempted a crossing of the Colorado River—which they called the Rio Tizon—another party of seven men was dispatched by him to seek a trail to the north. This second party was captained by one "Tomás Blaque." This man was not on Coronado's original muster roll, but had arrived late with an escort of soldiers from Mexico City. There is no question that Tomás Blaque was present; in a petition made some years later he stated that he had served in the pacification of New Granada in 1532 before

coming to Mexico in 1534 or 1535, and that he had enlisted with Coronado and served with the army until its return three years later.

"Tomás Blaque" was none other than Thomas Blake, a Scottish soldier of fortune, son of William and Agnes Mowat Blake. For twenty years he was the only man of British blood who was allowed to reside in Mexico, and he was also the only Englishman, so far as to known, to take part in any of the Spanish explorations in what is now the United States.

The northern route established by Blake's scouting expedition is defined in a map which the author discovered some years ago in the Archives de España at Madrid, in a packet of documents transferred from the Archives de los Indies at Seville, and thus overlooked by researchers for many years. The map, dated 1564, is titled "Mapa de los Indios del Norte de la Rio Tizon en los Provincias Internas de la Nuevo España, de la exactitud de lo referido a Senor Tomás Blaque, acerca de aquel pais, en Julio, 1540." The map is signed "Archivo General de los Indias, 1564."

The English translation of the map's title is as follows: "Map of the Indians of the North of the River Tizon (Colorado) in the Internal Provinces of New Spain, exactly as referred to by Senor Thomas Blake, who was near this country in July, 1540." The date of July 1540 may not be correct, however, for Cardenas did not set out to explore the Colorado River until 25 August, and Blake left the party to go northward nearly a month later. The earliest he could have arrived at the Green River would have been about 30 September or 1 October. The date of July, as used on the map, is probably calculated from Coronado's arrival at the Zuni village, where the parties separated.

The route indicated by the map, though vague due to their unfamiliarity with the terrain, shows a trail winding northward, then westward, then northward again, from the "Rio Tizon del Norte" across "terra del Sol" (Land of the Sun—i.e., desert, probably the San Rafael Swell) and across this desert eastward, thence north paralleling the present Utah-Colorado border to the "Rio de los Yutahs." This is probably the first recorded mention of the Green River, which the Spaniards later named the Rio Buenaventura.

The map indicates that the party made a crossing to the westward of the river and encamped at a place which coincides with the site of present-day Vernal, Utah. The site is indicated on the map as "Pueblo de los Indios y campo de la espedición." (Village of the Indians and camp of the expedition).

The map of the Blake expedition coincides in every detail with Ute Indian oral tradition which relates the story of the first white men ever seen by them. They claim that their ancestors were camped at the site of present-day Vernal when seven men with white skin, riding the first horses the Utes had ever seen, forded the Green River near present-day Jensen, Utah, and approached their village. They superstitiously believed that the men and horses were one being, spirits sent from the great Towats. This attitude had prevailed among the Aztecs who had greeted Cortes, and Fray Marcos de Nizza, during his first expedition of 1539, "pushed northward more than three hundred leagues and was welcomed by the Indians of the country, who greeted him as a messenger of heaven."

Blake and his Spaniards indicated to the Utes that they were looking for "money-rock" (i.e. gold), and expressed great interest when they noted that each brave carried a medicine bag which contained, among other religious items, a gold nugget. When their inquiries as to the source of the gold was met with silence, the Spaniards became more persuasive. They tortured a young brave to death, but still learned nothing.

The Spaniards then shot another young brave to death. The Indians, who had never before seen a gun, were terrified. They were convinced that the Spaniards were indeed white spirits with great powers. Coronado's men were armed with twenty-two harquebuses, the primitive forerunner of the musket. It was a formidable weapon, usually fired from a tripod. Loaded from the muzzle, often half a dozen lead balls were rammed in as a charge. A pan at the right side of the breech was primed with powder, and ignition and explosion might take as long as fifteen seconds after pulling the trigger. They were valuable more for impressing the Indians than as offensive weapons.

Still, the Utes remained silent as to the source of the gold. The Spaniards then tortured and killed one of the chief's sons, then another. Finally they learned that only the medicine man possessed the "Great Bear Medicine," and was therefore the only man who knew the location of the sacred gold, or was permitted to go there.

Under threat of death, the medicine man agreed to go to the gold mine and bring back some of the precious metal on a mule loaned to him by the Spaniards. The medicine man set out in a pouring rain and was, unknown to him, followed by two of the Spaniards with two more mules. When the medicine man returned with a mule-load of gold and learned that he had been followed, he was enraged. He stirred his people to anger, saying that these strangers must not have been sent from Towats or they would have known where the sacred gold was located.

When the two Spaniards returned with two more mule-loads of gold, the Indians surrounded them and demanded that their sacred metal be returned. The Spaniards attempted to shoot the medicine man, but their harquebuses, wet from the pouring rain, would not fire, and the medicine man took this to be a sign that his medicine was stronger than that of the white men. The Spaniards were disarmed and relieved of the gold, as well as most of their horses, and escorted to the river ford and warned never to return. It must be noted that the Utes, unlike their tormentors, spared the lives of the white men, belying the oft-repeated reports that Indians were "savages."

Shrewd and experienced as the Scotsman Thomas Blake undoubtedly was, he was fated to gain little gold through his service with Coronado. Shortly after his return he married Francisca de Ribera, widow of a prominent "old conqueror" who had been a nuncio and fiscal of the Holy Inquisition in Mexico. About 1550, like many another veteran of Coronado's expedition, Blake applied for aid from the crown because he "suffered great need." Blake was alive and residing in Mexico in 1556, when he was found there by Robert Tomson, an Englishman whose remarkable account of travels in Mexico and the West Indies appears in the writings of the English chronicler Hakluyt.

The names of the six Spaniards who accompanied "Tomás Blaque" to the Uintah Basin in 1540 have not been discovered, but there is no doubt that Blake was leader of the expedition, and thus must be credited as the first white explorer to visit what is now the State of Utah. This expedition occurred between 25 August 1540, when Cardenas started out to explore the canyons of the Colorado River, and November 1541, when he set out to return to Mexico.

Most present-day history books of the intermountain region credit the 1776 Dominguez-Escalante Expedition as the first to enter Utah. This is a strange claim to maintain considering how much evidence exists of the presence of the Spaniards in this region during the preceding two hundred years.

In 1848, Fray Juan Ortiz told officers of Stephen F. Kearney's American army at Sante Fe that as early as 1650 there had been a series of Spanish forts as far as five hundred miles up the Green River, and that at least two of these had been "near the headwaters of that stream." In that same year, according to Fray Ortiz, the Indians arose in open rebellion against the Spaniards and burned the forts, killing most of the occupants and driving the remainder of them from the country. In recent years, excavations by the University of Wyoming, in conjunction with others, has unearthed the remains of at least two old Spanish forts, one in Jackson's Hole and another in the Wind River Valley.

Nearly all accounts of expeditions north of Santa Fe were recorded by Franciscan or Jesuit priests, who were required by royal decree to accompany every party licensed by the king to pass into the "provincia's internas." Many smaller parties of Spanish miners passed into these regions illegally, and so no priest accompanied them to record their activities.

There were other early expeditions. Fray Geronimo Salmeron came into the region of the Great Salt Lake in 1621 and left one of the earliest descriptions of the great lake and the Indians who lived on the shore of Utah Lake to the south. Utah Valley became an important Spanish outpost in the northern mountains, and the hub of a trail which coursed up Spanish Fork Canyon eastward to the Uintah Basin.

The Spaniards explored nearly every desert range and mountain chain in the region long before the coming of the American fur trappers and traders. They followed the rivers and streams and penetrated into the most inaccessible places, and the quantity of gold and silver taken out of Utah during this period was staggering. Spanish mines have been found from the Kamas Valley and the Wasatch Range to the Green River at the eastern end of the Uintah Mountains.

In 1969, while exploring sites for information to be contained in our book *Footprints in the Wilderness*, Gale Rhoades and I discovered the foundation of an old Spanish fort in a meadow at the crest of Spanish Fork Canyon. The site was further authenticated by the discovery of Spanish symbols on nearby trees and our metal detector uncovered numerous mule shoes and a buried 12-pound "grapeshot" Spanish cannonball near a foundation wall.

Brown's Park, northeast of Vernal, was the site of another substantial early Spanish fort, probably one of those burned by the Indians during the Ute uprising of the mid-1600's. This region originally belonged to the Kohogue Shoshone Indians, who called it O-W i-U-Kuts (Big Canyon). Governor Juan Bautista de Anza's expedition of 1779 learned from the Utes of trails to west slope tributaries, including Brown's Park, which trails had been made by three Spanish civilians who had previously explored the region. The entire Uintah Basin region is replete with Spanish signs and symbols, some chiseled into rocks and ledges, others carved into the bark of pine and aspen trees, and even elaborate rock patterns laid out on the surface of the ground.

One early Spanish explorer to this region was Fray Alonzo de Posada who held a position of ecclesiastical importance at Santa Fe. In 1763 his party was sent by Governor Veles Cachupin to explore the country which is now the state of Colorado. Fray Posada wrote the *Informe,* a history of this expedition, to which Escalante refers when he arrived at the Green River near present-day Jensen, Utah, in 1776.

It was Posada who named the Green River the "Rio Buenaventura" in honor of Fray San Beunventure, which Escalante continues to use as a reference in his diary. When writing of the Green River at Jensen in his journal, Escalante states:

> This river of San Buenaventura is the largest that we have crossed and is the same one that Fray Alonzo de Posada says in his report, separates the Ute Nation from the Comanche, if we may judge by the description he gives of it, and the distance he says it is from Santa Fe.

Posada's records and reports were destroyed during the revolt of the Pueblo Indians in 1680; consequently the Dominquez-Escalante Expedition of 1776 has been credited with being the first white men of record to enter Utah. This is, of course, erroneous, but the significance of the Dominguez-Escalante Expedition cannot be discounted.

Fray Silvestre Velez de Escalante was a Franciscan Friar who came from Spain to New Mexico in 1768. He was in charge of the Mission of Our Lady of Guadelupe in Zuni, New Mexico, when he became obsessed with the idea that a northern route from Sante Fe to the missions in Monterey, California, would be more feasible than crossing the deserts of Arizona where the Hopi Indians were hostile.

The land of the Yutas, in present western Colorado, would be more advantageous. The Western Colorado Utes had been trading with the Spaniards out of Santa Fe since the early 1600s, and had gained access to both guns and horses since the re-conquest of the Pueblo lands by Don Diego de Vargas in the 1690s, and possibly even earlier. However, the Timpanogos Utes of central Utah, cousins to the Colorado Utes, had neither horses or guns when Escalante met them in 1776.

The Dominguez-Escalante Expedition was comprised of ten men, later joined by two Yuta guides whom they called Silvestre and Joaquin. Besides the two Fathers the party included: Juan Pedro Cisneros, chief magistrate of Pueblo de Zuni; Bernardo Miera y Pacheco, a retired military captain who acted as cartographer; Joaquin Lain, citizen of La Villa de Santa Fe; Lorenzo Olivares from La Villa del Paso; Andres Muniz, who knew the Ute language and served as interpreter; Lucretio Muniz, brother of Andres; Juan de Aguilar, born in Santa Clara, New Mexico; and Simon Lucero, a servant to Don Pedro Cisneros.

On 29 July 1776 the Dominguez-Escalante party set out on their historic 2,000 mile journey from Santa Fe through northwestern New Mexico, western Colorado, eastern and central Utah, northern Arizona and western New Mexico, returning to Santa Fe on 2 January 1777.

Escalante kept a detailed journal which affords us good descriptions of the route and peoples. On 13 September 1776 they arrived at the Green River. Escalante writes that "On the 13th, about eleven in the morning, we set out from El Arroyo del Cibolo over a plain lying at the foot of a small sierra which the Yutas and Lagunas call Sabuagari;…(we) came to a large river which, we named the San Buenaventura." The statement is important for two references. The "Arroyo del Cibolo" indicates the importance still attached by the Spaniards to the region as the location of the "Seven Cities of Cibola"; and, the fact that the "Lagunas" (the Utes who lived on the shores of Utah Lake) were familiar with landmark names in the eastern Uintah Basin is evidence of constant intercourse with their Uintah Ute cousins.

On 14 September, the day following their arrival on the Green River, Escalante noted in his journal the making of Spanish inscriptions and symbols on trees, a custom perpetuated by the Spanish miners at numerous locations throughout the Uintahs. Escalante's description is thus representative and conclusive evidence of this custom:

> At this place there are six big black poplars which have grown in pairs attached to one another, and they are the ones closest to the river. Near them is another one by itself; on its trunk, on the side facing northwest, Don Joaquin Lain dug out a small piece with an adze in the shape of a rectangular window, and with a chisel carved on it the inscription letters and numbers "Year of 1776," and lower down in a different hand "Lain" with two crosses at the sides, the larger one above the inscription and the other one beneath it.

Escalante's careful description of the placement of symbols indicates a general Spanish policy of marking specific sites for the benefit of those to follow. The primary purpose of these expeditions was a search for wealth, specifically gold, and such markings thus become important physical maps.

The Spaniards continued to explore the Uintah Basin region well into the middle of the Nineteenth Century, until the treaty of Guadelupe-Hidalgo ceded the territory to the United States in 1848. Even after this time, well past the year 1900, Mexicans continued to make illegal excursions into the Uintah Mountain region in search of the source of "El Sierra Madre de Oro."

Chapter Two

The Antonio de Reinaldo Story

THE BOOK *FOOTPRINTS IN THE Wilderness* outlines in detail the history of the Rhoades family and their connection with the famous lost mines, and so that aspect will not be repeated here, except where it is pertinent to do so. Suffice it here to say that Thomas Rhoades had discovered a number of gold mines in the Uintah Mountains other than the Sacred Mine (Carre-Shinob), which had first been shown to him in 1852. These additional mines, or some of them at least, were supposedly discovered by him through the means of several buckskin maps found on the bodies of eight Mexicans massacred by the Indians on Chicken Creek, near Levan, in 1857.

When Gale Rhoades and I published *Footprints*, we reported the story as we first learned it from family members, and it has remained relatively patent since. According to that account, the eight Mexicans had been returning from a trip to the mines with their burros loaded with gold. As they camped on Chicken Creek, the Utes caught up to them, killed the entire party, mutilated the bodies, and returned the gold to the mines.

The account continues by reporting that news of the massacre was brought to the attention of Brigham Young who dispatched First Lieutenant Thomas Rhoades at the head of twenty-one militiamen to investigate. This detachment arrived at the scene five days following the event, and they found the bodies in an advanced state of decomposition. One of the men allegedly discovered a small metal box half-buried in the sand near one of the bodies. Thomas Rhoades supposedly came into possession of it, discovering that it contained two maps (by other accounts there were as many as seven), which he kept. From these maps Thomas Rhoades eventually discovered some of the Spanish mines which he secretly worked.

The foregoing account was basically the accepted version at the time of publication of *Footprints*, and has remained the primary explanation of Rhoades' knowledge of the Spanish mines ever since. In its basic elements, the story is correct in details; but it is not the entire story, which is now told for the first time.

Since the publication of *Footprints*, true copies of the two maps obtained by Thomas Rhoades came into our possession. The original maps were burned into soft buckskin, about the size of a man's hand, and colored with inks or dyes of brown, blue and green. One of the maps contains the inscription "Antonio de Reinaldo, 1851," and the other "Antonio de Reinaldo Anos 1851-1853." The maps also contain written descriptions of the mines and landmarks, in Spanish.

Until now, however, the identity of Antonio de Reinaldo has remained obscure. It is generally assumed that he was one of the eight Mexicans killed by the Indians at Chicken Creek, but the reality proves otherwise.

The search for Antonio de Reinaldo began with a whim. Because the date of the first map was 1851, it occurred to me that these might be the same men who were brought to trial on 24 December 1851 for trafficking in slave children with Ute war chief Arapeen.

I searched both the Utah State Archives for the Territorial records concerning the trial, and the Bureau of Indian Affairs, Department of Interior, as well as the National Archives. The result was a list of the seven Mexicans brought to trial and the transcript of the trial record. Heading the list of names was none other than Antonio de Reinaldo! The list of names is as follows:

Antonio de Reinaldo Fernán Santiago Philip Perez

Juan de Meyo   Juan de Corso

Pedro de Santa   CruzAlvaro de Perón

Some or all of the foregoing slave traders, with the exception of Reinaldo, as we shall see, may have been among those massacred in 1857. It seems apparent from the evidence that the act of buying slaves from Arapeen was calculated to prevent returning empty-handed to Santa Fe after an unsuccessful trip after gold, or was a cover for their mining activities. There is a hint of this in the trial testimony. Judge Snow asks Fernán Santiago, through Ammon Tenney, the Spanish interpreter:

Snow: Has your expedition into this territory in any way involved mining activities or trading in valuable metals among the natives?

Santiago: We are not miners, but merchant traders, interested only in trading among natives for furs and buffalo robes. Occasionally, when trading is unsuccessful, we buy Piede children from Arropeen. It has always been the custom. My own grandfather traded in Piedes for the haciendas and mines of Mexico.

Of course they were miners, as well as traders, and Brigham Young well knew it, which is why they were driven from the Territory following the trial, warned never to return. The Utes were poor in buffalo robes, the buffalo having been killed off in their region, for the most part, by the year 1850. The only things the Utes had worth trading with an expedition all the way from Sante Fe was horses and Piedes slaves, and normally even these were brought to the Mexicans in the south by the Indians themselves. Gold had been their true objective, slaves an afterthought.

Most of the trial record deals with the issue of slave trading, and therefore is not repeated here. However, some of the facts which emerge are pertinent to our interest in the mines.

Isaac Morley (1786-1865) was my third great-grandfather, and so I was moderately surprised to discover his name among witnesses at the trial. He testified that the Spaniards had camped near his settlement at Manti on or about 10 December, having come down from "Sanpete Mountain by way of Salt Creek." He further testified that they "may have been the same (men) I saw camped in the mountains" earlier in the year. Morley was not asked about what he had been doing in the mountains, but later we will explore the reasons.

The testimony of Antonio de Reinaldo is in several places enlightening:

Snow: What is your name?

Reinaldo: Antonio de Reinaldo.

Snow: What is your usual profession?

Reinaldo: I am the aide-de-camp to the alcalde of Sante Fe.

Snow: Has the alcalde sent you here?

Reinaldo: No. I come as a private citizen. I am a member of a private trading company, organized to trade with the Indians. We have been among both the Navajos and the Yutahs for nearly two years.

Snow: If you have been trading in this territory for two years, how is it that you are found in no possession of either trade goods or Indian goods?

Reinaldo: We are only a part of a larger company. Twelve of our party have returned to Sante Fe with our goods. We remain here only to negotiate with the Yutahs for the coming year, in which we had planned to return. It was our purpose to purchase Piede slaves and return to Sante Fe before the heavy snows came.

Antonio de Reinaldo, we then discover, was aide-de-camp to the alcalde (mayor) of Sante Fe, an official of considerable rank inasmuch as the alcalde also served as military governor of all Mexican possessions emanating from the jurisdiction of Sante Fe. As second in command to the military governor, Reinaldo's only purpose for being in Utah Territory would have been in pursuit of gold.

Having learned that Reinaldo held a high political position in the Mexican government at

Sante Fe, the next step was to search the record of Mexican officials stationed there during this period. The results of that search produced the following information.

Antonio de Reinaldo was born in Spain in about the year 1820 (he was said to be 37 in 1857). He was of pure Castilian blood, his father being of the nobility and a grandee with large estates near Seville. In his early teens, Reinaldo's uncle secured a post for him at Sante Fe as a soldier in the guard of the alcalde, where he eventually worked his way up the political ladder to become aide-de-camp.

Reinaldo served as a soldier of the guard with his cousin, Juan Jose Hererra. The latter was a flamboyant and somewhat egotistical youth, inordinately proud of his noble Castilian blood which he lorded over his "lessers." Hererra considered himself a grandee and his father's employees as hidalgos (men of lesser nobility), whom he ordered about mercilessly.

Reinaldo and his cousin Hererra were at the height of their fortunes when called to serve in the Mexican War against the United States. In 1848, under the Treaty of Guadalupe Hidalgo, the Mexicans conceded defeat and ceded the entire northern territories, including Utah, to the United States government. The Treaty of Guadalupe-Hidalgo had another consequence, however; it took away the immense grants of land belonging to the grandees, including those of Reinaldo and Hererra, making them penniless overnight.

Antonio de Reinaldo and Juan Jose Hererra had planned to inherit their family grants and retire as grandees. Now suddenly, they were both poor, and they found this state of affairs unacceptable. Their mutual grandfather, Don Juan Reinaldo, had been a member of an expedition in 1831 led by Juan de Meyo, which came out of Mexico City via Santa Fe to retrieve gold from the Uintah Mountains for the Mexican government.

Hererra had acquired a map to this gold source from his grandfather, and in about 1849-50 he made a proposal to his cousin Antonio that they retrieve some of the gold for their own use. In only one of two trips, they reasoned, they could obtain enough gold to live like grandees in Spain for the rest of their lives.

Hererra himself would not accompany the first expedition. He had instead organized a gang of Mexican horse thieves, together with his brother Pablo and others, to raid wealthy American ranchers fastly settling around Sante Fe, to obtain proceeds with which to finance the expedition.

Antonio de Reinaldo and his companions arrived in Utah Territory either late in 1850 or early in 1851. Isaac Morley saw them encamped in the mountains in May or June, and by Christmas they were under arrest. They were driven out of the Territory by New Year's Day of 1852, and they left unburdened of either gold or slaves, having been warned never to return, and unless Reinaldo was telling the truth about another party of his men having departed earlier with their "trade goods," no gold was recovered in 1851.

By 1853, however, Antonio de Reinaldo was back in the mountains, and this time his expedition was apparently successful. His map of 1851 is simple, showing three mines in one area, an arrow pointing apparently to the only one which they mined that year. On the bottom of this map, Reinaldo wrote: "Explanation— these mines of gold and silver are in the high plateaus, two canyons from the east beyond the headland of the Mountain of the Timpanogos, and are hidden among a great many lakes. Here there is much wire gold and silver in a formation of rock crystal...Antonio de Reinaldo, 1851-   ."

The second map, dated "1851-1853," indicates much more extensive exploration. Reinaldo details rivers, streams, waterholes, peaks, trails, passes, plateaus, and mines, in some detail. The most important single delineation is that of "Huella de San Pedro"—the San Pedro Trail—which clearly traces the pedigree of Reinaldo's map to that of the 1831 "Juan de Meyo" map, which traces to an even earlier source. It is also noteworthy that a member of Reinaldo's 1851 party was "Juan de Meyo," who was probably a son or grandson of the leader of the 1831 expedition.

Apparently Reinaldo's 1853 expedition was successful. The Walker War was raging in the valleys of Utah Territory, and both the Mormons and the Utes were too occupied with killing one another to be concerned about Mexican traffic in the mountains. A notation in the records of Sante Fe show that Reinaldo resigned his office of aide-de-camp to the alcalde in 1855, the apparent reason being that he no longer needed the income, being described as "un hombre muy rico"—a very rich man.

There is no record of the names of the eight Mexicans killed at Chicken Creek in 1857, but it is evident that Antonio de Reinaldo was not among them. In the accounts of those registering for travel from Sante Fe to Mexico City in the month of December, 1857, is that familiar name "Antonio de Reinaldo y compania"—"Antonio de Reinaldo and company." The record clearly shows that he is our man, listing him both as former adjutant to the alcalde and as a member of the aristocratic class. Even though he was then en route to Mexico City, his final destination is listed as Vera Cruz, a port of embarkation for Spain. His name never again appears on record at Sante Fe.

Having made his fortune, apparently from the 1853 expedition, Antonio de Reinaldo was off to Spain to enjoy his wealth as a Spanish grandee. There appears to have been some intrigue and dissension between Reinaldo and his cousin Hererra. The latter was in the California gold-fields while Reinaldo was in the northern mountains, and when he returned he brought suit against his cousin for monies owed. The record is not clear on the reason or the amount of the suit, but it was apparently connected with financing the Uintah expedition.

Juan Jose Hererra, disgusted with his losses, obtained several other maps showing the location of Spanish gold in the high Uintahs. He organized an expedition of his own comprising his brother Pablo and five or six members of his gang, guided by an old forty-niner named "Uncle" Sam Bassett and his friend, Louis Simmons, who happened to be the son-in-law of Kit Carson. They made their headquarters at Joe's Spring in Brown's Park, and for the next few years prospected the Uintahs, apparently with small success.

Failing in his attempt to get rich by finding Spanish gold, Hererra—who came to be known as "Mexican Joe"—attempted to make his fortune by highway robbery, and was shot to death some years after his arrival. His brother Pablo met a similar fate in about 1878 in Brown's Park at the hands of the renowned gunman Cleophas J. Dowd.

Mexican Joe's map fell into the possession of a grizzled old reprobate named Jesse Ewing. By the use of one of the maps, old Jesse located one of the Spanish mines on the very fringe of Brown's Park itself, and by all accounts it was fabulously wealthy. However, before Ewing could develop it, he was murdered by his partner, a man named Coulter, over the attentions of a side-show contortionist named "Madame Forrestal," and the *Lost Ewing Mine* was relegated to the list of famous lost mines of the Uintahs.

In the meantime, Antonio de Reinaldo had drawn at least two maps to the locations of the source of his immense wealth and had given them to someone in his circle of acquaintances. Perhaps it was his companions of the first two expeditions, but if so it would seem extraordinary that they would need maps to the locations, having already been there. It seems as likely that Reinaldo had found new partners, who needed the maps for direction.

Whatever the case, an expedition of eight Mexicans was in the mountains of the north during the summer of 1857, loading their burros with Ute gold, even as Reinaldo awaited their return at Sante Fe. As they camped on Chicken Creek, leaving the mountains by way of Timpanogos (Provo) River, the entire party was killed by Indians, or so it was reported. It was likely to this event that Mormon V. Selman, a Mormon missionary to the Ute Indians, refers when he related:

> My father used to tell me of a time in the early days when a pack train came down the Provo River and camped by his place for a few days to rest up their small pack mules. He said they loaded these animals with a heavy pack load that did not appear to be very large, but it was all those mules could carry. The men kept an

armed guard at their camp and no one was allowed near. He said that they stayed a few days and then went south. A few days later there was a report that some Indians had killed those men down on Chicken Creek (Levan, near Nephi) and had stolen the mules, horses and whatever those animals were carrying in their packs. No one suspected that Indians would steal a pack train, so everybody decided that it was someone who had dressed up as Indians.

— [Journal of Mormon V. Selman]

Selman fails to speculate on who might have dressed up as Indians to perpetrate such a deed, but from independent sources we discover that Selman's statement was correct. It has long been the accepted version of this event that the Indians killed the Mexican miners and returned the gold to the mines. This has been a great injustice to the Indians, and at last the truth can vindicate them.

Brigham Young had warned Antonio de Reinaldo and his companions in 1851 that if they should return, the penalty would be prosecution or death. In the 1852 legislative assembly, at the instigation of Brigham Young, Isaac Morley had been successful in passing the anti-slavery bill, giving legal teeth to Young's efforts to keep the Mexicans out of Utah Territory. But still they came and took gold form the mines which Brigham Young now considered the property of the Mormon Church. It seemed that the only way to stop the Mexicans from coming was to teach them an object lesson; but it must be laid at the hands of the Indians to avert suspicion away form Church authorities because the federal government was already threatening punishment of the Mormons. By 1857, Albert Sidney Johnston was already on his way to Utah with an army to wrest control form Brigham Young and the Church over the question of the government of Utah Territory.

If any Indians did participate, they were likely members of Kanosh's band, for the gold was retrieved by the whites, and this the Utes would never have permitted.

The LDS Church archives contain a bit of carefully guarded evidence which verifies that Brigham Young was fully aware of the massacre, that the gold had been obtained for him and for the use of the Church, and further itemizes the amount of gold and the names of three of the participants in the massacre. The document is in the form of a hand-written receipt by Thomas Bullock, Brigham Young's personal secretary, dated 17 October 1857. The receipt is written together with numerous others in a bound volume of itemized entries at the Deseret Mint. The document reads as follows:

> Received this day at the Deseret Mint by the direction of Prest. Young, upon delivery of O.P. Rockwell, D.B. Huntington, and Brig. Gen. R.T. Burton, three loads of gold in form ore taken from Mexicans near Nephi. Load no.1 consisting of 162 pounds of high quality, in part refined. Load no.2 consisting of 107 pounds of gold unrefined. Load no.3 consisting of 97 pounds of unrefined ore containing high amounts of gold with silver and quartz. Consigned to John Neff for assay and valuation before being entered for process.

— (signed) THOMAS BULLOCK

The foregoing clearly indicates that Brigham Young authorized Rockwell, Huntington, and Burton to deliver a total of 366 pounds of gold to the Deseret Mint for processing for the use of the Church. John Neff owned a grist mill (which can still be seen in Salt Lake City's Liberty Park) which sometimes served as an assay house. Porter Rockwell was married to one of Neff's sisters, while Dimick B. Huntington's sister, Zina, was one of the wives of Brigham Young. Robert T. Burton was Brigadier-General of the militia.

Dimick B. Huntington was also Brigham Young's official Indian interpreter. The journal of William H. Huntington, Dimick's brother, under date of 21 October 1857, just four days after the gold was delivered to the Deseret Mint, states: "Dimick showed me two maps taken off the bodies of the killed Mexicans at Nephi. They are curious maps, etched on dried buckskin, with strange marks and writing in the Spanish tongue. Dimick says they are (i.e., contain) directions to the mines where the gold came from. He will turn them over to Pres. Young on Sunday."

Thus the story that Thomas Rhoades took the maps off the bodies of the slain Mexicans five days after the massacre is shown to be erroneous— unless he discovered additional maps at that time. What is apparent is that Dimick B. Huntington recovered two maps at the time of the massacre, which were turned over to Brigham Young a short time later; these were obviously the Antonio de Reinaldo maps "1851" and "1851-1853."

It thus appears that Thomas Rhoades obtained the two maps not from the slain Mexicans, but from Brigham Young himself. Brigham Young's motives are patently clear. He could not use the maps himself, having taken a public stand against mining in Utah, but there was one man who had unmolested access to Indian lands in the mountains—Thomas Rhoades. Rhoades must have felt certain that he could find these mines, and subsequent events show that he did; but it meant a partnership with Brigham Young. Gale Rhoades, in his last book, *Lost Gold of the Uintahs*, published posthumously, also reached the conclusion that Brigham Young "might have been an accomplice in this search" (p.30).

But inasmuch as Brigham Young could not openly involve himself in the search for gold, considering his public views against Mormons in mining, he conceived another plan. Isaac Morley was still a Territorial Legislator, serving his final term in the 1857-58 session. Among the last acts of his office was to sponsor a bill entitling private land grants.

It was common knowledge that the federal government had its eye on the Uintah Mountains as a site for a proposed reservation for the settlement of the Ute Indians. The best protection of the mines would be to encompass them by private land grants, ensuring that they would not fall into the legal hands of the federal government or the Ute Indians. Thus it was, with the sanction of the act by the Territorial Legislature early in 1858, that Brigham Young and Thomas Rhoades shared equally in a massive private grant which extended from the Kamas Prairie eastward to the headwaters of the Provo River, encompassing much of the area indicated on the Reinaldo maps. In the same year, Brigham Young dispatched Thomas Rhoades with a company of twenty-five men to establish a permanent settlement in the Kamas Valley. The settlement would constitute the "improvements" needed to legalize their claim to the grant.

At the same time, Brigham Young had not forgotten to reward his other loyal supporters. Huge grants of land were given to Isaac Morley, in conjunction with Apostle Franklin D. Richards and others, encompassing the environs of Utah Lake, while others were granted to Heber C. Kimball, Jedediah M. Grant, Wilford Woodruff, Bill Hickman, and others faithful to Brigham's causes.

During the ensuing years, Thomas Rhoades discovered and worked several of the mines illustrated on Antonio de Reinaldo's maps, all of which were in the Rock Creek- Moon Lake area of the high Uintahs. About 10 July 1859, twenty-three-year-old Caleb Baldwin Rhoades located two of the three mines shown on Reinaldo's 1851 map, which he called the "Pine Mine" and the "Rhoades Mine." Of the thirteen mines shown on Reinaldo's 1851-1853 map, Caleb Rhoades is believed to have located at least four.

At the time of Caleb Rhoades' death (2 June 1905), the Antonio de Reinaldo maps became the property of his widow, Sidsie Jensen Rhoades, who later relinquished the maps to Caleb's brother, John Joseph Rhoades, who later, upon his death (5 June 1935), passed the maps to his eldest child, Olive Ann Rhoades Westenskow.

By the year 1962 the maps were in such a deteriorated condition that they were carefully copied and the originals discarded. Mrs. Westenskow died on 14 October 1972, but in 1968, prior to her death, she relinquished the copies of the Reinaldo maps, together with other materials, to her nephew, Gale Rhoades, and to this writer, for our book, *Footprints in the Wilderness*. The maps were withheld from publication at that time, however, due to our on-going searches in the mountains.

The Antonio de Reinaldo story, in its entirety, was unknown even to my late cousin Gale Rhoades; it is here presented for the first time in print. Reinaldo had no idea of the chain of events his mining activities set into motion in Utah Territory. It was of little consequence to Reinaldo, who retired as a wealthy grandee somewhere near Seville, financed by one packload of sacred Ute gold from the high Uintahs.

Chapter Three

Keeper of the Yellow Metal

THE STORY OF THE SACRED GOLD OF THE Uintah Mountains could not be told without mention of Chief Walker of the Utes. To date, however, there have been few biographies written of this enigmatic man, and those which have been written are woefully inadequate. They are usually written from the perspective of the white man with its attendant bias, mis-truths and prejudices.

It is not the purpose of this narrative to correct this slight, except where it pertains to the topic of our interest. However, most of the information presented in this chapter derives directly from Ute sources, orally transmitted through interviews with elders of the tribe, or preserved in cultural traditions passed from one generation to another. The story of Chief Walker and his family and their connection with the gold of Carre-Shinob has never before appeared in print. It may offer heretofore unknown clues to the mystery of the lost Ute gold.

It is important to mention that much of the information on Walker and his family comes from an old Ute Indian named Tab-Wash, who was a son of Nauhnan, who in turn was a son of Chief Tabiona (Tabby), and thus Nauhnan was a nephew of Chief Walker. Nauhnan died some years ago near the age of 107, after passing these traditions on to his son, Tab-Wash, who in his old age became my good friend. The following account is based primarily on those traditions, supplemented by the historical record.

Chief Walker's great-grandfather was a man named Uin-pah-quint, who was born about 1725, and was a chieftain of the Uin-tah Yutahs residing in the Uintah Basin (in the Ute language "Uin-tah" means "Land of many trees"). In about the year 1755, Uin-pah-quint was challenged in his leadership of the Uin-tah Utes by his brother, Pah-yampa. Uin-pah-quint was deposed and forced to leave the Basin with a few of his loyal followers.

Uin-pah-quint removed to the territory of his cousins, the Timpanogos Utes, on the banks of the Timpanogos River (the Provo River; the Utes called it Tim-pan-ee), but because there was a shortage of food, the Timpanogos Utes soon urged them to move southward and establish their own settlement.

Uin-pah-quint moved his people to the mouth of the Pequi-nary-no-quint (Spanish Fork River; the Ute name means "Stinking Water," so-called because of sulfur springs nearby), a place which the Timpanogos Utes avoided, not only because of the stinking water, but because it was on the Spanish Trail. The Spanish miners frequently used this route to cross the mountains into the Uintah Basin. Here Uin-pah-quint and his band settled and grew in power and numbers until they soon rivaled their cousins, the Timpanogos.

Uin-pah-quint had several wives and many children. Three of his sons grew in stature and became chieftains over surrounding domains. The eldest son, Oquirrh, became the leader of a tribe which lived in the Tooele Valley, on the western slope of the mountains which today bears his name. Another son, Pah-vaun, moved farther south with his followers, who became known as the Pahvants, and settled near present-day Nephi, on Chicken Creek. The third son, in whom our narrative is most concerned, was named Pan-a-pitch. He established his tribe of followers in the valley which was to become known under his other name—Sanpitch or San Pete. San Pete was the grandfather of Chief Walker.

Pan-a-pitch, or San Pete, had been born in the Uintah Basin, on the banks of the Seeds-ka-dee ("Prairie Hen," i.e. the Green River), and was a boy of only three or four years when his father had been forced to leave their homeland. Pan-a-pitch had ridden the entire journey from the Seeds-ka-dee to the Timpanogos—150 miles—

tied to the back of a pony. Thus he was probably born about 1752.

Pan-a-pitch was a great warrior and his feats of daring made him legendary among the neighboring tribes. He made forays to steal horses from his northern cousins, the Shoshones, and ranged as far south as Santa Fe to sell Piede and Paiute slaves to the Spaniards. He had been a strapping youth of about twenty-four when the Spanish priest Escalante visited and traded with the Timpanogos.

Escalante had noted with particular interest that the Laguna Yutas (the Lake People, as he called them) wore gold trinkets, and Pan-a-pitch's people carried gold nuggets in their medicine bags. Pan-a-pitch boasted that his people were "keepers of the yellow metal," and knew the source of the sacred gold, but would not tell the Spaniards.

But Pan-a-pitch's boasts were recorded and carried back to Santa Fe. When next he visited there to sell Piede slaves, the Spanish took him captive and attempted to learn the secret of the gold from him, but he would not tell. They tortured him near unto death, but still he would not tell them, and so it was that the Governor of New Mexico devised a plan. If they could convert Pan-a-pitch to Christianity, they might convince him to reveal the location of the gold on the grounds that it belonged rightfully to the Catholic Church. For this cause the governor turned Pan-a-pitch over to the Provincial Minister of the Franciscans to be taken to a monastery in Mexico and there "converted," by force if necessary.

For about two years Pan-a-pitch remained a virtual prisoner in the monastery. He was shorn of his long hair, made to wear Spanish clothing, and taught the Spanish language, as well as the rudiments of Catholicism. He was fitted with a metal collar and chained to the floor at night. Many hours were spent at prayers, vespers and mass, and for every sin—real or imagined—he was compelled to do penance, the most humiliating of which to this proud brave was kneeling before a priest, kissing the priest's bare foot, and begging forgiveness.

After several years of captivity, Pan-a-pitch was able to effect his escape and returned north to his mountain home with an undying hatred of the Spaniards. For many years thereafter he would raid their territory and steal their horses, until his

warriors became the best-mounted and best-experienced in the region.

The Spaniards had given Pan-a-pitch a new name when he was "Christianized"—they called him San Pedro (Saint Peter). In time this was shortened to simply San Pete, though his people, wrapping their tongues around the syllables, called him Sanpitch. The place where his tribe lived came to be known as Sanpete Valley.

In time the Spaniards returned to the land of the Yutahs. It was in about the year 1815 that an expedition was launched from Santa Fe with a full military escort, because San Pete was still hostile towards the Spaniards. The famous chieftain was now about sixty-three years of age, too old to offer much resistance; still he refused to take the Spaniards to the source of the Ute gold.

In order to convince the obstinate old chieftain of their serious intent, the Spaniards turned their cannon on his tepee, blowing it to pieces, together with his favorite wife and at least one of his younger children. At last San Pete agreed to escort the Spaniards into the mountains and show them several gold sources, ever careful not to mention the Sacred Mine—Carre-Shinob. It was not voluntary servitude, however. San Pete was literally a prisoner of the threat of the virtual annihilation of his people if he refused cooperation. His was an act of bravery and not of betrayal.

The pack train of Spaniards, accompanied by San Pete and several of his sub-chiefs, proceeded up Salt Creek Canyon, over Sanpete Mountain, and through the Strawberry Valley to the Rock Creek area of the high Uintahs. At least three mines were revealed to the Spaniards, who made careful maps, mined enough ore to load their pack animals, and started back to Santa Fe. Before leaving the area of the mines, however, the Spaniards put to death old Chief San Pete and several of the Indian guides who had accompanied them. The bodies of the Chief and his companions were entombed in rock cairns near each of the mine sites, possibly as landmarks, for they appear as such on the later Reinaldo maps.

The Spaniards were unaware, however, that they had been followed into the mountains by members of San Pete's band, who witnessed the murder of their chief and hastily rode back to the

Sanpete Valley to organize the warriors for an ambush of the returning Spaniards.

San Pete's son, Moonch, then in his late thirties, was now chief of the Sanpete Yutahs due to the death of his father, and he ascended with the fire of vengeance in his eyes. Moonch led the attack upon the Spaniards as the latter reached a camp near present-day Nephi. A number of Spaniards were killed in the surprise attack, but the majority of them, having superior military arms and armor, managed to escape. Nevertheless, they were compelled to abandon the heavily loaded pack animals to the Indians.

Moonch chose the tribal medicine man with four or five others to assist him in returning the gold to the mines. They returned by way of Salt Creek Canyon over Sanpete Mountain (though the Spaniards had come back by way of the Provo River) to the site of the mines.

Each night, according to the Indian version, the medicine man would take a burro back to one of the mines, place the ore back inside the tunnel, and then take the burro off some distance and kill it—so that its spirit could not communicate with the other burros or with the spirits of the dead Spaniards (whose bodies were also thrown into the mineshaft). As added insurance, the hooves of the burros were cut off to prevent their spirits ever assisting further attempts by the Spaniards to remove the gold.

Moonch was now the undisputed leader of the Sanpete Utes. Like his father, he made repeated raids upon the Spanish territories, driving off horses and occasionally taking captives to sell as slaves. During one of his raids, Moonch captured a young Paiute woman named Tishum Igh, who had been raised and educated in a convent in Nevada by the "black robes" (Spanish priests). She spoke fluent Spanish, so Moonch kept her as one of his wives. She became the mother of Walker.

In fact, Moonch was father of a large number of sons, eight of whom were to achieve prominence: Sowiett, Kanosh, San Pitch (the younger), Grosspeen, Arapeen, Tabiona, Ammon, and Pan-a-Carre Quinker (who came to be known as Walker). Pan-a-Carre Quinker (which means "Iron Twister") was born about 1808, and so was about seven when his grandfather, San Pete, had

been murdered by the Spaniards. It established the basis of his lifelong hatred of the Spaniards.

In 1843, when Pan-a-Carre Quinker was about thirty-five, his father Moonch challenged Pah-rant for the leadership of the Timpanogos Utes. Pah-rant was Moonch's cousin, being a son of Pah-vaun, brother of San Pete. Pah-rant and his sons—Antonguer, Pah-sow-e-ett, Uin-ker-wendet and Tis-u-nah—with other Timpanogos braves, made a retaliatory raid on the Sanpetes, and Moonch was killed.

In that same year, Pan-a-Carre Quinker and his brother Arapeen made a daring foray into Pah-rant's village, and Pan-a-Carre Quinker single-handedly killed Pah-rant to avenge his father's death, and by so doing became undisputed war chief of the Sanpetes. The Timpanogos Utes also came under his subjection, even though Pah-rant's warlike sone, Antonguer, became their official chief.

However, long before he became chief of the Sanpete Utes, Pan-a-Carre Quinker had achieved renown, not only among his own people, but with the Spaniards and the white trappers who began penetrating the intermountain region. At the head of a band of hard-riding Utes, sometimes accompanied by his trapper friend "Peg Leg" Smith, Pan-a-Carre Quinker made raids on the large Spanish "estancias" of California, driving off huge herds of fine Spanish horses. At times, gathering horses from numerous ranches, he pushed herds as large as 6,000 through the Cajon Pass, becoming the wealthiest Indian chief in the American West. He came to be both feared and respected by the Spaniards.

Thomas L. "Peg Leg" Smith, the chief's lifelong friend, was born in 1801 on a 33-acre farm on Dick's River, between Crab Orchard and Lancaster, Kentucky. At the age of fifteen he ran away from home and began selling illegal whiskey to the Osage Indians at Natchez, Mississippi. He had a facility for languages and soon learned not only Osage, but Cherokee, Choctaw and Chickasaw as well. He had an Osage squaw and child, and lived among them as an Indian in all his ways.

Eventually Smith went up the Mississippi River with French trapper Antoine Robidoux to Illinois, where he learned the languages of the

Saux Fox and Potowatomie tribes. He wintered in 1822-23 in Nebraska with Robidoux, and on 11 March 1823 he departed for the Yellowstone country with William H. Ashley and Andrew Henry. He was twenty-two years old. Two months later he was involved in his first Indian battle, with the Arakaras near present-day Pierre, South Dakota. When he exposed himself to enemy fire to rescue a wounded companion, he established himself as a leader among the trappers. He bravery was never challenged.

Smith had his first encounter with Utes later that year when he went trapping along the Green River with two white men, Marlow and Hooper, and three Mexicans. The Utes attacked—primarily because of the presence of the Mexicans—killing one of the Mexicans instantly, and driving off the mules loaded with furs and supplies.

The two remaining Mexicans headed for Mexico, but Smith and his two companions trailed the Utes to their camp and boldly marched up to them and demanded the return of the mules and supplies. Astonished by their bravery, the Utes returned the stolen property, and the three men remained with the Utes while trapping that winter. This was Smith's first introduction to the Utes, but he had yet to meet Pan-a-Carre Quinker.

A few years later Smith was trapping along the South Platte River when his party was attacked by Crow Indians. He was shot in the ankle at close range, leaving nothing but jagged bones where his foot had once been. After the battle, nine Indians and three trappers lay dead. Smith was carried a mile or so away and given a drink of whiskey to ease his pain, but because they thought he was dying, they did little else for him. Smith took a butcher's knife and began his own amputation; when he passed out from pain and loss of blood, Milton Sublette finished the job.

The trappers carried Smith for two weeks on a travois. His leg was swollen with blood poisoning and he was unconscious. Believing he was about to die, his companions turned him over to a band of Utes and rode away. The squaws cleaned the wound and smothered the stub in roots, tobacco juice and horse manure. Smith survived, fashioned himself a wooden leg, which he tied to his real leg with leather thongs, and was as active as ever.

This band of Utes was the same to which Pan-a-Carre Quinker belonged. In fact, Smith took Pan-a-Carre Quinker's sister for his squaw, and the two men became fast friends. The Utes called him Wa-he-to-co, or "wooden leg."

It was near this time that the white trappers gave Pan-a-Carre Quinker the name by which he would ever after be known. It was generally pronounced "Walker" or "Walkara," for the whites could never pronounce the Ute term from which it derived—Yah-keerah, "Keeper of the Yellow Metal."

It was to his greatest friend, Isaac Morley, that Walker (for now we shall so call him) revealed the origin of his name. As a youth, he said, his name had always been Pan-a-Carre Quinker, the "Iron Twister," but he questioned his destiny and so went off alone into the high Uintahs to fast and pray to Towats for an answer.

Spirit Lake had always been a sacred place to the Utes. It was said that Towats, the Great Spirit, had once appeared there to the Old Ones. When Pan-a-Carre Quinker was born, his father, Moonch, had held him by the tiny foot and dipped him three times in the icy water of the lake to toughen him and to imbue him with the spirit of Towats. Now, as a man grown, Pan-a-Carre Quinker sought out a lofty precipice overlooking Spirit Lake to fast and to chant sacred songs and to pray to Towats.

At last Towats appeared to him in a vision and said to him, "No more will your name be Pan-a-Carre, but you shall be called Yah-keerah, the Keeper of the Yellow Metal." Towats showed him in this vision where the sacred gold of Carre-Shin-Ob ("Where the Great Spirit Dwells") was hidden in the mountains, and appointed him to be the keeper of its secret and protector of its sacred treasure—the relics of the Old Ones, his ancestors. He was told that when the "High Hats" came, he was to give the secret to them, and to them only.

At first he thought the "High Hats" were the "black robes" (priests) of the Q'uatz (Mexicans), for they wore tall pointed hats; but when he saw their cruelty to his people, he knew it could not be for them, for Towats had told him that the gold was to be used only for good—never for war or greed. When Jim Bridger, Kit Carson, Peg Leg

Smith and other mountain men came into the region, he thought it might be them, but they laughed that he thought they could be miners; they were interested only in beaver pelts.

Then came a strange occurrence. Shortly after becoming chief of his tribe, upon the death of his father in 1843, Walker went to Fort Uintah in the Uintah Basin to trade with the whites. While there he fell suddenly ill and was taken in by the trader—probably Antoine Robidoux—but he went into a deep coma from which he could not be stirred. Thinking him to be dead, the trappers turned him over to his people for burial.

However, just as suddenly, Walker recovered and awoke, to tell a strange tale. While he was "dead," his spirit had left his body. He had been above his body, he said, looking down upon it, when suddenly his spirit rose above the mountains like a soaring eagle, and he had flown northward to the Shoshone country, above the plains of Wyoming. There, high in the clouds, Towats spoke to him, saying, "Look down." When he looked, he saw a wagon train crossing the prairie,

wagons which he called "rolling wickiups," and there were many hundreds of them. They were being driven and escorted by men in "high hats" (silk and beaver top-hats) and these, Towats told him, were the men to whom he should show the secret. But not to just to any of them, but to one man among them, one of their leaders, a man of great good whom Towats showed him. "When will this man come?" Walker asked. "Soon," Towats replied.

On 14 June 1849, Chief Walker suddenly appeared in Salt Lake City at the head of a large contingent of Utes, to speak with Brigham Young about the intentions of the Mormons towards his people. As the pipe of peace was being passed around, Walker's eyes fell upon Isaac Morley.

"I have seen you before," the chief told the surprised Mormon patriarch. "I have seen you in a vision. You will come and live among my people. We will be brothers." On 28 October 1849, Isaac Morley set out for the Sanpete Valley with 244 colonists to settle in the midst of the Ute Indians.

Chapter Four

Isaac Morley—One of God's Footsteps

IN JULY 1852, AN AGREEMENT WAS ENTERED into between Brigham Young, President of the Mormon Church, and Walker, Chief of the Sanpete Utes, whereby the secret of the location of a fabulous source of gold, somewhere in the inaccessible reaches of the Uintah Mountains, would be revealed to the Mormon leader, under certain conditions. Only one man, mutually trusted by both sides, would be allowed to know the location of the sacred gold, and to go there to bring back gold for the use of the Church. The man chosen for this unusual mission was Thomas Rhoades. In the ensuing 150 years since that event, this famous gold source has been known as "The Lost Rhoades Mines."

However, more than two years before Thomas Rhoades first set eyes on the fabulous mine—as early as May 1850—another white man had been there, escorted personally by Chief Walker. That man was my third great-grandfather, Isaac Morley. His story is told on these pages for the first time; had it been told sooner, the sacred gold of the Uintahs might be known today as "The Lost Morley Mines."

Isaac Morley was born 11 March 1786 at Montague, Massachusetts, son of Thomas E. Morley (1758-1836) and Editha Marsh (1762-1836). He was well educated in the best schools of Salem, Massachusetts, but was endowed with a pioneer spirit that urged him, in 1810, to venture six hundred miles to the wilderness of the Western

ISAAC MORLEY

Isaac Morley, third great grand-father of author Kerry Ross Boren. Photogragh courtesty.

Utah State Historical Society.

Reserve, a tract of land in what is now the northeast section of the state of Ohio. He constructed a cabin and cleared the land where the town of Kirtland was soon after built, then returned to Montague to marry his childhood sweetheart, Lucy Gunn. Their wedding took place on 20 June 1812, just two days after Congress declared war against Great Britain.

Isaac Morley served as a fifer in the Ohio Militia under Captain Clark Parker, and Generals Wadsworth and Perkins, in the War of 1812, serving from 22 August until 2 October 1812, and again from 1 December 1812 until 27 February 1813, marching to Huron after the surrender of British General Hull.

Of nine children born to Isaac and Lucy Morley at Kirtland, seven grew to maturity—six girls and one boy. A cooper (barrel maker) by trade, Isaac was initially a Presbyterian, but in 1828 was baptized into the Campbellite church by Pastor Sidney Rigdon. Shortly thereafter, Morley, Rigdon and Lyman Wight established their own church, called "The Family," on Morley's farm near Kirtland. A number of families settled there in a communistic society called a "common stock family," sharing all things in common.

In September 1830, four Mormon missionaries—Oliver Cowdery, Parley P. Pratt, Peter Whitmer, Jr., and Ziba Peterson—visited Kirtland, converting many to the new faith. On 15

November 1830, Isaac Morley was baptized and confirmed a member of the Mormon Church by Parley P. Pratt.

In February 1831, the Prophet Joseph Smith came to Kirtland. He and his family lived in the Morley household for some time, until a log house was constructed for their use. Eventually, Isaac donated his entire farm to the up-building of the Church. He remained one of Joseph Smith's closest and most trusted friends until the Prophet's martyrdom at the hands of a mob at Carthage, Illinois, on 27 June 1844.

Isaac Morley followed the Saints throughout the years of their persecutions in Ohio, Missouri and Illinois. He was a prominent Church leader during this period, and founded the towns of Kirtland, Ohio, Far West, Missouri, and Yelrome (Morley, spelled backwards; now Lima), Illinois. He was a participant in many of the significant events of this period, and was imprisoned on several occasions as a Mormon leader hated by the Missourians. At one point he offered his life as a sacrifice for the Saints, but managed to make his escape from jail on the evening prior to his scheduled execution. His courage and integrity were never questioned.

As a colonel in the Nauvoo Legion, Isaac Morley played a pertinent role in suppressing the mob rule which culminated in the murder of Joseph Smith and his brother Hyrum. Afterwards, Morley's house, cooper shop and granary were burned to the ground (10 September 1845) and he fled with his family to Nauvoo. He was instrumental in the completion of construction of the Nauvoo Temple, and there, on 14 January 1846, with Heber C. Kimball officiating, Morley was sealed to two plural (polygamous) wives, Abigail Leonora Snow and Hannah Blakeslee Finch. On 22 January 1846, with Brigham Young officiating, Isaac Morley took four additional wives: Hanna Sibley, Nancy Back, Eleanor Mills and Harriet Cox. He took one other to wife—Betsy B. Pinkham—on 27 January 1846, for a total of eight.

Two of Isaac Morley's daughters, Cordelia Calista and Lucy Diantha, had been sealed as plural wives of Joseph Smith. Before his death, Joseph Smith had asked for the hand of Cordelia, but as she was in love with Frederick Walter Cox,

she declined. She was sealed to the Prophet posthumously, however, on 27 January 1846, by Heber C. Kimball, who married another of Morley's daughters, Theresa. Lucy Diantha Morley (my second great-grandmother) had been sealed to Joseph Smith in 1837, and on 15 September 1838, in Clay County, Missouri, she bore him a child, my great-grandmother, Caroline Delight (Allen).

On 3 February 1846, on the same day that Theresa Morley was sealed to Heber C. Kimball, the latter officiated in a special ceremony in the Nauvoo Temple whereby Isaac Morley and his wife Lucy were "adopted and sealed" to Brigham Young. On the following day, 4 February 1846, Isaac Morley bundled his family into a wagon, crossed the Mississippi River, and started westward with the migrating Saints.

On 3 January 1847, Lucy Gunn Morley died at Winter Quarters, Nebraska, after suffering for two months with typhoid fever. Isaac buried her in the "Mormon graveyard," situated in Florence, Nebraska, next to three of his grandchildren who died from lack of proper food and medical attention. These children belonged to my second great-grandmother, Lucy Diantha, and her husband, Joseph Stewart Allen.

On Wednesday, 7 April 1847, Isaac Morley made the first day's journey with Brigham Young and the original pioneer company en route to the Rocky Mountains. On the following day he was appointed to stay behind in charge of "Summer Quarters," where he remained until 25 January 1848, at which time he was appointed president of the second migration that year.

Isaac Morley's company, consisting of 1,229 souls, 397 wagons, and numerous chattels, left Winter Quarters on 1 May 1848, and after many hardships, arrived in the valley of the Great Salt Lake on 23 September 1848. Morley (who by now was called Father Morley by the Saints who revered him) settled first in Session's Settlement, a few miles north of Salt Lake City, but soon established his own community, "Morley's Settlement," which he later named Bountiful, a name taken from the Book of Mormon. On 16 February 1849, President Brigham Young sustained Isaac Morley as President of the High Council of the newly organized Great Salt Lake City.

On Thursday, 26 April, 1849, a regular fast-day service was conducted in the "Bowery." Even though a strong southerly wind prevailed, many Saints gathered to fast and pray and hear President Morley, Apostle John Taylor, and Patriarch John Smith (uncle of Joseph Smith) speak. During the meeting, the Nauvoo Legion was re-organized and was composed of two cohorts, four regiments in a cohort, two battalions in a regiment, and five companies in a battalion, with Major General Daniel H. Wells in command of the entire legion. Isaac Morley, who had been a full colonel at Nauvoo under Lt. Gen. Joseph Smith, was made lieutenant of a company composed exclusively of men over fifty years of age, called the "Silver Greys." Incidentally, Thomas Rhoades was commissioned First Lieutenant of Company B of the Nauvoo Legion.

Prior to 1 February 1849, the federal government refused to provide any form of government for the Mormons in Utah, being uncertain of their allegiance. Following the Treaty of Guadalupe-Hidalgo, on 2 February 1848, the United States claimed ownership of the northern section of Mexican Territory, which included Utah. The Mormons therefore accepted the responsibility of instituting a provisional government, and beginning on 4 March a constitution for the new "State of Deseret" was drawn up by a committee of ten men, with Albert Carrington as chairman. Isaac Morley proposed the name "Deseret" to Brigham Young, from a Book a Mormon term meaning "honey bee" signifying Mormon industry. The organization of the new state called for a governor; a legislature consisting of two houses— the senate and house of representatives; other state officials, and a judiciary. William W. Potter was appointed the first territorial marshal of the new provisional state. The first election was held 12 March 1849 at the Bowery, the constitution was adopted, and Brigham Young became Governor, Heber C. Kimball became Chief Justice, and Isaac Morley became a Senator.

Our interest in Isaac Morley, as far as the Rhoades Mines are concerned, actually begins when he was chosen to lead the first group of colonizers to settle among the Indians in Sanpete Valley. On 14 June 1849, Chief Walker appeared suddenly in Salt Lake city at the head of a large contingent of Utes, and demanded of Brigham Young to know the Mormons' intentions towards the treatment of his people. Brigham replied diplomatically, "No Indian will be turned from a Mormon's door as long as I remain their chief." Walker was pleased at this response, and suggested that they smoke the pipe of peace. According to Brigham Young, "When Walker had filled his pipe, he offered the Lord the first smoke, pointing the pipe and stepping toward the sun." After recognizing his sun god, Walker passed the peace pipe around the circle of Mormon leaders, and then with the Indians. When the pipe was passed to Father Morley, Chief Walker said to him, "I have seen you before. I have seen you in a vision. You will come and live among my people. We will be brothers."

About two months after the interview with Chief Walker, Brigham Young sent a party, led by Parley P. Pratt and guided by William W. Potter, interpreter, to explore Sanpete Valley and select a suitable site for settlement. The exploring party returned prior to the October 1849 general conference of the Church, and Pratt issued a favorable report for settlement. On the following day, in the first session of conference, the idea of sending a colony to Sanpete was presented to the general membership and unanimously approved. Because of Chief Walker's particular interest in him, Isaac Morley was appointed by Brigham Young to head the colonization effort.

Father Morley chose Seth Taft and Charles Shumway to assist him as ecclesiastical counselors over the families who accompanied them. Nelson Higgins, a veteran of the Mormon Battalion, was selected to take charge of the military responsibilities. The Nauvoo Legion loaned the company a cannon which was towed behind the last wagon. William W. Potter was again selected as the guide and interpreter.

Most of the colonizing families were not selected until the day of departure. On the departure date—28 October 1849—President Brigham Young spoke at a public meeting in Great Salt Lake City to recommend only healthy families enlist, for winter was fast approaching. By noon of that day, the requested thirty volunteer families began the trek to Sanpete, and while passing through Fort Utah (Provo), added twenty more families to the company.

Soon after their departure, the company was met by Chief Walker and some of his subchiefs, who offered to escort the colonists personally to their new home in Sanpete Valley. The Ute chief was sincere about the invitation, and wanted to make a show of his friendliness. He had told Brigham Young on 14 June:

> I was always friendly with the Mormons, as I hear what they say and remember it. It is good to live like the Mormons and their children. I do not care about the land, but I want the Mormons to go and settle it.

During the twenty-six day journey, Chief Walker rode by Morley's side, and the two men developed an abiding trust and friendship with one another. At night the Indians camped by themselves, but Walker frequently visited Morley's tent and they talked long into the night. Father Morley recorded his impressions of the Ute chief in his journal:

> Chief Joseph Walker is one of the most extraordinary of men. His English is quite good, in addition to which he speaks fluent Spanish, which he says he learned from his mother, a Pi-Ute woman who was raised by Spanish priests in a mission in the Sierra Nevada country, until stolen in a raid by Walker's father many years ago. He also speaks many Indian dialects, including the Ute, Shoshone, Navajo, Gosh-Ute and Pi-Ute, as well as some California tribes I cannot recognize...Tonight he came by my tent with an offering of roast venison shank. I took it as an excuse to talk, which he did until well after the midnight hour. We have become quite good friends, and I judge him to be a man of his word in all matters of honor...[*Journal of Isaac Morley*, ms. unpub., possession of the author]

At this early date, Chief Walker was still referred to by his Christian given name, "Joseph Walker." By his direction the colonists passed south to where the present city of Nephi stands, at

which point they turned east through Salt Creek Canyon, which opens to form the Sanpete Valley. The canyon offered the greatest obstacle yet, every abrupt turn giving the appearance of a dead end. With pick and shovel they filled in gullies and leveled projections, with the men walking and the women driving the teams. By the greatest of effort they were at last through Salt Creek Canyon and they pitched their tents for the first time in Sanpete Valley on 21 November 1849. Charles Shumway discovered a spring, ever after called "Shumway Spring," and camped next to it, suggesting to Father Morley that the location become their permanent settlement, but no decision was made that night.

The following morning, Morley called a council meeting to determine the exact location of the new settlement. He was not content with the location at Shumway Spring and felt constrained to proceed about three miles southward. Pointing a prophetic finger at an eminence rising in the distance, he said, "There is the termination of our journey in close proximity of that hill. God be willing, we will build our city (there)." Other men in the company were dissatisfied with the choice. Seth Taft gave vent to his feeling by exclaiming, "This is only a long, narrow canyon, and not even a jack-rabbit could exist on its desert soil!" But Father Morley was unshakable, saying, "This is our God-appointed abiding place; and stay I will, though but ten men remain with me."

The dissension and dissatisfaction among a certain faction of the pioneers stemmed from the difficult journey. Captain Higgins' infant daughter had died a few days after they left the Salt Creek Canyon encampment, and Sister Mary Lowery had severely fractured her ankle at the same camp. "Thop" Shoemaker, a well-liked young man, died shortly after the company arrived on City Creek.

By the evening of 22 November the pioneers reached the termination of their journey in close proximity of the hill. Here a second council meeting was held to conclude the matter as to where they would settle. Seth Taft, Nelson Higgins and several other men expressed anxiety at the desolation of the place, and tried to convince the company to continue farther south. After they had had their say, Father Morley once again arose and solemnly spoke, some have said with "little less than inspiration," saying, "We behold the stake driven by P(arly) P. Pratt in his exploration of this valley, this is our God-appointed abiding place."

Whereas individual families had scattered their camps, on 24 November Father Morley requested that every family locate on the south side of "Temple Hill." All but four or five families complied with the request, those few remaining on the banks of City Creek rather than to carry water in buckets 150 yards to the camp.

There was a compelling reason why Isaac Morley chose Temple Hill as the site of the new city. Chief Walker had pointed out the hill as being sacred to the Utes. His ancestors, he explained, the "Old Ones," once had an altar on the hill's crest where human sacrifices were performed. Morley inquired whether there were any remains of the stone altar still visible, but the chief said there was not. There were caverns beneath the hill, however, he said. Morley's curiosity was instantly piqued and he asked Walker to show him the caverns, but the chief balked: "Heap bad place," he said fearfully. "You no go there—never come out!"

"Why is it dangerous?" asked Morley. "Are there evil spirits there?"

"Worse," said Walker. "You will see when the warm weather comes." He would elaborate no further. Shortly thereafter he and his people departed while the colonists settled in for the winter.

Father Morley pondered the words of Chief Walker for some time. Something about the story of stone altars and sacrifice struck a familiar chord. A learned scholar of the Book of Mormon, he searched its pages for a clue. As last he found what he was looking for in Alma 1:15:

> And it came to pass that they took him; and his name was Nehor; and they carried him upon the top of the hill Manti, and there he was caused, or rather did acknowledge, between the heavens and the earth, that what he had taught to the people was contrary to the word of God; and there he suffered an ignominious death.

Father Morley, being devoutly religious and a strong adherent to the teachings of the Book of Mormon, recorded in his journal:

> …No sooner had I read this passage than I recognized the place as the very hill where the Nephites had sacrificed Nehor on the sacrificial altar for the sake of the preservation of the ancient Church. Here once an ancient temple stood, and here one day again would stand another in these Last Days…This was, even as Chief Joseph Walker said, a sacred hill, and so I called the place Manti, even as it was called in days gone by…

During the first winter at Sanpete Valley, the settlers lived in three types of shelters. A very few had time to erect log cabins before the snow became too deep for gathering logs. A few families turned their wagon boxes on end with canvas covers stretched across them for wind breaks, but they suffered greatly from the penetrating cold. The majority of the colonists, including Isaac Morley, made dugouts in the south side of Temple Hill.

On 13 December 1849, Chief Walker, who had left the colonists upon their arrival at the Sanpete location, returned with several hundred members of his tribe to establish a camp about one mile north from the place where the Mormons were located. The Indians also suffered greatly from the intense cold of that winter, saying it was the worst they could remember.

Although short of food themselves, at the suggestion of Father Morley the colonists permitted the Indians to retrieve the frozen carcasses of cattle which died regularly, which brought the Mormon leader even further esteem from Walker and his people. The cattle were dying faster than they could be saved, as snow lay three feet over the grass beneath. The men made a desperate attempt to save the livestock by uncovering pasture with hand shovels, but they became snowblind and had to be led to their labors by younger boys whose eyes had not been affected. Wily Chief Walker, who benefitted from the dead livestock, stood by watching silently, failing to mention to the colonists that the Indians had burned the dry grass shortly before their arrival. Of the 250 cattle brought into Sanpete Valley in November, only 100 remained alive when the snow melted.

In January 1850, Father Morley dispatched a party of twelve men, led by the experienced guide William W. Potter to bring supplies from Church headquarters. On their return they became embroiled in an Indian uprising at Fort Utah, led by Big Elk, one of Walker's renegade subchiefs who resented the encroachment of the Mormons. Following this battle, the supply party continued its journey, but soon became snowbound in Salt Creek Canyon. Tabionah (Chief Tabby), one of Walker's brothers, found the destitute men and led one of them, Elijah Barney Ward, to the Sanpete settlement.

Chief Tabiyuna (Tabby).

Courtesy Utah State Historical soiety.

President Morley and a few other men strapped snow shoes onto their boots and went to their rescue. The supply wagons remained snowbound until 1 March 1850, but in the meantime supplies were hauled on hand sleds back to the settlement in quantities sufficient to sustain the needs of the colonists. Morley noted in his journal:

> Contrary to the stories told about the Indian people being thieves, we have found them to be scrupulously honest in their every dealing with us. When they could have raided the supply wagons at Salt Creek Canyon and depleted our stores to their benefit, they instead maintained a guard over it in our behalf, and helped in every way to assist us, for the few rations we could spare them for their efforts. Chief Joseph Walker, while known to take advantage of any good opportunity to help his people, even to the extent of employing certain wiles, is otherwise a most honorable and trustworthy representative of his race, that even many of our own would do well to emulate...

On one extremely cold January night, two babies were born and wrapped in a single cow hide to keep them from freezing to death. Some discontent arose from the Shumway faction once again as to the conditions. Father Morley exhorted the settlers to diligence, faithfulness in their individual and family prayers, and good works."Put the Lord to the test and receive the blessing earned," he would say. One of the colonists boldly rejected the counsel, saying, "Neither God, angels or Brigham Young had anything to do in locating this place." When other more serious charges were brought against this transgressor, he was excommunicated from the Church on 27 January and fined twenty-five dollars.

On 20 February, Isaac Morley reported to Brigham Young:

> We are in as good circumstances as could be expected with the measles in our midst and living on "Mormon" fare (United Order— all things in common) which you well understand. The measles have made a general sweep through this part of the country and many of the natives have died. When Walker came within two days travel of our company, he sent for me. I met him eight miles out and gave medicine to twenty-four of his people on the first visit. Arropine's child, which was then dying, as I thought, lived until the next day and died on the way to this place. In obedience to counsel, I have attended them ever since. They have died, but only one under my care. Walker says that the Sanpitches would all have died, and many of his men, too, had we not been here. Four deaths have occurred in the camp since we arrived, namely Nelson Higgin's youngest child, Mr. Shoemaker's

son (about 17 years old), John Warner's child which died at birth, and Bro. Cable's daughter. The sick got better, but met with a relapse from exposure.

(Although hard times have prevailed,) the prospects are brightening and the thermometer this morning stands at 39 degrees F. ...We draw our wood on hand sleds a half a mile—good wood and enough of it, too. Pine trees are plentiful within four or five miles of us. We are erecting a school house 20 by 26 feet of beautiful pine logs, which I think will be finished in a few days.

Mr. Barney Ward arrived here yesterday, bringing the express from Gen. Daniel H. Wells, giving an account of the battle fought in Utah Valley the day before he left. We called a council and invited Walker, who came with his attendants. The case was made known to him through Mr. Ward. (Walker) said, "Let them fight it out; all is right; if your big captain does not interfere, I will not; all is right; the Utes are bad; they will not take my counsel; they have killed my son Battee. I feel bad. I want them (the Mormons) to make me some presents of guns, blankets, etc., and I will be satisfied. I want the Mormons to stay here and plant and sow, and do us good, and we will be friends. If the Utes will fight and be killed, it is all right."

We all parted with good feelings and friendship.

Chief Walker instructed Arapeen and the rest of his tribe in that region not to fight the Mormons, but to come and eat their bread, or "tiegup" (the Ute term for food acquired by

Chief Wakara (Walker).

Courtesy Utah State Historical Society.

persistent begging). Walker was willing to trade valuable furs, oxen or ponies for "tiegup," but Morley refused to accept them, giving him the supplies as a token of friendship. Morley wrote to Brigham Young: "It seems to be a trying time all around, and those who have the most wisdom can make a display of it for the most good."

Walker felt a deep sense of friendship and indebtedness to this extremely kind and generous man. He came to him one day and warned him about a band of renegade warriors in his tribe who wished to kill the Mormons. He admonished the colonists not to travel in groups smaller than eight or ten and always to be well armed.

During the latter part of February 1850, there occurred an incident which threatened to sever the close friendship between Chief Walker and Isaac Morley. The story has been preserved by Isaac Morley Allen, a grandson of Father Morley. The conflict arose over a tribal custom which Morley found unacceptable.

Chief Walker's mother, Tishum Igh, was a small, wrinkled old woman, who had reached an age when she was no longer productive, and had to be cared for by the rest of the starving tribe. According to tribal custom, she must die to make way for others. A common practice among the Utes was to lasso the oldest squaws in the tribe, and then lock them up to starve to death. On this particular occasion, Walker decided to kill his mother in order to end her suffering more quickly.

The chief brutally attacked her with his fists and a knife, each blow landing soundly on her skull, anyone of which might have ended a person's life; but Tishum Igh was a leathery tough old woman who had weathered many a hardship, and was stronger than the average soul. She managed to make good her escape by slipping from her son's grasp and hid in the bulrushes of Sanpitch Swamp for several days.

Father Morley found her there and tried to get her to come stay with him, but she would not; she did, however, accept some "tiegup" from him on which to subsist. Morley went directly to Chief Walker's wickiup and counseled him to take his old mother back and care for her. Walker sat in grim silence, his arms folded stubbornly.

"You have told me you wanted to be like the Mormons," Morley argued, "and adopt the Mormon way of life. Mormons do not kill their mothers, nor leave them to die of starvation. You have read the Book of Mormon; you said you believed its teachings. The Book of Mormon says we must have mercy upon the poor and honor our father and our mother. You must have mercy on your old mother and let her come back to your village."

"You know nothing of the customs of my people," Walker said sternly. "Do you think only Mormons know what is best?" Stubbornly then, he would speak no more, and Morley left. A few days later Tishum Igh crawled back to the wickiups where Walker let her eke out a tentative existence.

Nothing more came of the matter until about 1 March 1850, when Walker rode his white horse up to the door of Morley's dugout and demanded that the one-year-old son of Father Morley by his plural wife, Hannah Blakeslee Finch, be handed over to him. The boy, Thomas Simeon Morley (12 June 1849-9 March 1853), a big-eyed and curly-haired lad, was Father Morley's pride, a son of his old age, as Walker was well aware. Morley demanded to know why the request was being made, to which Walker replied that it was a whim of his squaw to have a boy.

"Take bread or beef instead of my papoose," Morley pleaded, but Walker would have none of it. Hannah Morley began to cry.

"You will give Walker the papoose," the chief said sternly, "or Walker will kill all of the Mormonee in Sanpete Valley." He leaped down from his horse and stepped forward to take the child from his father's arms. Hannah fainted.

"If you will leave my papoose with his mother," Morley pleaded, "and do no harm to the settlers in Sanpete, you may take my life if I have offended you."

"I do not care about your life," spat Walker. "Walker want the papoose."

His family pleaded with him not to give up the boy to Walker, but with tears in his eyes, Father Morley handed the child over to the chief, saying to his grieving family, "It is better to lose our baby than the whole settlement and the boy too." Walker took the crying child in his arms, leaped upon his horse, wheeled, and rode away with his waiting braves.

Father Morley encouraged his distraught wife to have faith that the Indians would not harm little Simeon. Hannah had no faith in the crafty Ute chieftain and was certain that her baby would be killed or would die of exposure, but together they prayed throughout the long night for their son's safety. Two weeks passed and not a single Indian was seen in the area. Then, at day-break on 13 March 1850, Walker and his band rode into the settlement and directly to Morley's dugout.

Little Simeon, dressed in buckskins, his face painted white with red stripes, and wearing a headband with a single feather in it, was tied onto the back of a small pony. Walker, in contrast to his attitude of a fortnight earlier when he had taken the boy, now wore a broad smile on his handsome, high-cheekboned face.

"Walker bring your papoose home," he said, "All is right."

"Why have you brought him back to us?" asked Morley, hugging the boy tightly in his arms.

"Your squaw feel bad," replied Walker. "We bring him back." Walker's squaw was quick to explain to the boy's mother, "He laid in my arms all night and sleep tight."

"You keep the pony for your papoose," Walker added. "All is right."

And all was right. Morley was well aware that the wily chieftain had used the incident as a kind of test, and when the Mormon leader sent no militia to recover the child, it was concluded that Morley was a man of honor who could be trusted, and who lived the precepts he taught. Now Walker had another surprise in store for Morley: he announced that he was ready to be baptized for the remission of his sins, and had convinced his brother Arapeen and others to do likewise.

On 13 March 1850, Chief Walker and his brother Arapeen waded into the ice-choked waters of City Creek and submitted to immersion under the trusted hands of Isaac Morley. Walker became the first of his people to be confirmed a member of the Mormon Church. Several other distinguished "Lamanites" entered the baptismal waters on 20 March, after which President Morley wrote to Brigham Young:

> The door is opened and they are coming in, with expression of good feelings, and kindness as could probably be expected from uncultivated minds. A stone from the quarry needs polishing to become useful, and we believe there are some here that may be made, (with watchful care) to shine as bright gems in the Temple of the Lord, yes, stars that may spread their twinkling light to distant tribes...We feel to say that there never was a mission opened with brighter prospects to the scattered children of Ephraim than the one in which we are engaged, and shouldn't be willing to leave unless called away by as good authority as that by which we were sent here. Did we come here to enrich ourselves in the things of this world? No. We were sent to enrich the Natives, and comfort the hearts of the long, long, oppressed. Let us try the experiment and if we fail to accomplish the object, then say, boys come away. Amen.

Charles Shumway and a few other brethren arrived in Salt Lake City on 23 March, bearing this letter written by Father Morley. On the following day, a special Sabbath meeting was called in the Bowery where the letter was read to the congregation. The clerk who took minutes of the proceedings recorded that, "The (Manti) settlers, notwithstanding their limited supply of provisions, could not refrain from administering to the Indians, who would sometimes cry with hunger."

Shumway addressed the meeting and supplied in more detail the condition of the settlers in Manti. President Young called for assistance in the form of cattle, wagons, and any other neces-sity that could be gathered and dispatched to their suffering brethren. The supplies reached Manti by mid-April and were greatly welcomed by the colonists emerging from their first terrible winter season in Sanpete Valley.

While Charles Shumway was in Salt Lake City, in private conference with Brigham Young, he complained that Morley paid more attention to the needs of the Indians than he did the settlers under his charge. But this complaint had little effect on the Church leader, for the First Presidency wrote its Third General Epistle on 12 April, in which reference was made to the Sanpete settlement by saying, "The citizens have laid the foundation of a great and glorious work." The Presidency dwelt on the accomplishments under Morley's direction and prophesied that those who persevere to the end in following the counsels of heaven will be a thousand fold richer than those who leave to search for gold, as many Mormons were then planning.

By this time spring weather had arrived early in Sanpete Valley. By 23 March the snow had nearly disappeared and the colonists discovered that water had soaked three feet into the ground. They began digging irrigation ditches, ploughing and planting.

Then, on an evening of a certain warm day, the settlers were disagreeably confronted from every direction by a loud hissing and rattling from snakes. Upon awakening from hibernation, hundreds of rattlesnakes had made their way unnoticed from caves situated above the dugouts in Temple Hill, and were suddenly in the colony.

Rattlesnakes are most dangerous when awakening from a comatose hibernation because they are temporarily blind and will strike at anything that moves. The spotted serpents were seen twisting and coiling over practically every rock on the hillside, and many were already under foot. The men immediately armed themselves with pine knot torches and began the battle of extermination. One settler killed thirty in a matter of a few minutes, and the total of the first night's slaughter was over five hundred!

The extermination continued for several evenings before the crisis ended. Since rattlesnakes travel during the early evening, it was not uncommon for the colonists to awaken in the morning to find a rattlesnake curled on the foot of the bed or in a cupboard. "They invaded our homes with as little compunction as the plagues of Egypt did the palace of Pharaoh," wrote one settler. While horses and cattle were bitten, not one settler was poisoned by the invading horde.

Chief Walker rode into the camp at the head of a contingent of his band to gather dead snakes, which the Utes considered a delicacy. Approaching Father Morley, Walker grinned broadly. "You still want to visit caves in hill?" he asked.

Morley's close friendship with Walker was proving a strong protection for the settlers of Sanpete. On 17 April 1850, Isaac Morley wrote a letter to Brigham Young and the quorum of Twelve Apostles, explaining that Walker and Arapeen were chastising and killing Indians who persisted in killing Mormon cattle. Arapeen shot and killed Toy-a-ump, one of his fellow tribesmen, for butchering two oxen belonging to the Mormons. A young man named John Baker, who guarded the supply wagons, gave two of the Utes some gunpowder as a token of friendship, and was murdered by them as a reward. When Morley informed Walker of this incident, he became livid with rage, swearing to avenge young Baker's death upon the perpetrators.

After joining the Church, Chief Walker found himself losing control of his fiery warriors who now considered him a "squaw" and a puppet in the hands of the Mormons. Walker's brother, Pat-sow-e-ett (Sowiette), with other chiefs, challenged Walker's leadership, and he became constantly fearful of attack. On 21 April, Sowiette returned from a raid into Utah Valley where he killed two horses, two mules, and six cattle belonging to Mormon settlers. But Sowiette was not only killing the cattle of the Mormons, but those of Walker as well. Walker came to Morley one day and asked him if the Mormons would execute Pat-sow-e-ett, Un-ker-wen-det and Tis-u-nah, so he could sleep in peace.

Chapter Five

The Mormon and the Money-Rock

THE BOND OF FRIENDSHIP AND TRUST between Isaac Morley and Chief Walker was at its apex at the time of Walker's baptism. Then, sometime shortly after this event, Chief Walker came alone to Morley's newly-built log cabin and asked to talk to him in private. Morley sent his family away to a neighbor's house while he spoke in secret with the solemn chief. Morley recorded the event in his journal—an event destined to change the course of history.

> ...Walker appeared to be very nervous and uncertain. He never seemed comfortable indoors, and at first I attributed it to this, but there was something different in his demeanor that I could not discern the meaning of. "I will show you something," he said, removing a small buckskin pouch tied on a long leather thong about his neck. He dumped the contents onto the table-top. Even in the dim light I could see that the pile of thumb-sized rocks were gleaming with yellow color, and I recognized it immediately as being as pure gold as I had ever seen. Walker called it "money-rock," and I was quite surprised at his casual attitude towards the great fortune before him.

Morley asked the chief why he allowed his people to suffer want if he had so much wealth at his disposal, to which Walker replied that the gold belonged to Towats, and was therefore sacred. The place where the gold was hidden was protected by Towats, he said, and Indians were forbidden to go there.

Walker recited the long history of the gold of Carre-Shinob, then informed Father Morley that he had once seen a vision in which the great Towats had appeared to him, telling him that when the "high hats" came, he should give the gold to them. He had also seen Morley in his vision, he said, and Towats had told him that this was the man to whom he should reveal the secret. "I will show you where is money-rock," he told the Mormon leader.

Walker offered the gold to Morley for his own use and for the betterment of the Mormon settlers in Sanpete Valley, but he declined to accept any gold for himself; for one thing, Brigham Young had threatened to excommunicate any Mormon who pursued the gold fields; for another, he considered himself Morley's friend, and "...did not feel as though I should profit by our friendship."

Assuming that Walker had access to gold other than that which he displayed from the pouch, Morley convinced the chief that if such a source did indeed exist, it should be given to the Mormon Chief, Brigham Young, for the benefit of all the Mormons. Inasmuch as the Mormon Chief was a prophet, a shaman, of the great Towats, said Morley, he should be the one to rightfully possess the gold.

Walker reluctantly agreed to provide the gold to Brigham Young, under certain conditions, but first he would take Morley to Carre-Shinob, both to verify its existence to him and because Towats had commanded it. Morley protested that he was growing too old to go traipsing around the mountains, but Walker was insistent; they would go, he said, as soon as the snow melted in the high country, which, due to an early spring thaw, should be sometime in May. In the meantime, preparations would be made.

Isaac Morley wrote promptly to Brigham Young; the letter is undated, written in apparent haste, probably sometime before 20 March, and was one of the sealed letters which Charles Shumway delivered into Brigham Young's hands on 23 March. The letter is on file in the archives of the Mormon Church, inaccessible to the public. Its contents are revealed here for the first time:

…Thinking this to be a matter of the utmost urgency, and for your eyes only, I remit this letter among those sealed as matters of intelligence concerning the Natives of this place. Walker has this day come to see me, bringing with him a pouch of what appears to be the purest gold, in the form of nuggets uniformly the size of the nail of the thumb or larger. He reports these to have come from an ancient mine somewhere high in the mountains to the east of this place, and has offered to take me there, and to give me the gold on the basis of our friendship. He tells a marvelous story of a vision, in which the spirit of Towats appeared to him, making him the keeper of the "money-rock," as he calls it, until the Mormons came, at which time he was told to give it to them. He perceives, somehow, that I am the man that Towats chose to have the gold, but I have managed to convince him that you, as the great Mormon Chief, should have it, and he is willing that it should be so…

I firmly believe in the truth of Walker's statement that such a mine does exist somewhere in the mountains, and I am willing to go with him there to verify it, if you see it in your wisdom for me to do so. Walker says the trip will take two or three weeks, as soon as the snow melts in the mountain passes. The snow goes daily here in the valleys, and should be gone in the high country before a month or two has passed…

The door is opened for a marvelous work in these last days, and an expression of good feelings from Walker has given us the prospect of filling the bellies of the Saints with food and our temples with decorations befitting the Lord of Solomon. If the mine is as rich as Walker purports it to be, then might our temple rival even that of Solomon's in its richness…

I would never permit others to enrich themselves, nor would I enrich myself, at the expense of the Natives who daily perish from cold and hunger and disease. It is my fervent hope that the Lord of Hosts has chosen me as a means to bring forth this wealth for His purpose, that His people, red and white alike, may be relieved of their suffering…

Walker will do nothing until hearing from you, which I pray will be by return messenger, for it is the nature of the uncivilized mind to forever change…

In retrospect, it appears that Morley was making allusions to the mines in his "open" letter to Brigham Young of the same date, read to the Saints in the meeting at the Bowery on Sunday, 24 March 1850; therein he alludes to the Indians being made "to shine as bright gems in the Temple of the Lord." Moreover, he states: "Did we come here to enrich ourselves in the things of this world? No. We were sent to enrich the Natives…"

It is noteworthy that not long after receiving Morley's letter, Brigham Young delivered his directive against Mormons seeking after gold, saying, "I hope that the gold mines will never get closer than 800 miles, as even now a few have caught the gold fever. I have counseled them and other saints to remain in these valleys and make improvements, to build comfortable houses and raise grain."

But Brigham Young did not direct Isaac Morley to remain in the valleys. While there is no known copy of Brigham Young's response to Morley, we get a sense of it in an excerpt from Father Morley's journal, dated 14 April 1850:

> Today received a letter in hand from Pres. Young and the First Presidency, commending me for the progress of the Sanpete settlement and requesting shingles for the Council House of Great Salt Lake City…Pres. Young has written to Walker, and I have sent word for him to come in that I may read it to him. Having full authority from Pres. Young to proceed to the mine, I will make the necessary preparations with Walker when he arrives. He is anxious to leave for the mountains soon, as Sowlett and other members of his tribe daily threaten his life.

Around the first of May 1850, Walker notified Morley that he would be ready to go to the Sacred Mine within one or two weeks, but that first Father Morley must come to the Indian camp, several miles north of the Mormon settlement, to undergo a "purification" rite. They could not go near the gold of Carre-Shinob unless precautions were taken to ward off evil spirits which might follow them, or might be waiting there. "Walker told me," wrote Morley, "that evil spirits sometimes take the form of a panther, and follow their trail; a bear, however, is considered to be a sign of the protection of Towats."

A sweat lodge had been erected near a spring in a grove of pines. The leading Utes of Walker's band, including his brother Arapeen, had gathered to participate in the cleansing, though not all of them would accompany them on their sacred journey.

Inside the lodge, cold water was poured over heated rocks to create steam, and the men, stripped to their skin, went inside. Father Morley, unaccustomed to displaying his nakedness publicly, was the last to enter. As he stood before the circle of solemn Utes, he noted that they were looking intently at his genitals. He asked Walker if something was wrong.

"You are different," the chief replied, "Not like us." He pointed at Morley's penis.

"It is called circumcision," Morley explained.

"Did you have accident?" Walker inquired curiously. "Mebbe a wound in battle?"

Morley explained that it was a religious custom, to cause all good and righteous men to look like Jesus.

"If Jesus had this done, then it is good for Utes to do it and look like Jesus," Walker reasoned.

"I think baptism is enough," Morley counseled. Walker appeared to be offended. He insisted that if Jesus looked like this, and Morley had it done to look like Jesus, then Walker, as a great chief of the Utes, should look like this too. At last Morley agreed that it was the right thing to do.

Walker retrieved his hunting knife and handed it to Morley, urging him to perform the ceremony, but Morley declined, saying he had no experience in such matters. Walker then turned to his brother Arapeen, who backed away uncertainly, his eyes wide with fear. Walker realized that, as chief, he would have to set the example, and he was determined to do so.

"I will be the first to look like Jesus," said Walker, pinching his foreskin between his thumb and finger. With a quick slice of his knife, he cut it free. "He stood there," wrote Morley, "a broad grin on his face, with blood trickling down his bare legs, holding the trophy aloft for all to see—his badge of courage."

Chief Walker proceeded around the circle of men, beginning with Arapeen, and as they held their foreskin taut, he sliced each one away. The braves endured the ceremony without a single protest, not wanting to be less courageous than their chief. Walker collected the foreskins—23 in all—and stretched them around willow rings to dry. "Thereafter," recorded Morley, "each man carried the strange trophy in his medicine bag, as a sign of favor from Towats."

Two weeks later, everything had apparently healed sufficiently for Walker to make the journey into the high Uintahs, for on 13 May 1850, Morley wrote in his journal: "This morning before sunrise, I left Sanpete (Valley) in the company of Walker, Un-gas-ton-igats, Poonch, and Arropine for the sacred mine of the Indians." This affords us the identity of at least four Utes who knew the location of the Sacred Mine.

Isaac Morley recorded the route taken out of Sanpete Valley as being through Salt Creek Canyon and "eastward over Sanpete Mountain." Unfortunately, being unfamiliar with the country thereafter, he leaves us few recognizable names of places; however, his journal offers some interesting descriptions of the route taken:

> …(from Sanpete Mountain) we turned northeasterly, traveling all of one day and into part of one night, so that after dark I saw but little in the way of landmarks. On the morning of the third day, leaving our night camp in a grove of aspen, we emerged from a large ravine which wound like a snake for several miles onto a dry plateau. Here, for the first time, I beheld the snow-crested peaks of the Uintah mountains (which Walker calls—"Winty") to the north, which I had observed several years since to our south while crossing the Plains near Bridger's Fort…

> On the evening of the fifth day we camped near a cold stream which tumbles off the mountains in levels, like stairs, where Poonch made a willow trap and caught us several trout for supper. Next to our camp was an old trail between trees with curious markings on them, which Walker said were carved there by the Mexicans in the time of

his grandfather, who the Mexicans called "Saint Peter" or Pedro...

Walker recounted an interesting story of a party of these Mexicans who brought gold from the Indian mine on burros into the valley south of Sanpete some three years since—about the time the Mormons first arrived in Zion. The Mexicans were all killed in their camp and the gold returned to the Indian mine along this very trail. After the gold was thrown back into the bowels of the mine, the Indians took the burros away and slew them, in order to keep their spirits from divulging the mine's location. As I was told this story, I could not refrain from wondering, or at least pondering, that if they would dispose of a burro for any uncivilized reason, how easy would it be to do the same to a white man like myself, worth much less to them than a burro? At night my prayers reflect my fears, and I am always surprised when in the morning I awaken alive and well...

On the sixth day we arrived at a large alpine lake, after meandering through timber for many hours. We skirted the south shore and climbed a low pass between two large buttes protruding above the timber line, and covered, as is most of this high country, with layers of rocks. Beyond the pass we traveled all day through alternating meadows and trees, the meadows being deep and wet from melting snows...

On the seventh day we crossed the largest crest and dropped swiftly down the northern slope, past some vermillion cliffs to our right (east), then through heavy timber for two hours. We emerged at the foot of a large formation which I named "The Two Sisters," where a fault has rended the cliffs, leaving a huge crack between two large formations resembling, I thought, women, but Walker prefers to think of them as bears, guardians of the entrance to the sacred Indian mine...

Entering between the Two Sisters, we left our horses in a lush meadow, and ascended what appears to be an ancient trail, which climbs abruptly to a promontory whereby one can see the country both north and south for many miles with unobstructed view...

The entrance to the Indian mine lies just beyond this place, but Un-gas-ton-igats, Arropine, and Poonch would go no further, having a superstitious aversion to the mine itself; and so, following close behind Walker, who alone dared go further, I found myself soon ascending the steepest trail of our journey, where no horse could ascend or descend, but which might have been negotiated by a burro or mule...

[The author has chosen to omit further description from Isaac Morley's journal concerning the mine in the interest of the Ute Indian people].

By the first week of June 1850, Isaac Morley had returned to Sanpete Valley, in possession of 58 pounds of almost pure gold. On June 9th he ordained Chief Walker an Elder in the Melchizedek Priesthood, the first of his tribe to be so honored.

On 19 June, William W. Potter, Barney Ward, Nelson Higgins and M.D. Hamilton arrived in Salt Lake City from Manti with four loads of ten thousand shingles each. The Church-owned *Deseret News* of 22 June records their arrival:

> Bros. M.D. Hamilton, Potter, and others arrived from San-Pete on Wednesday, bringing shingles and lumber, in search of a little more flour, &c. They report health, peace, and prosperity; late frosts; and crops doing well.

Potter brought with him something more than shingles; in his charge was the 58 pounds of gold to be delivered personally to Brigham Young. Potter, was next to Morley himself, the most trusted man in Walker's circle of white friends. Not long before, William Potter and Barney Ward had discovered gold on the Sevier River, but President Young had suppressed news of it, fearing a gold rush. Now he was entrusted with another secret concerning gold which, if revealed, would surpass anything that California had experienced since the discovery of gold at Sutter's Mill.

Brigham Young put the gold to good use. During the summer of 1849, one dollar bills had been issued and signed by Brigham Young, Heber C. Kimball, and Thomas Bullock, clerk. The paper currency was based upon a promissary note, the Church having nothing in its treasury with which to support it.

Late in the fall of 1849, at about the time Isaac Morley led the colonizers to Sanpete Valley, Thomas Rhoades arrived from California and paid a tithing of $17,000 in gold dust gleaned from Sutter's Mill. With this gold dust, Brigham Young began the coinage of gold coins, best known as "Mormon Money." John M. Kay and Willard Richards, under the supervision of Thomas Bullock, established the "Deseret Mint" in the home of Dr. William Sharp, dentist. The gold coins produced were cast in the values of $2.50 to $20.00, and were engraved on one side with an emblem of "clasped hands," surrounded by the official engraving title and value amount, while the obverse was engraved with the "all-seeing eye," surrounded by the logo, "Holiness To The Lord."

By late in the year 1850 and continuing for several years thereafter, an abundance of these gold coins began to circulate, and there was great speculation about the source of the metal used. The Church remained silent, and continued silent on the topic for nearly 150 years.

On 7 July 1850, Isaac Morley officiated at the dedication of a new bowery in Manti, at which Chief Walker attended with over 200 members of his tribe. During the course of his speech, Father Morley gave instructions to the settlers regarding future dealings with the Indians, and challenged Walker's people to accept baptism. So great was their esteem for Morley by this time, 120 Utes were baptized under his hands on this occasion, "causing all the Saints to rejoice."

On 28 July 1850, the First Presidency wrote a letter to Orson Hyde in Kanesville, giving details of a recent visit from Father Morley, which included a flattering account of Manti's prospects for an abundant harvest. Three days later, on 31 July, George Albert Smith wrote to Orson Pratt advising him of Brother Morley's visit, adding that "He is in favor of keeping up the settlement, and wishes to have its numbers increased."

Brigham Young left Salt Lake City on 31 July for a personal visit at Sanpete, where he arrived on Sunday, 4 August, averaging 27 miles a day with a meeting at Fort Utah en route. To welcome the Church leader, Manti's only cannon was fired in salute from atop Temple Hill.

On the day following his arrival, Brigham was escorted by Morley and others to sample the trout fishing, and in the afternoon he officially christened the settlement, giving it the name "Manti" as suggested by Morley. President Young also dedicated the hill above the settlement as a future site for a temple, based upon Morley's opinion that it was once the site of an ancient Nephite temple.

At two o'clock Wednesday afternoon (7 August), a special picnic preceded festivities at the Sanpete Fort (a cluster of cabins, tents and wagons built sufficiently close together to provide protection). At 5 p.m., after an hour of heavy wind and rain, the meeting was moved into the multi-purpose school, chapel, and city hall. Brigham Young was the first speaker, followed by Heber C. Kimball, Newell K. Whitney, and Isaac Morley. Brigham Young's entourage left Manti on 8 August, and arrived in Salt Lake City on 12 August.

The foregoing account is the official version, recorded 12 August 1850 in Brigham Young's "Journal History." However, Morley's private journal informs us that Brigham's trout fishing trip was a ruse which afforded him an opportunity to council privately with Chief Walker. William Potter served as the interpreter, for though Walker spoke English, he generally preferred to negotiate in his own language for the benefit of his sub-chiefs. The Mormon leader and the Ute chieftain discussed the possibility of bringing more gold out of the mountains for the use of the Church. Young explained that the gold would be used for a sacred purpose for which Towats would be pleased, for adornment of a temple in His honor, and to make a statue which would stand atop the House of Towats in Salt Lake City.

Chief Walker was happy to please Towats and the great chief Brigham, but he imposed specific conditions on further retrieval of gold from the Sacred Mine. The location of the gold would be revealed to only one man, mutually trusted by Brigham Young and Chief Walker— not even Brigham Young was to know the location of the mine. The penalty of death would be imposed upon the man chosen to retrieve the gold should he reveal the location to any other person without permission from the Utes; any white man who attempted to follow the chosen man would also suffer death. Finally, the Indians would at no time assist in the removal of the gold, and the man chosen must take only as much as was needed in one trip at a time—no mining operation would be allowed.

Brigham Young accepted the conditions, and Walker immediately nominated Isaac Morley as the man to retrieve the gold, and Brigham concurred that he would be the logical choice, but Morley himself declined, saying that "my advancing age (he was then 64) making it unlikely that I could endure such rigorous journeys as the mission required." Brigham then asked for more time to find a man who would be acceptable to both parties, and the meeting concluded with gifts being presented to the chief and his entourage.

The semi-annual conference of the Church began on 6 September, about one month earlier than usual, wherein President Young outlined the propriety of strengthening the Manti settlement. Isaac Morley had come up from Manti and was the first speaker in the opening session. After expressing gratitude for the privilege of meeting with the main body of the Saints, he declared: "My heart is full of blessings for the people...I want a company of good men and women to go to Sanpete, and I do say that no man shall dwell in that valley who is in the habit of taking the name of God in vain."

As soon as Father Morley had concluded his address, President Young stood and inquired: "I have it in my heart to ask the congregation, if Father Morley shall have the right and privilege to select such men as he wishes to go there?" The assembly carried the motion and moved that he select one hundred men, with or without families, which motion was carried. Brigham Young, who now expressed uncommon interest in Morley's settlement because of the gold connection, then said to the congregation:

> It is a good a valley as you ever saw; the goodness of the soil cannot be beat. There is only one practicable road into it, and that is up Salt Creek. The inhabitants there are No. 1; and when I was in that valley, I prayed to

God that he never would suffer an unrighteous man to live there.

Within one year's time, Manti was the fourth largest city in Utah Territory. On 6 February 1851, Manti, Great Salt Lake City, Ogden, and Provo were officially incorporated. Much of the success of its growth was due to benefits accrued from the gold of the Sacred Mine. Not all of the initial 58 pounds had been used for coinage; a certain allocation of the gold had been set aside for improving the Manti settlement, as Chief Walker had originally intended.

It began with a letter from Brigham Young to Isaac Morley dated 23 December 1850. After informing Morley that horse thieves were headed his way, driving forty stolen horses to California, Brigham stated that plans were under way to run a stagecoach from Salt Lake City to Manti. He requested that a good state road be built through Salt Creek Canyon, and that a sturdy bridge be built over Salt Creek.

While some of the foregoing project expenses would be defrayed by tithing and donated labor, another project was almost entirely financed by sacred gold. Manti's first grist mill was completed in January 1851, with Brigham Young purchasing two-thirds of the necessary materials and Isaac Morley the remainder. Prior to that time, all grinding had been done by hand with a large coffee grinder. On 24 February Isaac Morley and his counselors surveyed block No. 103, and excavation for the first county court house began.

While on his second visit to Manti, President Young organized Sanpete into the fourth stake of Zion in the Great Basin Kingdom. Isaac Morley was called to be the first stake president over the Sanpete stake.

After the snow of the second winter melted, Brigham Young called upon Father Morley with a difficult request; he wanted him to make another trip to the Sacred Mine. The gold of the year before was nearly expended, he said, and the Church was still heavily in debt from the migration, which was still continuing from the states and abroad. A man had not yet been chosen to make the trip, and Walker would approve of no other but Morley in the interim. Still reluctant, Father Morley at last agreed to one more trip when Brigham appealed to his sense of religious duty. He records the event in his journal under "1851" without mentioning the month, but other events which transpired that year indicate that the trip must have taken place in early summer, probably May or June.

The second trip to the mine was mostly uneventful, even though before they started, Arapeen had voiced an objection that was over-ruled by Walker. The return trip proved more eventful when they encountered the camp of Spaniards led by Antonio de Reinaldo; though they were able to skirt the Q'uatz and elude them, the encounter had raised an alarm in Brigham Young, who could see his fabulous gold source disappearing before his eyes. By the end of the year, Brigham would have the Spaniards on trial for violating his newly-enacted anti-slavery statue, rushed through the Territorial Legislature by Representative Morley.

Both Walker and Arapeen were on friendly terms with the Spaniards, but Arapeen was especially involved with them in the lucrative slave trade. With Spaniards in the vicinity and Arapeen acting unusually belligerent, Brigham Young thought it prudent to show him a little special attention; he asked Father Morley to have a house built for Arapeen. The chief's brother was pleased with the gift and directly moved in, though other members of his tribe thought it strange that Arapeen should live in the white man's "wooden wickiup."

Arapeen's house was not the only one built that year. Under Morley's supervision, a large two-story council house was built of limestone, and a number of one-story and two-story adobe houses were also completed, including a new one for President Morley and his family.

On 18 September, Governor Young published a proclamation stating that Isaac Morley was elected a member of the Territorial Legislative Council. While attending the first council of the legislature in Salt Lake City, Father Morley helped pass a bill preserving Salt Lake City's original charter, and a second which transferred the territorial capital to Fillmore, Utah. Governor Young stated the purpose for the latter was to encourage colonization in southern Utah; in

reality, it was to separate escalating federal government intervention from Church affairs.

President Morley reported that Reinaldo's Spaniards were in the Sanpete area on 10 December, purchasing Indian children from Arapeen for the purpose of selling them in Mexico. If Arapeen succeeded in his effort to over-ride the authority of his brother, access to the mines might be denied the Mormons and given over to the Spaniards.

Brigham Young was Governor of the Territory (at an annual salary of $1500) and Indian Agent (with an additional salary of $1,000: the equivalent of the two salaries, at today's values, would surpass $25,000, and Young held numerous other offices at comparable salaries), with considerable jurisdiction on such matters. Stephen B. Rose, the Indian sub-agent, led a company of armed men from Salt Lake City to arrest the slave traders and bring them back for trial. Special instructions were dispatched to Morley from Governor Young. He was asked to prepare a factual report as a testimony against the Spaniards. Major Rose was successful in making the arrest and placing the captive children in his custody. By 23 December, Rose and Morley reached the Governor's office in Salt Lake City and conferred with Brigham on plans for the trial. On the following day, Judge Z. Snow was selected to preside over the court, his views being in conformity to the will of the governor.

Arapeen came to court to testify for the defense. He said that he was in favor of the slave trade, for this activity had been his principal means of revenue for many years, long before the arrival of the Mormons and their law. The Piute boys, whom Arapeen sold, brought an average of one hundred dollars, while the girls, being in greater demand, brought twice as much.

Brigham Young's plan was successful, at least as far as driving the Spaniards from the Territory was concerned; from that time forward—especially after the Chicken Creek Massacre in 1857—few of them were seen in Utah. But Arapeen refused to comply with Judge Snow's edict and persisted in stealing children from the Piute tribe. Buyers for the slave children were now scarce, however, and Arapeen became desperate and angry at his plight.

Arapeen brought some of his newly acquired slaves to the Provo River where Daniel W. Jones was camped with a few other Mormon men. Since Mormons were responsible for outlawing the slave trade with the Spaniards, Arapeen argued that Jones and his companions should buy the children from him. Jones instead lectured Arapeen on his evil ways and the tempestuous Indian became provoked. Grabbing one of the slave children by the heels, he dashed its brains out on the rocks. He then tossed the bloody little corpse at Jones' feet, who stood in total shock and disbelief at what he had just witnessed. Arapeen angrily spat his logic at Jones: "You have no heart," he ranted, "or you would have bought (the child) and saved (his) life."

The day following the court trial with Arapeen and the Spanish slave traders was Christmas. At President Young's request, Isaac Morley remained in Salt Lake City to participate in the holiday celebrations. During the ensuing six weeks Morley remained in Salt Lake City he attended to many Church duties and participated in several parties sponsored by the saints. A large party was held in a carpenter's shop on Christmas day, at which many of the General Authorities spoke. Community singing and music from the brass band culminated in the benediction offered by President Morley, who expressed the thankfulness of the Saints for the freedoms they currently enjoyed.

On 4 February 1852, a business meeting of the General Authorities was conducted in the "bath house," another gathering place; a brass band escorted the brethren to this location. Brigham Young led the discussion, and Isaac Morley offered the invocation. After the meeting, many of the Saints joined the brethren and band members,

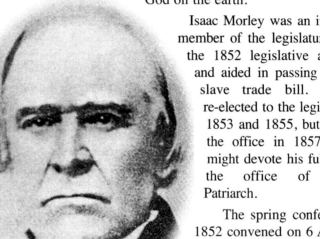

Thomas Rhoades.
Courtesy Utah State Historical Society.

and danced until midnight. The following day, President Morley departed for Manti.

While in Salt Lake City, Morley attended two solemn prayer meetings held by the General Authorities in the Endowment House (a building utilized for performing sacred ordinances until completion of the Salt Lake Temple). All in attendance wore holy temple clothing. At the first meeting, President Young swore Isaac Morley to a solemn and sacred oath, "that I would never reveal the secret, or the true location of the sacred Indian mine, or the nature of its contents, or the use thereof, on the penalty that my blood should be shed and my life be forfeit."

At the second meeting, each of those in attendance were granted an opportunity to thank the Lord for establishing the kingdom of God on the earth.

Isaac Morley was an influential member of the legislature during the 1852 legislative assembly, and aided in passing the anti-slave trade bill. He was re-elected to the legislature in 1853 and 1855, but resigned the office in 1857 that he might devote his full time to the office of Church Patriarch.

The spring conference of 1852 convened on 6 April and concluded on the 10th. As Church Patriarch (alternate to Patriarch John Smith), Isaac Morley sat with the General Authorities, and was the first speaker in the afternoon session on 9 April; the following afternoon, he gave the benediction which concluded the conference.

About one month after the April conference, President Young came to Manti where he remained two days as the first stop on a tour of the settlements of southern Utah. He was accompanied by Thomas Rhoades, who had been appointed to the office of Treasurer of the Church the preceding March, prior to general conference at which he was sustained in the office. On 13

May 1852, when Brigham Young left Manti, he invited Father Morley to travel with his company, ostensibly to familiarize him with conditions existing in that part of Mormon county. Morley returned from the tour on 9 June.

The purpose of Brigham Young's tour was two-fold: to visit the southern settlements, and to bring together Isaac Morley with Thomas Rhoades, the man he had selected to bring the gold from the Sacred Mine. As the only white man who had actually been to the mine, Morley could offer important information to Rhoades on the latter's up-coming duties. Moreover, they met with Chief Walker and elicited his approval of Rhoades as the man who would bring gold from the mine. This meeting between Young, Morley, Rhoades and Walker in early June was tentative, however, and subject to final arrangements yet to be worked out. Walker wanted Brigham Young to intercede as mediator to bring peace between the warring Shoshone and Ute tribes, and Brigham wanted further assurances from Chief Walker that he would not change his mind once the agreement was made to regularly retrieve the gold.

After returning to Salt Lake City, Governor Young concentrated immediately on a plan whereby peace might be established between the Ute and Shoshone tribes. The governor summoned Chief Antlers of the Shoshones to Salt Lake City, and gave Isaac Morley the assignment of bringing in Chief Walker for the negotiations. The talks continued at length until at last the two chiefs came to an agreement and passed the pipe of peace. The peace was concluded by 21 August 1852.

Even prior to the concluded peace, Chief Walker, being pleased with the negotiations, granted his permission for Thomas Rhoades to retrieve the gold. Brigham insisted that Chief Walker swear an oath on the Book of Mormon that he would not rescind his agreement nor permit anyone else to know the secret of the Sacred Mine; to which the chief agreed on the condition that Brigham Young, Thomas Rhoades, and Isaac Morley do the same. The oaths were performed in July, in the Endowment House, all of them dressed appropriately in temple garments—including Walker.

Thomas Rhoades made his first trip to the Sacred Mine shortly thereafter. All that is known about this initial trip of Rhoades' was that it took 14 days and that the first load of gold "was pure; and weighing about 62 pounds."

Less than a year after the treaty had been formalized between Walker and Antlers, the Ute Chief declared war again, this time against the Mormons. It began with Walker's resentment toward the legislature action which forbade slave trading with the Mexicans. Isaac Morley had been a sponsor of the anti-slavery bill, and Walker was not ignorant of that fact. On a day in 1852 the angry chief rode up to Morley's house in Manti astride his favorite white horse and called President Morley outside.

"I thought you were Walker's friend," the chief said hotly.

"I am your friend," replied Morley calmly.

"Then why does my friend make Mormonee law which say Walker no more sell Piedes to the Q'uatz?" he demanded to know.

"Because slavery is not the Mormon way," Morley replied.

"And Walker will not stop selling slaves to the Mexicans," Walker said. "That is not our way." He whirled his mount and rode away. Morley wrote directly to Brigham Young to warn him about Walker's volatile tirade.

The chief's ardour might have cooled if other irritants had not provoked him to war. The final incident which sparked his anger against the Mormons occurred on 17 July 1853 when James Ivie, who lived in Spring Creek in Utah Valley, struck a belligerent brave over the head with a broken gun barrel, killing him. Angered because the Mormons would not turn Ivie over to him for justice, Walker declared war on the settlers. Outbreaks, stirred by Arapeen, then occurred all over the Territory. At Manti, Father Morley ordered the settlers into the newly constructed fort.

In a speech given at the Tabernacle in Salt Lake City, at ten a.m. on Sunday, 31 July 1853, Brigham Young told the congregation:

> How many times have I been asked in the past week, what I intend to do with Walker. I say LET HIM ALONE,

SEVERELY. I have not made war on the Indians, nor am I calculating to do it. My policy is to give them presents, and be kind to them. Instead of being Walker's enemy, I have sent him a great pile of tobacco to smoke when he is lonely in the mountains. He is now at war with the only friends he has upon this earth, and I want him to have some tobacco to smoke.

Much has been made of Brigham Young's magnanimity towards Walker and the Ute Indians, but when considered in perspective, he could do little else, with the richest gold source in history at stake. To that date, some 200 pounds of pure gold had poured into Church coffers.

Though the Walker War raged for several months throughout much of the Territory, with many killed on both sides, it is a tribute to the respect Walker held for Morley that no attacks were made upon Manti, in the very center of Walker's realm. By 8 April 1853, many of Walker's people were already at war, but Walker was trying to maintain the peace. On that date Chief Walker asked Father Morley to deliver a message to Brigham Young: "Tell Brother Brigham we have smoked the tobacco he sent to us in the pipe of peace: I want to be at peace, and be a brother to him."

Brigham Young's private response to Father Morley reveals his personal philosophy, unmasked by diplomacy: "That is all right, but it is truly characteristic of the cunning Indian. When he finds he cannot get advantage over his enemy (he will) curie down at once, and say 'I love you.'"

Within days of making the statement, Brigham Young traveled to Manti to confer with Morley about using his influence with Walker to curb depredations throughout the Territory. About midnight on 29 April, while Young was still in Manti, three Indians crept into the fort where they were fired upon by an alert guard. The frightened Indians ran directly over to Father Morley's house where they told him they had come with a message from Walker, that both of the chiefs, Walker and Arapeen, wanted peace with the Mormons. Brigham Young came to interrogate the three Indians, whom he believed had been sent to

assassinate him, or at least to spy. He counseled the braves not to tell lies, then sent them home with presents of shirts and tobacco for both Walker and Arapeen. His message to the two chiefs was, "Behave yourselves."

Isaac Morley traveled to Salt Lake City on 22 July 1853 to obtain ammunition for the settlers at Manti. En route he learned that there were Indian uprisings near Payson and Nephi. A number of cattle had been stolen by Indians in Nephi, and had been located and brought back to town by Charles Hancock, a scout (and brother of Benjamin Hancock, Bishop of Payson, great-uncle of the author). When Morley left, the Indians, who were lurking around Nephi, had not attacked. James C. Sly, however, was wounded by his own night guard when Sly crawled up to test the guard, who challenged Sly for a sign, but failed to hear the counter-sign. Morley reported these occurrences to Brigham Young when he reached Salt Lake City.

There was a period of time in the fall of 1853 when tension arose between Brigham Young and Isaac Morley, beginning with Brigham's apparent suspicion that Morley was partial to the Indians' point of view in the recent troubles. Morley was a very powerful man; probably no one in the Territory held more influence besides Young himself, and Morley was the only man who could handle the San Pete Utes. His knowledge of the mine and the sacred gold of the Uintah's made him an ever present threat in Young's mind, no matter how faithful Morley had proved himself to be. Young began mentioning his suspicions in private councils and Morley caught wind of it. The report was that President Young had said that perhaps Morley was too old to serve another term in the territorial legislative council. Sixty-seven-year-old Isaac Morley immediately wrote to Brigham Young, asking, "In what duties have I failed?" His letter was dated 5 November 1853.

On 15 November, Brigham Young responded by writing: "Permit me to say that I was some what surprised that one of your years, judgement, and experience should allow himself to be affected and weighed down by mere reports." He notified Morley that had he felt any need to replace him in the legislature, he would have notified him in person, as he had always done in matters of consequence.

The next legislative body was scheduled to assemble in Salt Lake City on the second Monday of December 1853. "I do not wish you to even dream of resigning," Young wrote. "Bring your certificate of election and take your seat in the assembly." But Governor's Young's suspicions that Morley held too much influence with Walker and his Utes, and had become a liability, expresses itself clearly in the concluding paragraph of his letter to Morley:

> I have reflected upon your age, circumstances, and probable feelings and feel today that it would please me much if you would arrange your affairs with the view of returning and living with us here in this city at the earliest reasonable date.

Father Morley was ever obedient to the man he considered to be a prophet, and not unaware of the consequences of disobedience.

Upon reaching Salt Lake City in December, Brigham Young invited Father Morley to discuss the matter of moving his family back to that city. Morley wanted more time, but Brigham pushed his demand by deciding that Isaac should send for part of his family immediately. They also discussed Morley's friendship with the Indians, but what was said is not recorded.

The discussion took place on 12 December 1853; the following Sunday morning, Isaac Morley occupied the pulpit in the Bowery to address the Saints on the subject of "Indian Activities in Sanpete." In the afternoon, Brigham Young spoke to the theme, "Be Ye as Perfect as You Can," wherein he made allusion to Father Morley and the Indians by stating:

> (This principle of perfection) will apply to every man...including Brother Morley who spoke to you this morning. If he has done the best he could in the late Indian difficulties in the district where he lives, and acted according to the spirit of revelation in him, he is as justified as an angel of God!

Bishop Hoagland of the Salt Lake Fourteenth Ward invited Parley P. Pratt, of the Quorum of Twelve Apostles, and Patriarch Isaac Morley to be the guest speakers at the Ward's annual Christmas meeting which commenced on Monday, 26 December, at 11:00 a.m. Pratt spoke on the subject of "The Importance of Education," while Father Morley spoke on the theme, "The Love and Brotherhood of Man."

Following the April 1854 general conference of the Church, Isaac Morley returned to Manti to put his business affairs in order. He paid his respects to his old friend, Chief Walker, who was camped on Meadow Creek, saying that Brother Brigham had called him away.

"But Sanpete is your home," Walker lamented. It was a great tribute to say this now, after the great war which had been calculated to drive the Mormons out. Morley had convinced him to make peace the previous summer.

"I am your brother," Morley assured him. "I shall return."

Morley wrote in his journal:

> There were tear in Walker's eyes. He was ill, and thought we might never see one another again. I told him that Towats would never allow brothers to be parted, and that should either of us die, or us both, we would meet again in the Lord's Heaven. He seemed pleased and comforted at that. "When Walker die," he said, "my brother Morley will speak to Towats when I am buried?" I told him I would. We parted with an embrace, which thing is not customary with Walker. He is the most unforgettable man I have ever known.

Upon leaving Manti, Isaac Morley made preparations of his own. He made a request of his son, Isaac Morley, Jr., that after his own death his body be returned to "lovely Manti" for interment at the foot of Temple Hill. On 23 July 1854, three months after his return to Salt Lake City, one of Isaac's wives, Harriett Lucinda Cox, died at Manti at the age of thirty-one.

On 20 December 1854, Wilford Woodruff, Loren Farr and Isaac Morley, Utah legislators serving on the Territorial Revenue Committee for taxes, roads, bridges, and ferries, met in joint session with members of the House of Representatives to report what they regarded as the needs of the Territory. Governor Young gave the keynote address, followed by Heber C. Kimball. Isaac Morley spoke next to the assembly, reporting the findings of his committee.

Then occurred one of the most amazing events in Isaac Morley's long and eventful life. On 29 January 1855, after a protracted illness, Chief Walker died at his camp on Meadow Creek in Millard County. His body was tied to the back of his favorite white horse and was escorted by a long procession of mourning, wailing, gourd-rattling Utes up Meadow Creek to the top of the mountain. Walker had requested that his body be buried on the highest mountain in Ute country, that he might even in death be exalted above all other Ute chieftains.

Only a day or two thereafter, several Ute Indians rode into Salt Lake City looking for Father Morley. They informed him of Chief Walker's death, saying, "You come." Several of the brethren, including Heber C. Kimball, cautioned Morley that Walker had often expressed the desire to have several Mormons killed and buried with him, to accompany him on his journey to the land of medicine dreams. Nevertheless, without hesitation, Morley hastily departed with the Indians, saying that he had given his promise to Walker to consecrate his grave and commend his soul to God.

Upon the death of Walker, his brother Arapeen succeeded to the chieftainship of the Sanpete Utes, and a shudder of dread went through the Mormon settlers as they hastily gathered in the forts and prepared for war.

It was a different Arapeen, however, that Isaac Morley met in his wickiup on Meadow Creek (for Arapeen had since abandoned his fine house in Manti to rejoin his people). He was docile and friendly, obviously still in mourning for his recently departed brother. He had just returned from burning Walker's wickiup, so that his dead brother's spirit could not come back to haunt it. He was fully aware of the burden now placed upon his hoary old head. He revealed to Morley the cause of his change of heart.

Shortly after Walker's death, said Arapeen, as he had been preparing for war against the Mormons, he had experienced a sudden weakness which had sent him to his bed of buffalo robes.

There came to him then, he said, a vision of his dead brother who told him not to make war with the Mormons because they were a good people. He had argued with his brother's spirit: The Mormons had stolen the Indian's lands. Walker had told him that the land did not belong to either the Utes or the Mormons, but to the Great Spirit who had created it. Now, Arapeen told Morley that he was ready to deed the whole of the country of Sanpete to the Mormon Church.

Walker had given him two messages to deliver before he died, Arapeen added. The first was for Brigham Young. On the very day that Walker died, gifts had arrived from Brigham, and Walker believed that the Mormon Chief must possess great medicine to have known that he was about to die. The gifts, of course, had merely been a token of good will, arriving by coincidence during the Chief's final illness. Nevertheless, Walker cherished Brigham Young's letter, which had accompanied the gifts, and the chieftain asked his brother that it be buried with him. Moreover, he instructed Arapeen to honor his vow and, after his death, permit Brigham Young to bring gold from the Sacred Mine, under the agreement that only Thomas Rhoades could have access to the site.

The second message from Walker was for his faithful friend Morley. Walker reminded him of his promise to officiate at his burial, and see to it that he was buried in his temple garments, beneath his best, beaded buckskin suit. Morley assured Arapeen that he would honor his vow. Walker had also asked Arapeen to tell his white brother this: that for the rest of Morley's days on earth, the spirit of his red brother would walk at his side.

It was early in February when Isaac Morley set out up Meadow Creek accompanied by Arapeen and a few of the subchiefs. Even though it had been a relatively mild winter, the snow lay deep near the summits of the mountains, and their progress was slow. According to Indian custom, they traveled in absolute silence.

Even before they reached the crevice in the mountain rim where Walker's body lay entombed, Father Morley heard the crying. At first he thought it was someone mourning for the dead chief, but the mourners had long since departed, and as they neared the place he realized that the crying was emanating from the burial crevice, which had been walled up with rocks. The sounds came from two Piede slave children—a boy and a girl—who were placed there to accompany Walker on his journey to the spirit world. They were left alive, entombed within the grave, to slowly starve to death, their crying calculated to scare away evil spirits which might try to steal Walker's spirit on its three-day journey to the great beyond.

As Father Morley opened his Book of Mormon to prepare for the service, Arapeen stopped him. The final resting place would not be in the crevice tomb, he said; this place was merely a decoy, to prevent Walker's enemies from molesting his remains. Walker had requested to be entombed with his ancestors at Carre-Shinob!

Morley protested that he was nearly seventy years of age, too old to make such a rigorous journey in the dead of winter. They would make the trip later, Arapeen told him, after the snows had melted; for now, he wanted Father Morley to say a Mormon prayer to drive away evil spirits and protect Walker's tomb until his body could be moved. His body had been packed with ice and snow to preserve it until the reburial.

In compliance with the request, Father Morley knelt in the snow and began to pray. Arapeen, uncertain about what to do, at last kneeled next to him, and one by one the subchiefs followed suit. It was a most unusual scene, 'midst the pathetic crying of the two unfortunate children. Afterwards, Morley wrote in his journal:

> Never has my heart been rended more than when I heard the pathetic crying of those children, and could do nothing to alleviate their suffering, nor secure their release. According to Indian custom, they must frighten away the evil spirits and protect the soul of the chief: to remove them or rescue them from starvation and freezing would have precipitated another war and the annihilation of the settlers. I could do nothing in the end but ease my troubled conscience with the knowledge that the deaths of two children would save the lives of dozens or hundreds of our people, and I was comforted in my belief that their tender sacrifice would ensure their eternal salvation. So I left them there, in the hands of the

Lord, and in the company of my dead Ute brother, Chief Walker of Sanpete...

Settlers around Meadow Creek reported hearing the pathetic crying of the children for several days following the burial of Chief Walker, but as in the case of Father Morley, they dared do nothing to save the children, knowing it would incite the Sanpete Utes to war.

Brigham Young objected to Morley's participation in the Indian affairs, and as Indian Agent for the Territory, had the authority to prevent it; but Morley reminded him that breaking his solemn promise to Walker might end Arapeen's sudden peaceful inclinations, and Brigham reluctantly capitulated.

Thomas Rhoades, the only other white man now permitted near the Sacred Mine, was indisposed by illness during 1855, and could make no trips into the mountains. His nineteen-year-old son, Caleb Baldwin Rhoades, was chosen to accompany Morley and the Ute tribal burial party on the pilgrimage to Carre-Shinob to inter the body of the chief. Caleb Rhoades was required to take the same oath as his father, and as Morley had taken, and had to meet the approval of Chief Arapeen. All things being in readiness, with utmost secrecy enforced, Father Morley and Caleb Rhoades departed Salt Lake City sometime late in April, and by the first week of May arrived at Meadow Creek.

At Meadow Creek the two white men joined Chief Arapeen, his brother Tabby, and five other Utes—Un-gas-ton-igats, Cessapoonch, Fuchawana, Un-gaco-choop, and Rabbit—and repaired quietly to the temporary crevice grave of Chief Walker on upper Meadow Creek. The rocks were removed from the opening and entrance gained.

It might be convenient at this place to mention that noted Utah historian and author, Charles Kelly (who was a mentor of this writer), discovered this walled tomb on Meadow Creek during the 1930s; on opening the grave, expecting to find Walker's remains, he found instead an empty chamber.

The journal of Isaac Morley contains an interesting accounting of the chief's grave. In addition to the body of Chief Walker, the tomb contained the bodies of two of his favorite wives, who had been killed in order to accompany him on his supernatural journey: nearby lay the two bodies of the unfortunate Piede children who had starved to death in each other's arms. In addition there were the carcasses of fifteen of the chief's best horses: most chiefs were buried with one or two, but Walker had been the greatest horse thief in the West—it was fitting that he die wealthy in horses. There were the chief's personal possessions: bows and arrows; his favorite hunting knife; two fine rifles and a pistol; a can of tobacco; beadwork and a grand feathered head-dress; a tin of Jim Bridger's firewater, laced with pepper and brown sugar, as Walker liked it; some corn and venison jerky, to prevent his hunger on the long medicine journey; and numerous other items such as robes, blankets, a mirror, and much more. The most bizarre of the contents of the grave, however, were the bodies of two of Walker's numerous children, in a grotesque sitting position against one wall, as though in perpetual vigilance. Each of the bodies had a "medicine arrow" protruding from the breast—a colored arrow with special eagle feathers on the shaft.

The chief's greatest treasures were clutched in either hand: the Book of Mormon given to him by Isaac Morley, and the letter from Brigham Young, received on the day he died. Around his neck, on a leather thong, hung his medicine bag, containing gold nuggets from the Sacred Mine, together with other items granting "powerful medicine."

The body of Chief Walker, still frozen, was strapped to the back of one of his favorite mounts, and the other bodies and relics similarly packed, the caravan proceeded to the Sacred Mine.

This was Caleb Rhoades' first view of the Sacred Mine. The story that he may have accompanied his father to the mine two years earlier is dispelled by information contained in Morley's journal, which makes it clear that this was Caleb's initial visit.

A distinction must here be made between *Carre-Shinob* and the *Sacred Mine*. Carre-Shinob ("Where the Great Spirit Dwells") is a series of nine great caverns in which reposes the treasure of Montezuma, as well as other ancient artifacts, and the remains of numerous "Old Ones," former leaders of the Aztecan-Yutah nation. The Sacred

Mine is one of seven ancient caves from which the sacred gold was mined, and from which, according to Indian belief, their ancient race emerged from the underworld.

Chief Walker was interred—in a sitting position—within a chamber of Carre-Shinob, where also reposed the bones of his grandfather, Sanpete, and many other of his ancestors. Like Sanpete, Walker was adorned with golden Aztecan artifacts—mask, breastplate, anklets, bracelets, necklaces and rings. Because of the superstition prevalent among the Utes, only Fuchawana, a shaman, entered the burial chamber with the two white men.

Near the end of the final arrangements, after Father Morley had knelt in prayer to consecrate the final resting place of his old friend Walker, he began to have concerns that perhaps because young Caleb Rhoades had been brought along, they might not be allowed to leave. Other than Thomas Rhoades, they were the only white men who knew the great secret, and it had long been Walker's wish to have several Mormons accompany him to the great spirit world of Towats, and to Morley's mind it seemed more than coincidental that two Mormons had been selected by Arapeen to assist in the burial.

When the final ceremony concluded and the two men stepped outside into the bright sunlight, only Arapeen and Tabby were to be seen. Arapeen instructed the two men to go to the Sacred Mine itself, collect the gold needed for Brigham Young, and return by themselves to Salt Lake City; the Indians were going south, he said. Then, to Morley, Arapeen said, "You no come here anymore." "Don't worry," Morley replied, "I am too old."

Isaac Morley remained an active legislator in Utah Territory for another two years, until 1857, at which time he declined the nomination for another term. His decision was partly based on Brigham Young's continued pressure for him to resign and become full-time Church Patriarch—a less political position under Church control—and the massacre of the Spaniards at Chicken Creek, for which he held himself partly responsiblebecause he had reported the Spaniards presence to Brigham Young which brought about their trial and subsequent deaths. He administered patriarchal blessings to the Saints scattered throughout Utah Territory. Many diaries of this era contain references to the blessings administered upon the heads of Mormon pioneers.

On 12 October 1859, Patriarch Morley and his wife, Harriet Lenora Snow, sister of the great Mormon poetess Eliza R. Snow, and future Church President Lorenzo Snow, arrived with M.M. Shelton and Jacob Hamblin at the home of John D. Lee in Washington County. Morley had pronounced a blessing upon Lee's head in 1836, and Lee now remarked that every promise of that blessing had come to pass but one—that Lee would shed his blood as a sacrifice to the Saints: in 1877, Lee would be executed by firing squad for his participation in the Mountain Meadow Massacre.

Morley never ceased his colonizing enterprises. A firm believer in the "United Order," he helped to found the Muddy Mission in Nevada, and the communal town of Orderville in Kane County, and North Bend (later called Fairview) in Sanpete County.

In March 1864, while living with his daughter Lucy Diantha Allen and her family in North Bend, Isaac Morley developed severe rheumatism. As he lay in his sick bed for some months, another Indian war—the Black Hawk War—broke out in Utah. Once more the Utes rose up against the Mormon settlers, and Father Morley's mood plunged into a despair from which he never recovered. While the Black Hawk War raged around him, Isaac Morley died at his daughter's home on 24 June 1865. He was seventy-nine.

Isaac Morley, Jr., traveled to North Bend and retrieved the body of his father to Manti where funeral services were held two days later; Father Morley's remains were laid to rest at the foot of Temple Hill.

Lucy Diantha and her husband, Joseph Stewart Allen, set out from North Bend by wagon to attend the funeral. En route, their team suddenly stopped in the middle of a stream, and no amount of urging or force would induce the horses to continue. In frustration, they returned to North Bend, foregoing the funeral. The next day they learned that a band of Black Hawk's braves had hidden themselves on the opposite bank, waiting to ambush and kill them.

Apparently, Chief Walker was walking with Father Morley....

Chapter Six

The Dream Mine

ONE DAY IN THE YEAR 1886, after returning from a Mormon religious service in the little community of Leland, Utah, John H. Koyle was inspired by the preacher's sermon on manifestations and testimony and determined that he would pray until he had either a manifestation or a testimony of his own.

Koyle dreamed that he saw his cow, which had been lost for several days, in a familiar place in the lower field, with an injured horn which was bent until the point of it was sticking into the animal's eye. A voice came to him in this dream, saying: "If you find your cow at this place tomorrow, will you believe that the Restored Gospel is true?"

The next morning before going down to the lower field, Koyle reported the dream to his wife, and later he discovered the cow, just as the dream had related to him. He spoke aloud, saying: "God—now I believe!"

Three years later, John H. Koyle served a mission for the Mormon Church in East Tennessee. His mission president was J. Golden Kimball, a son of Apostle Heber C. Kimball. In a prophetic dream, Koyle saw a mob pursuing Kimball to take his life, and Kimball heeded the dream and was able to avoid the approaching mob which materialized just as Koyle had predicted.

"Bishop John H. Koyle, Prophet of the Dream Mine, had the gift of prophecy to a higher degree than anyone I have ever known. His remarkable gift first came to my attention when he predicted World War I, and said that the 145th Field Artillery of Utah boys would be called to the colors, but would never see action on the front."

So begins a summary of the life of Bishop Koyle by Norman C. Pierce, donated to the Utah State Historical Society.

"Another remarkable prediction was in July of 1929, when he predicted the stock market crash 4 months to the very day ahead of it. He not only told various groups about this, but he warned his banker, Henry Gardner, who was also his landlord and stake president, to be careful with his loans because after October 29th, he might not be able to collect some of them because of the big financial crash that would come at that time.

"One day as he was passing the bank, Mr. Gardner hailed him in, saying, 'Bishop Koyle, come on in here; I have a bone to pick with you. I have been over-cautious about our bank loans because of what you said, and now four months have gone by, and nothing has happened. What have you got to say for yourself now?'

"Koyle paused a moment and then replied, 'Bro. Gardner, I've got one more day. If you still have a bone to pick with me after tomorrow, just call me back in again.' Of course, the next day the newspapers carried big headlines about the Wall Street Crash of October 29, 1929, in which it is estimated that investors lost over 40 billion dollars, and the whole nation went into the Great Depression."

Koyle made some startling predictions that influenced many people to follow his advice. In about 1930 he predicted every election for president for a span of some forty years. He predicted the outcome of the Hoover-Roosevelt election, and stated correctly that Roosevelt would go back into the White House more times than any other president.

Yet, his predictions also failed in certain areas. For example, he predicted that the Republicans would lose "four or five" elections—which they did—and the "Elephant (Republican Party) would go over on its side and become buried in a landslide," and that this would be the last presidential election. He prophesied that there would not be another election due to the chaos and tribulation which would follow.

But there are those who believe that Bishop Koyle's prophecy of the collapse of the government was not meant to be the immediate future, but is yet to be fulfilled. Koyle stated emphatically that the president would die in office at this time, and a search would be made throughout the United States to find a man able to cope with the financial crisis, when every bank in America would fail except one, and gold would become worth more than $100 an ounce. The bank that survived would be the one backed by a tremendous store of gold bullion. At this time, he said, Kennecott Copper Company would be shut down and not re-opened.

Koyle warned Utahns that they would know as the time approached by certain signs: there would be a severe winter in the country, followed by a wet spring and dry hot summer, at which time the Dream Mine would "turn out," although he predicted that another mine with which he was associated in Mountain City, Nevada, would turn out before the Dream Mine. At that time Utahns would take their gold to Denver to get it coined, but east of Denver all would be in chaos, the rails rusty, no care of the highways, and refugees would be coming in by foot to the protection of Utah's valleys. This was in keeping with a Mormon prophecy of the latter days.

Koyle predicted many other things for these last days, including the invasion of the United States by Russia and China, but that they would be stopped by "divine intervention." He predicted a famine, even in Utah, and foresaw the time when a bushel of wheat would cost a bushel of gold. He predicted that Cities of Refuge would share their resources in a communal society (ala Isaac Morley's "United Order"), and where there would be no rioting and mob actions like those which would prevail throughout the rest of the country. After seven years the tribulation would end and only about ten percent of the people would survive to greet a new age, governed by Christ himself.

It was Bishop Koyle's belief that the Dream Mine would be the source of wealth which would preserve the righteous seed and afford them the means of rise above all other people. This, of course, is the identical philosophy behind the Rhoades Mines—and soon enough the connection between the Rhoades and Koyle mine will be made clear.

John H. Koyle professed that on a night in late August of 1894, he had been visited by a heavenly messenger, an exalted personage from another world, who was attired in a brilliant white garment. This personage informed Koyle that he was named Moroni, and was the same resurrected Nephite prophet who had visited the Prophet Joseph Smith in 1823 and revealed the location of the gold plates from which the Book of Mormon was translated.

"Moroni" further revealed to Koyle that he had shown Joseph Smith a cavern filled with great ancient treasures and relics of the Nephite people, and much gold. Then this messenger allegedly conducted Koyle "in the spirit" from his home in Leland, Utah, to the crest of a high mountain where, at a certain point, they entered directly into the stone of the mountain itself without the slightest resistance, and traveled downward towards the core.

The heavenly messenger took Koyle along a cream-colored seam which led downward nearly a thousand feet into the mountain, and he told Koyle that this would be the seam Koyle would have to follow if he accepted the divine calling to dig a mine for the gold. At the end of the thousand foot seam they came to a hard capstone, beneath which was a large mass of white quartz containing beautiful leaf gold.

At 175 feet below this capstone, at the very heart of the mountain itself, the messenger led Koyle into *nine spacious caverns,* part of an original mine worked ages ago by a vanished and ancient people. Here in these caverns were artifacts of this people in the form of gold ornaments, one entire room filled with gold coins in vases three feet high, and stacks of gold and brass plates with engravings on them which the messenger said was the history of this ancient civilization which would come forth one day when a worthy man would be shown these things. The center of the caverns were supported by huge stone pillars, covered with pounded leaf gold, into which were carved and painted hieroglyphics of curious workmanship.

The heavenly messenger revealed to Koyle that he had been chosen to open the mine, but that it would not come forth until certain prophecies had been fulfilled. It would be opened at a time of world-wide crisis when the people would be in need of relief, and so he was told it should one day be called *The Relief Mine*.

The purpose of the gold would be to redeem Zion, said the messenger, and he predicted it would come about in a day when horseless carriages streaked the highways at great speeds and with brilliant lights, and these vehicles would replace the trolley cars in Salt Lake City.

Bishop Koyle reported this "divine experience" in these words:

> When I was taken thru the mine for the first time in 1894, after being shown the body of rich ore beneath the capstone, I was told that the ancient inhabitants of this land had one time discovered these riches, and had mined out these nine large caverns which form the southwest portion of the great body of gold ore. Then the values had been shut off from them, and would also be shut off from us, too, if we became lifted up in pride and hardhearted, and stiff-necked, using this wealth for our own self-gratification only.
>
> The messenger then showed me how this great wealth could be lost to us. "Look!" he commanded, and immediately there followed a tremor of the earth, and a shifting took place in front of us.
>
> "Now set your men to work," he said, and I saw that dig as we would, we could find nothing but valueless rock. The white ore filled with gold, which had been there but a moment before, could no longer be found. "Now you can see," said the messenger, "how easy it is for the riches of the earth to be taken from you; yet there is much more than you can take out in several generations."
>
> The messenger then showed me the nine large rooms from which the ore had been mined. The pillars standing in the middle of the rooms supporting the roof were also filled with gold and beautifully carved and engraved. There was other gold, both mined and refined and coined and there were implements and relics which they had left

there, as well as great treasures—and many precious records containing the word of God in great power...

> This messenger talked to me freely, and answered my questions as one man would talk to another. He was exceedingly anxious that all the details of the mine be fixed clearly in my mind, and as we went along, he pointed out all of these ore bodies so plainly that I can never forget them, nor where they are located. He promised me success according to my faithfulness. It was clear to me that this heavenly messenger was the Angel Moroni, the same who was and is the custodian of the gold plates of the Book of Mormon. [Norman C. Pierce treatise on Bishop Koyle, Utah State Historical Society]

The story is almost identical in detail to that reported by the Prophet Joseph Smith a generation earlier. The visitations of the Angel Moroni to Smith allegedly occurred three times, and Koyle's alleged visitations occurred three nights in a row, exactly repeating themselves (as in the case of Smith), from about 25 August to 27 August, 1894.

For comparison purposes, note the following account by Brigham Young, claiming that there was a secret cave inside the Hill Cumorah:

> When Joseph got the plates, the angel instructed him to carry them back to the hill Cumorah, which he did. Oliver (Cowdery) says that when Joseph and Oliver went there, *the hill opened, and they walked into a cave,* in which there was a large and spacious room. He says he did not think, at the time, whether they had the light of the sun or artificial light; but that it was just as light as day. They laid the plates on a table; it was a large table that stood in the room. Under this table there was a pile of plates as much as two feet high, and *there were altogether in this room more plates than probably many wagon loads; they were piled up in the corners high along the walls.* The first time they went there the sword of Laban hung upon the wall; but when they went again it had been taken down and laid upon the table across the gold plates; it was unsheathed, and on it was written these words: "This sword will never be sheathed again until the kingdoms of this world become the kingdom of our God and his Christ." [Journal of Discourses, 19:38]

Heber C. Kimball also spoke of this cave:

> How does it compare with the vision that Joseph and others had, when they went into a cave in the hill Cumorah, and saw more records than ten men could carry? There were books piled up on tables, book upon book. [Journal of Discourses, 4:105]

Mormon writer Edward Stevenson added some information above this cave which sounds remarkably similar to the claims made by Bishop Koyle:

> It was likewise stated to me by David Whitmer in the year 1877 that Oliver Cowdery told him that the Prophet Joseph and himself had seen this room and that it was filled with treasure, and on a table therein were the breastplate and the sword of Laban, as well as the portion of gold plates not yet translated, and that these plates were bound by three small gold rings, and would also be translated, as was the first portion in the days of Joseph. When they are translated much useful information will be brought to light. But till that day arrives, no Rochester adventurers shall ever see them or the treasures, although science and mineral rods testify that they are there. At the proper time when greed, selfishness and corruption shall cease to reign in the hearts of the people, these vast hoards of hidden treasure shall be brought forth to be used for the cause and kingdom of Jesus Christ. [*Reminiscences of Joseph Prophet,* Edward Stevenson, Salt Lake City, 1893, pp.14-15]

According to Koyle, on the third visit by Moroni in 1894, the messenger reported that it was time for Koyle to begin his mission to open the mine. As a sign, the visitor told him that his neighbor would strike water in an artesian well the next day at exactly high noon, and that is precisely what happened. They also removed the drill at four o'clock in the afternoon, just as the messenger had predicted. This was convincing to Koyle and he prepared for his mission.

The messenger had instructed Koyle to take his friend, Joseph Brockbank, with him to the mountain, and the two of them went there on 3 September 1894. Brockbank saw a spot of ground that appeared to have a halo over it and they found white ore at a depth of three feet, so they staked a claim on the mine.

Within days, Koyle was back to his farming, but when his chickens began to die suddenly, his wife warned him that it was the Lord's way of reminding him of his calling, and that if he didn't work on the mine, the children might be next to die.

On 17 September 1894, Koyle returned to the mountain with five friends and the long years of work which were to follow were initiated, and the Dream Mine was born.

Numerous experiences were incurred in the digging operations of the Dream Mine which cannot be recounted here. Suffice it to say that , guided by Koyle's dreams, tunnels were driven into the mountain above Water Canyon. None of the work ever met with success. At least three men lost their lives as a result of working the mine. Lee Gardner in 1912; Reid Weight on 17 September 1934; and David Kunz in 1939.

The Koyle Mining Company was organized with 114,000 shares of stock on 4 March 1909, on a fifty year charter, with John H. Koyle as President and Director, J.D. Creer as Vice President and Director, W. James Bowen as Secretary, Treasurer, and Director, and George Hales and B.F. Woodard, Directors.

At about 5 o'clock on the morning of 10 January 1914, Bishop Koyle was lying awake in his bed contemplating a remarkable dream he had just had, when all of a sudden—as he reported—a powerful vibratory influence enveloped him, lasting for several minutes. The event occurred three times, becoming stronger upon each recurrence until, after the third time, two men dressed in grey clothes, having white hair and beards, approached his bedside.

One of the two men did all the talking. He declared that they were two of the three Nephite Prophets (to whom the Lord had granted immortality until the Second Coming, according to the Book of Mormon) who had been given the divine custody of the Dream Mine. They had come to warn him that vicious and malicious rumors were being spread about him to the effect that high Church authorities would soon join in the persecutions against him, but they admonished him to stand faithful to his mission.

Their visit, said Koyle, lasted fully two hours, but they instructed him that he could only reveal what was said to him during a certain half-hour of the conversation. The remaining hour-and-a-half he was never to reveal to anyone except member of the Mormon Church hierarchy, if they would listen to him. If they would not listen, then the third Nephite Prophet would deal with the Church "in due time."

The Church authorities were not only willing to listen to Bishop Koyle, they condemned him openly for his alleged revelations and set out to end them.

In about 1910, Mormon Church President Joseph F. Smith made a visit to the Mormon colonies in Chihuahua, Mexico, and predicted that these members would be the next to have a temple built for them. Bishop Koyle, however, believed that the so-called "Manifesto of 1910," which prohibited polygamous marriages world-wide in the Church, and more specifically in Mexico, where these families had gone to avoid persecution, precluded them from any blessing.

Koyle revealed his dream wherein he saw Mexican soldiers driving these Mormon colonists from their homes and out of Mexico, being allowed to carry only one piece of baggage with them. Koyle said that if this occurred, there would not be enough Saints in Mexico to support a temple.

Word soon reached President Smith that Bishop Koyle was calling him a false prophet, which was not exactly what Koyle had said. But then, in 1912, Koyle's dream was literally fulfilled when the forces of General Francisco Madero and Pancho Villa drove the Mormons from their homes, allowing them to carry only one piece of baggage with them. The fact that Bishop Koyle had been right did not appease the Church officials, but instead made them even more determined than ever to denounce him.

Apostle James E. Talmadge prepared a newspaper article called "THE WARNING VOICE" which appeared in the Church newspaper, the *Deseret News*, which stated, in part:

When visions, dreams, tongues, prophecy, impressions, or an extraordinary gift of inspiration conveys something out of harmony with the accepted revelations of its constituted authorities, Latter-day Saints may know that it is not of God, no matter how plausible it may appear...No person had the right to induce his fellow members of the Church to engage in speculation or take stock in ventures of any kind on the specious claim of divine revelation of vision or dream, especially where it is in opposition to the voice of recognized authority, local or general...The history of the Church records many pretended revelations by impostors or zealots who believed in the manifestations they sought to lead other persons to accept and in every instance, disappointment, sorrow and disaster have resulted therefrom. Financial loss and sometimes utter ruin had followed. We feel it is our duty to warn the Latter-day Saints against mining schemes which have no warrant for success beyond the professed spiritual manifestations of their projectors and the influences gained over the excited minds of their victims. We caution the Saints against investing money or property in shares of stock which bring no profit to anyone but those who issue and trade in them.

Pressure was also exerted on Koyle from the local level of the Church. His stake president approached him and informed him that unless he abandoned all mining operations forthwith, he would be excommunicated from the Church.

J. Golden Kimball, one of the Apostles of the Church and former mission president whose life Koyle's dreams had saved, came to his defense and wrote letters of encouragement and support. Two other Apostles eventually came to his support—Matthais F. Cowley and Anthony W. Ivins. These men were able to keep Bishop Koyle within membership status.

For virtually the remainder of his life, Bishop Koyle put every effort into the Dream Mine. The years passed and no major strikes were ever made, yet he persevered, fully confident of his eventual success.

The State of Utah entered the campaign against Bishop Koyle in an effort to close down his activities. The State Securities Commission called upon the University of Utah's resident expert geologist, Dr. Frederick J. Pack, to visit the Dream Mine and made an appraisal of it. *The Deseret News* of 20 January 1933, carried the full story under the headlines: *"SUIT AGAINST DREAM MINE LOOMS—Securities Board Orders Charge in Dream Mine Case."*

Dr. Pack's report stated, in part: "In my judgment the Koyle Mining property offers no encouragement whatsoever for the future—evidences of commercial mineralization are wholly lacking. The 'ore' bodies recently discovered are shown by assays to be worthless…"

Bishop Koyle countered with assay reports showing returns of from 40 cents to $444 a ton, but the *Deseret News* refused to print these, so Koyle took them to the rival *Salt Lake Telegram*, where they were published together with Koyle's reply to Dr. Pack on 24 January 1923.

Koyle and his mining company were taken before the state tribunal on several occasions in the state capitol, but no evidence of fraud could ever be proved against them.

For several years, faith in the Dream Mine dwindled, but by 1939 it had rekindled again, and investors had constructed a new home for Bishop Koyle near the Dream Mine itself, so that he could be close to the work. Here, in the full basement of the home, Thursday night meetings were held to determine the course of the mining efforts, but they also turned into a sort of religious and spiritual service, filled with testimonies and inspirational manifestations of faith in the Dream Mine venture. These meetings so inspired investors that new ones were recruited and the work was pursued with greater vigor and enthusiasm than ever before.

In 1944, Mark E. Petersen was made an Apostle of the Church, and Bishop Koyle remarked that this man would become the worst enemy the Dream Mine ever had. The statement proved to be prophetic, for on 7 January 1847, after several years of attacking Koyle and the Dream Mine in the press, Koyle was called before the Church Court sitting in High Council. They gave him an ultimatum: either total repudiation of the Dream Mine or excommunication.

Bishop Koyle was now in his 84th year and his membership in the Church was important to him. He weakened in his commitment to the promise he had made to the Nephite visitors many years ago, in 1914, that he would never write anything or sign any statement concerning the mine. On 7 January 1947, he signed the following repudiation:

TO WHOM IT MAY CONCERN:

I, JOHN H. KOYLE, do sustain the President of the Church of Jesus Christ of Latter Day Saints as the Prophet, Seer and Revelator of the Lord in this day.

I do believe that the President of the Church of Jesus Christ of Latter Day Saints alone has the right to receive divine guidance for the People of this Church as a whole, and am willing to sustain the First Presidency of this Church in all things, including their stand and instruction with regard to the so-called Dream Mine, of which I am the principal leader.

I hereby repudiate all statements which I have made against the advice of the First Presidency of the Church of Jesus Christ of Latter Day Saints as pertaining to this Dream Mine and my conduct of it, and I hereby repudiate all spiritual claims I have made with respect to the mine.

I appeal to all of my followers to join with me in this repudiation of claims to divine guidance in connection with this mine and to regard this mine as a business venture without any religious significance. I also ask all stockholders in this mine to harmonize their thinking with the published statements of the First Presidency of the Church of Jesus Christ of Latter Day Saints with respect to the Dream Mine and to honor and sustain the First Presidency as the only ones chosen of the Lord to give divine direction on any subject pertaining to the Church at large.

I ask my followers likewise to retract all statements they may have made to the effect that the Authorities of the Church of Jesus Christ of Latter Day Saints have been mistaken with regard to our mine.

I appeal to all stockholders in this mine to rally around the Authorities of the Church of Jesus of Latter Day Saints and give to them their undivided loyalty, which I now hereby do.

I voluntarily do this of my own free will and choice.

—(signed) JOHN H. KOYLE

The following day after the document was signed, it was rushed to the presses of the *Deseret News* where it was published in bold print on the front page of the second section in full-size reproduction, which included the signatures. It was no coincidence that Apostle Mark E. Petersen was the editor of the *Deseret News*.

Within a few days of the repudiation, Bishop Koyle became repentant of his actions and began systematically to break every promise he had made in the repudiation. He had promised to give up the Thursday night meetings but he now re-instituted them, stronger than ever before. All of his loyal followers were there to offer support and a stronger conviction than ever before of the divine nature of the Dream Mine.

On 18 April 1948, John H. Koyle was excommunicated by the Mormon Church. On 17 May 1949, John H. Koyle passed away. Among his last words were these:

> Woe unto any man who fights and persecutes John H. Koyle and the Dream Mine, for they are fighting and opposing the work of the Lord! Anyone who does it will have to answer for it before the Eternal Courts of Heaven: and some of them will be called home to answer for it before the Eternal Courts of Heaven: and some of them will be called home to answer for it sooner than they expect!

The Golden Knights

ON 22 AUGUST 1842, WHILE REFLECTING upon the "faithful few" who had remained loyal to him "in every hour of peril," Joseph Smith recorded the following sentiments concerning his close friend Joseph Knight:

> (He) was among the number of the first to administer to my necessities, while I was laboring in the commencement of the bringing forth of the work of the Lord, and of laying the foundation of the Church of Jesus Christ of Latter-day Saints. For fifteen years he has been faithful and true, and even-handed and exemplary, and virtuous and kind, never deviating to the right hand or to the left. Behold he is a righteous man, may God Almighty lengthen out the old man's days; and may his trembling, tortured, and broken body be renewed, and in the vigor of health turn upon him if it be Thy will, consistently, O God, and it shall be said of him, by the sons of Zion, while there is one of them remaining, that this was a faithful man in Israel; therefore his name shall never be forgotten.

Joseph Knight was born 3 November 1772 at Oakham, Worcester County, Massachusetts. In 1809 he moved to Bainbridge, Chenango County, New York, and in 1811 to Colesville, Broome County, New York, where he remained for nineteen years. He operated a farm, grist mill and carding machine, and he frequently employed young Joseph Smith. A strong bond of friendship developed between them. While Joseph Smith was involved in the translation of the gold plates to the Book of Mormon, Joseph Knight sent provisions from time to time to assist in the work. Indeed, when Joseph Smith obtained the gold plates in September 1827 (according to his own account), Joseph Knight was visiting at the Smith home near Manchester, New York, and Smith used Knight's horse and carriage to retrieve the sacred plates on that occasion.

Joseph Knight and his family were baptized into the Church in June 1830, shortly after its organization. His family moved with the Colesville branch of the Church to Kirtland, Ohio, in 1831, and a few months later went with them to Independence, Missouri, where he became a pioneer settler. Joseph Knight died 3 February 1847 at Mt. Pisgah, Iowa, during the Mormon exodus from Illinois.

Joseph Knight married Polly Peck, who was born 6 April 1776 at Gillford, Windham County, Vermont, and died 7 August 1831 at Kirtland, Ohio. Joseph Smith recorded her death as follows: "On the 7th, I attended the funeral of Sister Polly Knight, the wife of Joseph Knight, Son. This was the first death in the Church in this land (i.e., Ohio), and I can say, a worthy member sleeps in Jesus till the resurrection."

Newell Knight, son of Joseph and Polly, was born 13 September 1800, at Marlborough, Windham County, Vermont, and moved with his family to New York when he was nine years of age. He lived with his father until he was twenty-five. On 7 June 1825, he married Sally Colburn, and established a carding mill and operated a grist mill.

From Newell Knight's journal, published in the *Juvenile Instructor* in 1883, he relates the following:

> On Sunday, April 11, 1830, the first public discourse preached by a Latter-day Saint was delivered by Oliver Cowdery at the house of Peter Whitmer in Fayette (Seneca County, New York). During the same month the Prophet honored me with a visit.

At this time Newell Knight received a great manifestation which was the first recorded "miracle" in the Church, causing many to be converted. At one of the meetings held in his home, Newell Knight was asked to give the prayer and he found himself speechless. He then left the house and went to a place nearby to kneel and pray by himself to discover the cause of his lack of faith.

In the course of praying, Newell was overcome by a power which robbed him of speech and mobility. When he was at last able to move, he made it back to his home where he was greeted with concern by his family and friends, for he showed signs of being "possessed" by a demon. He rolled on the floor and uttered strange, unintelligible sounds.

Newell was taken to his bed and he called for Joseph Smith to give him a blessing which would exorcise the devil which possessed him. Joseph, with some uncertainty, having never before encountered such a challenge, pronounced the blessing, and Newell suddenly levitated from his bed and stuck to the beams of the ceiling! After a few minutes he lowered to the bed and felt refreshed, showing no after-effects. He was then able to participate in communal prayer and he was baptized into the Church at Fayette the last week in May 1830.

At about the same time, Joseph Smith was arrested and taken before a court at Colesville to be tried for "glass-looking" and "money-digging"—seeking to find treasure beneath the ground by means of peeping into a "seer stone" and then dowsing rod. Joseph Knight provided legal help for the Prophet, and Newell Knight was a witness in his behalf.

Newell labored as a missionary with Hyrum Smith and Orson Pratt in the fall of 1830 and in the early part of 1831 he moved the Colesville Branch of the Church, of which he was the leader, to Ohio, where the Prophet and the main body of the Church had relocated.

For the next several years, Newell and his family suffered the persecutions which followed the Saints. On 15 September 1834, Sally Colburn Knight died, and on 23 November 1835, Newell was married to Lydia Goldthwaite by the Prophet Joseph Smith. Some sources list this as the first marriage solemnized by Smith, but he had performed the marriage ceremony that united my second great-grandmother, Lucy Diantha Morley, to Joseph Stewart Allen, on 2 September 1835, some two months earlier. By Sally Colburn,

Newell had one son, Samuel; by Lydia Goldthwaite he was the father of six: Sally, James, Joseph, Newell, Lydia and Jesse.

When Joseph Smith was martyred on 27 June 1844, the Saints, under the leadership of Brigham Young, decided to go West. Newell and his family left Nauvoo, Illinois, on 17 April 1846, he having been appointed captain of the first company of fifty by Brigham Young. The companies wintered on a plateau above the Niobrara River. Newell's wife Lydia recorded the following in her history:

> On Monday morning, January 4th, 1847, Newel (sic), whose health had been failing, said, "Lydia, I believe I shall go to rest this winter." The next night he awoke with a severe pain in his right side, a fever had set in, and in spite of all that loving hands could do, he grew worse. I felt at last that I could not endure his sufferings any longer and that I ought not to hold him here. I knelt by his bedside and with my hands upon his pale forehead, asked my Heavenly Father to forgive his sins; and that the suffering of my companion might cease, and it was appointed unto death, and could not remain with us that he might be quickly eased from pain and fall asleep in peace. Almost immediately, all pain left him and in a short time he sweetly fell asleep in death without a struggle or a groan, at half past six on the morning of the 11th of January, 1847.

Jesse Knight, son of Newell and Lydia, was born at Nauvoo, Illinois, 6 September 1845, and died at Provo, Utah, 14 March 1921, in his 76th year of age. As a boy he was extremely poor, giving all that he earned to the support of his widowed mother.

Jesse's early mining ventures netted him his first fortune, and eventually he diversified his investments. To secure control of all his holdings he effected the organization of the Knight Investment Company. The company was organized on his 61st birthday, 6 September 1906. It was capitalized for $100,000, distributed into one hundred thousand shares with the par value of $1.00. He gave 10,000 shares to each of his living children and 50,000 shares went to his wife and himself. All of his property, real and personal, went into his holding company and all future business was transacted through it, directed always by Jesse Knight.

More than eighty corporations were eventually brought into the Knight Investment Company. On 28 May 1910, the Knight Consolidated Power Company was organized with a capital stock of $2,000,000 divided into 10,000 shares with a par value of $200 per share. There were seven plants, six of them located in canyons of Utah as follows: two in Mill Creek, two in American Fork, one in Santaquin, and one in Snake Creek; the seventh was at Hailstone on Provo River. These plants were constructed mainly to provide service to Jesse Knight's various mining concerns, including his mines and smelter at Tintic.

On 12 October 1912, the Knight Investment Company disposed of these plants to the Electric Bond and Share Company. Jesse drew a draft on that company for $1,892,083.75, of which his share was $1,032,214, giving him an immediate profit of $300,000. Jesse immediately had his treasurer make out his tithing of ten percent to the Church, and a check for $30,000 was made out, bearing the date of 16 October 1912. Jesse was prompt to pay his tithing.

At the same time as the Knight Consolidated Power Company was organized in 1910, Jesse organized the Bonneville Mining Company. Securing title to a large tract of ground on the mountainside just east of the later Columbia Steel Plant, a tunnel was driven a distance of over one mile with the object of striking ore or developing underground water sources. Jesse justified the doubtfulness of this venture by saying it would give employment to many men who had worked for him at Tintic but were now unemployed because of age or infirmity. He maintained ownership of the land upon which the Columbia Steel Plant was later built.

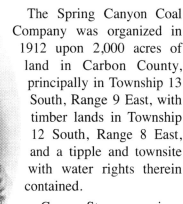

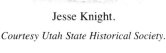

Jesse Knight.
Courtesy Utah State Historical Society.

In June 1910, Jesse Knight purchased the Provo Woolen Mills, an institution organized 1 June 1869 under the direction of Brigham Young. Jesse Knight, in connection with Church interests, continued the operation until a disastrous fire on 19 July 1918 closed its functions.

Again in 1910, Jesse organized the Ellison Ranching Company, capitalized for $1,000,000 divided into 10,000 shares of $100 each. The corporation, managed by Ephraim P. Ellison, consisted of a number of fine ranches in Nevada. In 1930, during the depression, the company almost collapsed, but was able to continue.

The Spring Canyon Coal Company was organized in 1912 upon 2,000 acres of land in Carbon County, principally in Township 13 South, Range 9 East, with timber lands in Township 12 South, Range 8 East, and a tipple and townsite with water rights therein contained.

George Storrs was given management authority of the company and the town which grew up around the coal mines was called "Storrs" in his honor. Jesse Knight, who owned the town, refused to allow saloons and gambling houses in Storrs and to ensure that rule, hired the notorious former outlaw Matt Warner to maintain order. Warner, one-time member of Butch Cassidy's Wild Bunch, was a personal friend of George Storrs, Warner having served time in the Utah State Prison, and Storrs having been warden of that facility shortly after Warner's release in 1900. Both Warner and Storrs had been partners with Caleb B. Rhoades and F.W.C. Hathenbruck in their efforts to mine one of the gold sources on the Uintah-Ouray Reservation a few years before.

The Spring Canyon Coal Company began shipping in May 1913, and soon became about the fourth largest in output in Utah's coal mines.

In 1913, settlers in Duchesne County in eastern Utah organized the Blue Bench Irrigation District No. 1, consisting of about 8,000 acres. They had issued bonds in the sum of $155,000 to build an irrigation system, but after three years of failure, they appealed to Jesse Knight in 1916 for help. Against the wishes of the Knight Investment Company board members, Jesse put money into the venture. He brought 3,500 acres under cultivation and purchased 10,000 sheep which he ranged in the nearby Uintah Mountains on his grazing land and on grazing permits secured for more land. One of the men who worked for Jesse Knight on the Blue Bench Irrigation project was my uncle, Alma Leroy "Roy" Boren.

Jesse Knight turned over bonds consisting of $100,000 worth of Blue Bench Irrigation District No. 1 to Brigham Young University as an endowment fund. Until the Blue Bench ranch project was abandoned in 1930 because of the depression, the irrigation district made payments on the interest and principal of these bonds as they fell due.

The Knight Trust and Savings Bank—later the First Security Bank of Utah—was made trustee for the fund. Eventually, several university dormitories—the Allen Hall for boys and the Amanda Knight Hall for girls—were erected from this fund.

The Knight Trust and Savings Bank was organized in 1913 on the corner of University Avenue and First North streets in Provo, Utah. The capitalization of the bank was $300,000, and on 25 July 1931 it joined the First Security Banking System.

In 1914 the Knight Sugar Company of Raymond, Alberta, Canada, decided to move their sugar plant to Utah. Eventually it was located at Cornish, Utah.

In 1917, Joseph J. Cannon with some others had secured possession of a million-acre tract bordering on and lying to the west of the Magdelena River in Colombia, South America. Hyrum S. Harris, a Spanish-speaking attorney, found that the original title to the land lay in a Spanish grant dating from the sixteenth century which was still valid.

Capital would be required to develop the land, and these men turned to Uncle Jesse Knight. From H.M. Curran, and American timber forester, Jesse learned that there was an estimated six billion feet of marketable timber on the land, as well as having rich soil and luxuriant grass which would support numerous cattle. There were also prospects for oil and mineral wealth.

On 30 June 1917, the American-Colombian Corporation was organized with a capitalization of $100,000, divided into a million shares with a par value of ten cents each, and it became an affiliate of the Knight Investment Company.

Joseph J. Cannon was the first manager, and they first undertook the enterprise of raising cattle, importing 28 purebred Hereford bulls to improve the native stock. The operation was eventually taken over by W. Lester Mangum, Jesse's son-in-law, and later still by Jesse H. Knight, son of Raymond Knight and grandson of Uncle Jesse Knight.

In 1917, Jesse Knight organized the Springville-Mapleton Sugar Company and the Tintic Drain Tunnel Company. The latter, organized 19 September 1917, with the avowed purpose—according to a circular soliciting stock subscriptions—to "launch a new epoch in the mining industry of the famous Tintic District; make possible deep mining by un-watering the whole southern region, thus indirectly adding millions of dollars of wealth to the State of Utah and directly by making money for the company."

Knight's proposal was to extend the tunnel into the mountain about five miles, draining the Diamond Mining District around Silver City, making possible the operation of mines which had been closed because of excessive water. After running a tunnel for one-and-one-eighth miles into the mountain, the project ceased for lack of funds, and Jesse Knight personally bought back the stock he had induced people to buy.

The Tintic District history began when the entire Tintic Valley was granted to Rust and Nebeker for grazing by Juab County. In 1869 the first discovery of gold was made in the "Sun Beam Lode" located 13 December 1869 by William Jasper Harris, Joseph Hyde, S.J. Worsley, S.B. Moore, F.M. Beck, and Joseph Bates, Jr.

In July 1896, Jesse Knight entered Tintic mining with the discovery of the Humbug Lode. After hitting the bonanza of the Humbug, he obtain control of the Beck Tunnel, the Colorado Mine, and Uncle Sam's claims. The town of Knightsville was named in his honor. On 24 July 1908—Pioneer Day—the Knight Smelter opened at Tintic. In 1916 Jesse Knight formed the North Standard Mining Company, and on 19 September 1917 he opened the Tintic Drain Tunnel project.

It is said of Jesse Knight that he was standing under a pine tree on the eastern slope of Godiva Mountain, looking down the valley of Tintic, when he heard a voice say aloud: "This country is here for the Mormons."

It was upon this same mountain that Jesse spoke to his son, J. William Knight, saying: "Will...I want to tell you something. We are going to have money...all the money we want as soon as we are in a position to handle it properly. We will also someday save the credit of the Church."

Chapter Eight

The Golden Saviors of Zion

THERE IS A POPULAR STORY ABOUT JESSE Knight having saved the credit of the Mormon Church. For the sake of clarifying the account, following are presented the letters which were written concerning the subject, as quoted from the book *The Jesse Knight Family* by Jesse William Knight, son of Jesse Knight.

April 2, 1930

Dear Mother:

In the spring of 1896, just prior to discovering ore in the Humbug Mine, father said to me one day as we were walking up the mountainside that he felt sure that he was going to find ore in the ground and we would have all the money we wanted and that some day we would save the credit of the Church.

This remark did not meet with my judgment at that time and I had some little argument with father about it, saying that he did not know how much we would want, nor did it look possible for us to save the credit of the Church when it was owing a million dollars or more. Our own ranch was mortgaged and we did not know how to meet that obligation. But notwithstanding this, father said he hoped I would remember what he said; he said he did not wish to quarrel or argue with me about it and only wanted me to remember what he had said.

Soon after this, however, ore was discovered in the Humbug Mine, in the year 1896. I have been unable to find the date of the first shipment, but the second lot shipped October 24, 1896, brought a net return of $11,189.05. The shipment, which was very high grade, assayed as follows:

Gold, 3.80 ounces, silver, 175.10 ounces; lead, 24.0%.

Money accumulated very rapidly, and as I had heard father say that he had received a letter from President Woodruff at a certain time regarding help given the Church to save its credit, Leon Newren and I put in a part of a day trying to find among the old papers this letter from President Woodruff to father, but we were unable to find it. (Note: this letter was subsequently found and is presented below.)

I had just left the building after the search when I met President Joseph B. Keeler on the street, who said to me before I had time to tell him what was on my mind, that he wished to tell me the details about father making a certain loan to the Church; and strange as it may seem, his story, which he subsequently wrote in the form of a letter, answered the very question that was in my mind, and which I had hoped would be answered in the letter from President Woodruff, for which we had searched. I am enclosing you herewith a copy of the letter from President Keeler which goes to confirm very positively the statement which father made to me about saving the credit of the Church.

Your son,

J. Wm. Knight

March 31, 1930

President J. Wm. Knight

Provo, Utah

My Dear Brother Knight:

I was very much interested in our conversation in regard to an unusual occurrence that transpired November 22 and 23, 1896, in which your father, President Woodruff, Trustee-in-Trust for the Church, and myself participated. The details of the event, which I here briefly relate originated in a request made by President Wilford Woodruff at a Special Priesthood Meeting following the general October semi-annual Conference of the above named year. As you know such meetings are composed of General Authorities of the Church, Presidencies of Stakes, Bishops of Wards, and other officials. At that time I was Bishop of the Fourth Ward, Provo, and your father and his family resided there.

In the Priesthood meeting above noted, many topics were presented, discussed and disposed of in the usual way. Just before adjournment, however, President Woodruff arose and made a special request, namely: that when the Bishops present returned to the respective wards they would visit members who were possessed of means and who might be able to lend money to the Church for a short period, in any sum large or small, on which interest would be paid as well as the principal. He explained that the Church was in very straightened circumstances financially. This condition was brought about in part, he said, on account of the Federal Government confiscating Church property and through other oppressing anti-Mormon laws passed by Congress by which the peace of the people had been greatly disturbed, property of the Church wasted, and the industries of the then Territory depressed and hindered. He presented this matter, he said, because right now there were some very pressing demands on the Trustee-in-Trust, and the credit of the Church was at stake.

This particular request went entirely out of my mind until the afternoon of Sunday, November 22, 1896. I was returning home from our Tabernacle services; and when within a short distance of my home a voice said to me—a voice as audible as that of a person—"Jesse Knight will lend the Church $10,000.00." That was all. Then it was that I distinctly remembered the remarks of President Woodruff bearing on this subject. I immediately changed my course and went to the home of "Uncle Jesse," and found him in his parlor reading. After a few preliminary greetings, I rehearsed to him what had transpired in the meeting, and

what President Woodruff had said about the Church being financially embarrassed. But before I could ask him whether he would make the loan, he said instantly, "Yes, I'll lend the Church $10,000.00 and I'll see the Cashier this afternoon and have a check ready for you tomorrow morning, and you may take it down to Salt Lake." That was at a time when there was but one train a day to Salt Lake. So, early in the morning, he met me at the station and handed me an envelope containing the check.

As it happened, President Woodruff, with his counselors, George Q Cannon and Joseph F. Smith, and several of the Twelve were present in the President's office when I arrived. After viewing the contents of the letter, President Woodruff was very much pleased; and it appeared to me that a great weight was lifted off his mind. At the request of President Woodruff, I spent several hours there and took lunch in the office with him and several of the brethren.

A letter was formulated to Brother Knight and was given to me to hand to him. When I arrived at Provo he was at the depot to meet me. I did not know the full contents of President Woodruff's letter, but Brother Knight remarked to me a few days later that President Woodruff had said that the check was the means of saving the credit of the Church. Brother Knight also remarked to me some months later that was one of the best loans he had ever made.

Very sincerely your brother,

Joseph B. Keeler

(Note: the actual letter from President Wilford Woodruff to Jesse Knight reads as follows:)

Office of

The First Presidency

of the

Church of Jesus Christ of Latter-day Saints

Box B

Elder Jesse Knight,

Provo,

Dear Brother:

I am just in receipt of your check for $7,000, per hand of Bishop Keeler, which makes $10,000 in all which you have kindly advanced to me as trustee in trust for the Church. I feel that this kindly act on your part is in answer to my prayers to the Lord to open some door of relief whereby we may be enabled to meet pressing demands upon us. I feel very thankful to you, and feel with every sentiment of my heart to say, God bless you and prosper you.

With kind regards,

Your Brother,

Wilford Woodruff.

P.S. My note in your favor for $10,000, at 8 percent is hereby enclosed.

Heber J. Grant, who was at the time a member of the Quorum of Twelve Apostles and later President of the Church, asked Jesse Knight for $5,000 to assist some Church members who had gotten financially involved in a failing venture. Jesse declined to loan any money to the men, stating that it was a private venture on the part of the men and was their responsibility, having little to do with the Church.

Apostle Grant then turned to another man and asked him for the same donation, adding that he should pray about it. Jesse Knight overhead the request and asked Grant why he had not asked him to pray about it. "Because you refused alto-gether to do anything," Grant replied. Jesse was somewhat offended, declaring that he, too, believed in prayer, and he said he would go straight home and pray about it. After praying, Jesse felt inspired to double the amount, and when he prayed again the next morning, he was still impressed to do so, and he sent his check for $10,000, together with a check for $1,000 from Reed Smoot, Jesse's close friend.

When Jesse Knight next encountered Heber J. Grant, he said with a smile, "When you ask me for another contribution, I'll pay it without stopping to pray." Shortly thereafter the First Presidency sent the following telegram:

Salt Lake. September 3rd, 1898

To Jesse Knight and Reed Smoot,

Provo.

God bless you and yours forever. May you and all your loved ones have a great abundance of peace, prosperity and happiness in this life and may you all enjoy an eternity of bliss in the life to come is the profound and heartfelt prayer of your brethren in the Gospel.

LORENZO SNOW

JOSEPH F. SMITH

HEBER J. GRANT

The following letter from Heber J. Grant to Jesse's son refers to the above incident, adding some of the detail:

Church of Jesus Christ of Latter-Day Saints

Heber J. Grant, President

Salt Lake City, Utah

February 15, 1923

Elder J. William Knight

Provo, Utah

My dear Brother Knight:

One of the most remarkable and wonderful things, to my mind that ever happened to my life was when your father sent me $10,000 to assist in saving the honor and good names of President Joseph F. Smith, Francis M. Lyman and Abram H. Cannon, in connection with the Utah Loan & Trust Company of Ogden. Brother Reed Smoot sent $1,000.00 the same day...

Senator Reed Smoot.
Couresty Utah State Historical Society.

Sincerely your friend and brother,

Heber J. Grant

On the surface, the above account seems reasonable and even plausible. The involvement of several of the Church authorities in dubious banking schemes certainly was cause for concern, and the $10,000 sent by Jesse Knight and the $1,000 sent by Reed Smoot aided a great deal in salvaging their good names from that particular deal, but it can in no way be construed as "saving the credit of the Church." A mere $11,000 would not have even paid the interest on what the Church then owed.

The Mormon Church was approaching bankruptcy. If they had possessed the funds, they would have extracted the $10,000 from existing accounts, rather than broadcast for help and solicit it from the likes of Jesse Knight. The debts of the Church at that time must have been at least several millions of dollars.

The Edmunds-Tucker Act of 1887 formally dissolved the corporation of the Church of Jesus Christ of Latter-day Saints, the entity holding title to most Church-run businesses and properties, such as their banks, their cooperative store, their industries and land holdings.

By the 1890s, the Mormons were making trade-offs with the federal government, and agreed to abandon polygamy and to dissolve its political arm, the People's Party. In return, they requested statehood for Utah in 1896, amnesty for previously persecuted Mormon polygamists, and most importantly, the restoration of Church property.

Church historian Leonard Arrington wrote:

The Raid had finally culminated in the long-sought goal of statehood, but had produced capitulation in many areas of Mormon uniqueness, not the least of which was the decline in economic power and influence of the church. The temporal Kingdom, for all practical purposes, was dead—slain by the dragon of Edmunds-Tucker.

Heber J. Grant had gone to Wall Street in the 1890s to seek financial aid, arranging loans from New York banks; in so doing he, in effect, mortgaged the Church. Therefore, the above account of Jesse Knight's generosity by giving $10,000 to the Church was a personal gesture to save the general authorities from embarrassment in a private financial venture, and not to save the credit of the Church. If he did indeed save the credit of the Church, it must have been in some other fashion.

In addition, there is a gross discrepancy in the whole account. According to Joseph B. Keeler, the donation of $10,000 was made by Jesse Knight on 22 November 1896 to President Wilford Woodruff, but the letter of gratitude, signed by Lorenzo Snow, Joseph F. Smith and Heber J. Grant, was not written until 23 September 1898, nearly two years later! One must logically question whether or not they were written concerning the same donations or other offerings of a later and perhaps more significant amount. Woodruff's letter to Knight is undated.

The entire affair takes on a new significance when we discovered that the "other" man to whom Heber J. Grant applied upon Jesse Knight's first refusal was none other than Caleb Rhoades!

The following letter, written by Caleb B. Rhoades to Reed Smoot, dated 23 October 1901, clarifies this to some extent, while adding other more enigmatic mysteries:

Reed Smoot,

Provo, Utah

My good Friend:

In my haste to write to you last time I neglected to enclose the information you requested regards to my present indignation of the actions of Bro. Jesse Knight and his interference in my efforts to secure the Indian lease.

...I do not need to inform you, since you were a party to that information at that time, that Bro. Jesse Knight brought out significant amounts of ore from that mine against the warnings to the contrary that he should do it. You will remember that these are the amounts he gave to Pres. Woodruff just before his (Woodruff's) death nearly six years ago, *to save the credit of the church.*

...Pres. Grant (Heber J. Grant) knew about these things as I am sure you will remember, and he could testify to them, if he would, but they (i.e., the general authorities) are not about to do that while this thing is unsettled with the government. I don't blame them for

not wanting to get involved, but on the other hand they are involved, and between them and Bro. Jesse Knight's recent efforts against me, I am left in a hard place.

...I do not worry that Bro. Jesse Knight will ever reveal the location of the mine or that he will use it for any purpose other than that which his conscience dictates. I am more concerned with his attitude towards me which our friendship has never merited in the past...*I will not go near the sacred mine again* because I know he has agents everywhere and in the government. I say these things to you not to accuse because you have been a friend to both of us but instead to permit you to understand my feelings about Bro. Jesse Knight's recent bid to overcome the mining lease. I hope you are still a friend and in support of our efforts for which we keep you in mind always...

...I might talk to Bro. Jesse if the opportunity arises and it might occur when I visit at Diamond (probably Diamond City at Tintic) within the month...

Yours truly,

Caleb B. Rhoades

That Reed Smoot had more than a passing interest in the Rhoades mines is attested to by the following document:

FOR VALUE RECEIVED, I hereby sell, assign, transfer and set over, to Reed Smoot, all my right, title and interest in and to that certain lease between the Indians of the Uintah Indian Reservation, in Utah, and myself and Caleb B. Rhoades; and also my right, title and interest in and to capitol stock subscribed by me in the articles of incorporation of the Rhoades Mining & Milling Company, and which articles, with my assignment, have been deposited with H.S. Young, Cashier of the Deseret National Bank, to be used and filed and said company incorporated when the said lease is approved by the Secretary of the Interior of the United States, or prior thereto, if a majority of the parties interested therein so desire.

I hereby authorize the filing of said articles and the substitution of the name of Reed Smoot for my own whenever it appears in said articles, and hereby authorize and direct the officers of said corporation, when formed, to transfer and deliver to said Reed Smoot all stock to which I would have been entitled in said company if I had not made this assignment.

And I hereby authorize the said Reed Smoot, to sign all papers, documents, receipts and releases in my name, whenever the same is necessary, to perfect in him the interest hereby assigned by me to him in said lease and in said corporation.

Witness my signature this 24th day of April, A.D. 1901.

F.W.C HATHENBRUCK

Signed in the presence of:

ELIAS A. GEE

[see *Footprints in the Wilderness* at page 270]

Reed Smoot was the most powerful U.S. Senator Utah ever sent to Washington. It is notable that he was, at the same time, a member of the Council of Twelve Apostles of the Mormon Church. He was, consequently, romanced by many different persons seeking the benefit of his considerable influence. Ironically, it was Smoot's high tariff on the trade bill—the highest in U.S. history—that is said by many to have been the cause of the Great Depression of 1929-30, after which he was never again re-elected to office.

It is apparent that Reed Smoot was part of a swiftly developing plot. Hathenbruck apparently needed the aid of Smoot badly in order to sign over to him his interest in the Rhoades mine.

Senator Reed Smoot's vested interest in the mines is documented by certain references in the following correspondence:

Salt Lake City, Utah, June 12, 1901

Hon. Reed Smoot

Provo, Utah

Dear Friend:

I believe you have the Articles of Incorporation of the Rhoades Mining

Company, which I would be very glad to have at your earliest convenience.

The lease has not yet been approved but there seems to be every prospects of its being approved, at an early day.

With kind regards, I am,

Very respectfully yours,

J.H. Moyle

Salt Lake City, Jan. 20th. 1902

Mr. G. Taylor

Dear Sir:

I just learned that you have served papers to vacate—(I just returned from the Las Vegas Desert)—I am surprised at that, and have written [illeg.] Smoot to see you at once, for [illeg.] to your satisfaction. I am regrettably detained here a few days, hence I ask a few days delay from you.

Hoping this will meet your approval, I remain

Respectfully,

F.W.C. HATHENBRUCK

New York, July 21st, 1902

Mr. F.W.C. Hathenbruck

Provo City, Utah

My dear Doctor:

[Discusses the Florence Mining Company and the concern of Hathenbruck and Rhoades that they and others will prospect the reservation under cover, and informs Hathenbruck that certain people are defaming his (Hathenbruck's) character.]

Upon the receipt of this letter, let me know definitely just how much money it is going to take to satisfy Reed Smoot, and also definitely state whether you will go into this project, leaving the matter entirely in my hands and giving us your best knowledge and experience in the matters concerning which the company is interested...

Yours &c.

H.C. HENDERSON

By

M. BENTON (dictated)

Provo Commercial & Savings Bank

Provo, Utah, Oct. 14/03

Mr. F.W.C. Hathenbruck

Dear Will:

I received your letter Sept. 26th and have read carefully and note that you expect to furnish me well enough to know that I do all I can for any person whose rights are jeopardized. I shall take your letter with me to Washington and any other information you can furnish me and do what I can to secure justice for all parties concerned. With best wishes, I remain,

Yours truly

REED SMOOT

United States Senate

Washington, D.C., January 14, 1904

Mr. F.W.C. Hathenbruck,

Provo City, Utah

My dear Sir:

I am just in receipt of your letter of January 10, 1904, and have read the same with considerable interest...I certainly hope that you will be successful in obtaining a good large sum of money from the Florence Mining Company people, for you certainly have worked hard and a long time.

I desire to thank you for the interest you have shown in my behalf, and wish you a successful future.

Yours very truly

REED SMOOT

Frederick William Claudius Hathenbruck was born in London, England—date unknown—and was raised by an aunt in Prussia. He had received degrees in geology and medicine from Heidelberg University. He migrated to the United States and came West to the Territory of Utah as a member of Johnston's Army (probably as physician) in 1857. He resigned his commission to marry Rozilla Rebecca Sauncecie and settled in Provo, Utah, as proprietor of the "F.W.C. Hathenbruck and Company Store," a mercantile venture.

Hathenbruck had worked for the Denver & Rio Grande Railroad Company as a topographer and later, having lost his right arm in a mill accident, he reverted to his medical profession and operated a mercantile store in Provo, where he dealt extensively with the Ute Indians and spoke their language fluently. When he died at Provo in 1925, he was nearly destitute and reduced to selling sewing machines.

Caleb Rhoades had first approached Hathenbruck in regard to a partnership arrangement in the early fall of 1894. The good doctor was interested in the project, but only upon Rhoades' proving to him beyond any doubt that the fabulous mines did exist. Without hesitation, Caleb took him to the reservation and showed him two of the mines.

In later years, Hathenbruck would recall that journey vividly. Traveling by horseback along stream beds under cover of darkness to avoid detection by the Indians, he recalled that one of the mines was easily accessible while the other one was not. Near both mines he found old pieces of broken harness, buckles and buttons from decaying Spanish uniforms. Hathenbruck took ore samples from both mines which he later had assayed, the results showing that the mines contained both gold and silver in excess of $20-$26 thousand to the ton!

Agreements were then drawn up between Caleb Rhoades and F.W.C. Hathenbruck, signed by both parties, and a new partnership was formed. Hathenbruck lived a full year among the Indians (1896-97) in the effort to gain their full support for the Hathenbruck and Rhoades Mineral Lease, and the majority of the following seven years (1897-1904) in Washington, D.C., trying to secure approval of the lease from the Secretary of the Interior. For the latter effort, he desperately needed the help of Reed Smoot.

On 18 December 1897, the Hathenbruck and Rhoades mining lease, covering a large area of the Uintah-Ouray Indian Reservation, was signed and approved by 114 tribal members at Whiterocks, Utah. Hathenbruck and Rhoades needed only the approval of the Secretary of the Interior and the opening of that portion of the reservation to locate the mines and begin production.

Within days of the signing of the lease, newspapers throughout the region picked up the story, and the existence of the mines was quickly made public. The *Salt Lake Herald* reported, in December of 1897:

"CALEB RHOADES MINE"
THE MYSTERIOUS BONANZA OF THE
UINTAH RESERVATION
WIRE GOLD AND SILVER
FABULOUS VALUES IN THE WHITE
AND YELLOW METAL

Mineral brought in by F.W.C. Hathenbruck... Application made for a Strip four miles square.

Mr. Hathenbruck is just in from the Uintah Indian Reservation, in the northeast portion of Utah, where the Herald readers will know he is interested in the resurrection and rehabilitation of the famous old Caleb Rhoades gold mine, concerning which so much has been written and said during the past few years.

The Rhoades mine is accounted as being one of the richest propositions in the state of Utah, and while the reports regarding its fabulous wealth have probably been added to with each succeeding year, there is no doubt that it is a bonanza, and better than a Klondike, at least Mr. Hathenbruck thinks so, and he is straining every nerve to acquire a foothold in this ancient producer of the precious metals, for its exact location, although clothed in mystery for many years, is now known...

A Herald representative had a pleasant interview with Mr. Hathenbruck yesterday... According to Mr. Hathenbruck... "The ledge is well defined, and the pay streak is from three inches to three feet in width. There is what we call barren rock in the ledge, but even this assays 35 ounces in silver and $4 in gold, while the pay streak goes as high as $150,000 in gold and silver to the ton, the gold contents of the mineral predominating." Mr. Hathenbruck then got his grip and showed the Herald man a number of samples of ore from the mine and they were magnificent, the mineral being almost solid tellurium, and was covered and streaked through and through with wire silver and gold that was beautiful to look at. Mr. Hathenbruck also stated that the Caleb Rhoades ledge was full of just such mineral as this, and he produced an assay certificate showing the results obtained from half an ounce of ore, the values of which were 1,800 ounces of silver and $17,000 in gold to the ton.

The following document written by Hathenbruck explains some of the intrigue then developing over the mines:

State of Utah

County of Salt Lake

}ss

F.W.C. Hathenbruck, being first duly sworn, says, that he with Caleb B. Rhoades, obtained a lease from the Indians on the Uintah Indian Reservation some years since which lease is now pending before the Interior Department of the United States. That while said matter was so pending in the year 1899, H.C. Henderson, an attorney of New York City was interested with F.W.C. Hathenbruck and his associates in securing the approval of said lease by the Secretary of the Interior of the United States, and said Henderson represented to affiant that Mr. Sherman, Representative from the State of New York and Chairman of the Indian Committee of the House of Representatives, was acting in the interest of affiant's said lease and that said Henderson had secured the services of said Sherman. That affiant met said Henderson, Sherman, Representative Ward of New York and a Mr. Hooker at the Manhattan Hotel in New York City during said year and had an interview with them at said hotel, during which affiant was assured that said Sherman would do all he could to secure the approval of affiant's said lease, and would not let any measure pass the House detrimental to the interests of said lease.

Affiant was introduced to said Sherman first by Nathaniel McKay, who was also acting in the interests of affiant's said lease. That without any notice to affiant or his associates, said parties ceased to act in the interest of affiant's said lease and became interested in the lease subsequently obtained by the Florence Mining Company through which they hope to secure the Rhoades Mine on said Reservation, and which was located previous to the creation of said Reservation by said Rhoades.

That during the spring or early part of the summer, 1897, affiant met Mr. Myton, now Indian Agent on the said Indian Reservation and then a member of the Allotment Commission of the Uncompahgre Indian Reservation at Fort Duchesne at which time and place said Myton stated to affiant that if affiant would allow said Myton to come in on the ground floor on the said lease of said Rhoades and Hathenbruck, meaning to him an interest therein, that he would do what he could, and, in fact, secure the approval of the said lease, but that if such was not done, he would see that the lease was not approved.

Affiant said that he would submit the matter to Mr. Rhoades and during the summer and as near as affiant can state, the month of July, 1897, said Myton met affiant and said Rhoades on 2nd South Street between Main and State Streets in Salt Lake City, Utah, at which time said Myton asked affiant if he had spoken to Mr. Rhoades about the proposition he had made relative to said lease, affiant said that he had. Then said Mr. Myton wanted to know what we were going to do about it. Mr. Rhoades said that he would not accept Mr. Myton's proposition, whereupon, Mr. Myton said "You will never get your lease approved."

F.W.C. Hathenbruck

Subscribed and sworn before me this 25th day of April, 1902.

RAY VANLOTT

Notary Public

(seal)

We refer the reader to the letter of H.C. Henderson to F.W.C. Hathenbruck, dated 21 July 1902, which states, in pertinent part: "...let me know definitely just how much money it is going to take to satisfy Reed Smoot..." In the same letter, Henderson states:

> It is my desire, of course, to have as much accord with both yourself and Rhoades as possible, and I want you to feel and Rhoades to feel that although the Florence Company has the power to enter the reservation, ignoring any claim of either, yet it has no desire or intention to do so, but that it expects to have both you and Rhoades act in perfect accord with us in the matter if it is possible to have you do so. The Secretary of the Interior has made no effort, as yet, to negotiate with the Indians, and when he will do so I do not know, but we do not need to wait for these negotiations unless we see fit...

Even before Hathenbruck had arrived in Washington, D.C. to submit the Utah lease to the Secretary of the Interior, special interest groups had organized to defeat the measure.

These men—many of them anonymous government officials—set up "puppet" corporations which manipulated both the law and the Indian Commission, all to the intent of defeating the Utah lease in order to have their own leases approved covering the same tract of land for the purpose of securing the Rhoades Mine.

Hathenbruck reported to the *Salt Lake Herald* newspaper under date of 3 February 1905:

> I went at once to Washington to secure a ratification of my treaty by Secretary of the Interior Cornelius N. Bliss. I found that my troubles were by no means over; that I had people to deal with more uncertain than the Indians. I had won on the reservation, but that was only part of the battle. Secretary

Bliss showed me a letter to him from George Q. Cannon [Reed Smoot's companion politician from Utah, and an Apostle of the Mormon Church] in which that gentleman said that the men at the head of my scheme were poor and ignorant and unable to swing a proposition worth from $50,000,000 to $100,000,000. Mr. Bliss said he would recognize my claim before any other on the reservation but he said he was going to resign, that he did not like the work.

Bliss resigned and Hitchcock came in and my lease was pigeon-holed. One of the hardest workers against me was (Major) Dick, who is now United States senator from Ohio. He was a lobbyist then and a particular friend of H.P. Myton.

I had not been long in Washington before I discovered that I must have help if I expected to win. The pressure was too strong against me unless I could secure the influence of men high up in Washington. A meeting of a number of prominent men from New York was arranged to be held in the Manhattan Hotel in New York City and I went over from Washington to attend that meeting. The result of it was that I agreed to turn over a portion of my interests in exchange for help in getting my lease ratified by Secretary Hitchcock.

Jesse S. Sherman, Warren Hooker, Judge H.C. Henderson and William Ward were to give their assistance. They were all congressmen from New York at the time. Sherman was the chairman of the committee on Indian affairs, and for that reason had much influence. Others became interested later. Among these were Judge Thoman of Chicago, Postmaster General Henry C. Payne and Colonel George F. Timms. The New York parties (later) organized the Florence Mining Company.

The upshot of the whole matter was that my lease was never ratified by the Secretary of the Interior; but when the law passed providing for the opening of the Uintah reservation, 640 acres of consecutive mineral ground in the reservation was to be given the Florence Mining Company *before* the opening. It is not easy for me to recognize the justice of this arrangement. If the matter is ever opened up for investigation there will be some disgraceful revelations.

In retrospect, the events surrounding the period from about 1896 until the opening of the reservation in 1905 were these: the Rhoades Mining Company was formed and on 18 December 1897, Rhoades and Hathenbruck signed a lease with the Ute Indians and submitted it for approval with the Secretary of the Interior.

But even before it could be considered, political machinations began behind the scenes and involved some of the most influential men in mining and government circles, in both Washington and in Utah, as well as elsewhere. They manipulated both the Secretary of the Interior and the Indian Commission and were able to get the Rhoades lease "pigeon-holed" while they organized the Florence Mining Company and soon thereafter the Raven Mining Company. They obtained a judgment against the Rhoades Mining Company denying them entry to the reservation on the threat of arrest, while the Florence and Raven companies had free access to Indian lands. Their lease was ratified by the Secretary of the Interior, even though it was not signed in open council on the reservation as the law required.

The end result was that no investigation was ever held and the Florence and Raven companies raped the reservation lands of mineral prospects, but never located what they had originally set out to find—the Lost Rhoades Mine. The American Asphalt Company also gained access, as did several others. The basis for the leases were equally as flimsy: all had simply taken a small group of Indians to Washington where they had them sign a lease which was then ratified by the Secretary of the Interior, in violation of the law which required the signing to be in open council on the reservation.

Mindful of this fact, Utah Congressman Sutherland introduced a resolution to the House of Representatives on 23 June 1902 for the relief of Caleb Rhoades. From the *Congressional Record* (volume 35, page 7277), House Joint Resolution 204 reads as follows:

JOINT RESOLUTION

Resolved by the Senate and House of Representatives of the United States of America in Congress assembled, That the Secretary of the Interior is hereby authorized and directed to grant to Caleb B. Rhoades, his heirs and assigns, preference right to make five contiguous mineral entries, under the mineral laws of the United States, not to exceed one hundred acres of land, within the Uintah Reservation, in Utah, which entry shall cover the mineral discoveries and locations made, designated, and worked by him and his deceased father prior to the establishment of said reservation: Provided, That upon inquiry and due hearing had thereon by the Secretary of the Interior he shall determine that said discovery and location was made prior to the establishment of said reservation: And provided, That said grant shall take effect only in the event of the agreement of the Indians to the opening of said reservation as provided by the Act of Congress entitled "An Act making appropriations for the current and contingent expenses of the Indian Department, and for fulfilling treaty stipulations with various Indian tribes, for the fiscal year ending June thirtieth, nineteen hundred and three, and for other purposes," approved May twenty-seventh, nineteen hundred and two, and that said locations shall be designated and marked upon the ground at least thirty days prior to the opening of the lands of said reservation to settlement.

The bill was introduced into the first session of the 57th Congress on 23 June 1902. It was thereafter referred to the House Committee on Indian Affairs, where it died.

But the intrigue only begins at this point. The letter of Caleb Rhoades to Reed Smoot dated 23 October 1901, indicates that Jesse Knight was one of those interfering with Rhoades' attempt to get the Indian lease ratified. This indicates that Knight was one of the shadowy figures behind the Florence and Raven mining companies.

In all of these matters the influential Reed Smoot was ever present, first on one side, then on the other. Henderson's letter to Hathenbruck dated 21 July 1902, intimates that Smoot was prone to bribery, and the notarized document of Hathenbruck dated 24 April 1901, giving over his lease to Smoot, indicates that he was one of the "prominent" men who met with Hathenbruck at the Manhattan Hotel in New York City, to whom he was compelled "to turn over a portion of my interests in exchange for help in getting my lease ratified..." Unfortunately, Hathenbruck had no way of knowing that Smoot was secretly working for the interests of Jesse Knight.

Caleb Rhoades had known Jesse Knight intimately for many years and had even been involved with Knight in several coal and copper mining ventures. Rhoades had lived at Diamon City in the Tintic District (where Knight later developed the Humbug Mine) from 1865 until about 1874, at which time he moved to Salem, Utah, not far from Koyle's Dream Mine.

It is interesting to contemplate that Caleb Rhoades, Jesse Knight, and John H. Koyle were all friends and associates at some time in their lives, and had a common connection in their association with Senator Reed Smoot.

However, by the year 1896, Caleb Rhoades and Jesse Knight had become deadly rivals, if not enemies, for the same quest—the source of the golden bonanza on the Uintah-Ouray Indian Reservation.

Chapter Nine

Gunfighters, Ghosts & Gold

IN JULY 1896, JESSE KNIGHT STRUCK his bonanza at the Humbug Mine at Tintic. It was the first of many such major discoveries that eventually made him extremely wealthy. But earlier in the same year, before the strike, Jesse Knight was anything other than wealthy; in fact, he was barely paying his debts.

The Mormon Church was also nearing bankruptcy and the general authorities had approached Jesse Knight seeking financial aid. But Knight had not yet struck the bonanza at Tintic, and so the question must be posed why the Church authorities would seek out Jesse Knight for aid. If Knight had access to wealth at that point, where did it come from?

The answer can be found in part in the collected family history of the Twitchells, who intermarried with the family of Jesse Knight, provided to the authors by descendants of James Twitchell, Sr.:

> Uncle Jesse Knight often told us the story of his Dream Mine, which he said was located somewhere northwest of Vernal in the Uintah Mountains. He said that one day in about 1885 he was standing on a hilltop over-looking the Uintah-Ouray Indian Reservation where he had gone to build an irrigation canal, when he was overcome with a tremendous weakness which caused him to sink to the ground to his knees. While he was in this position he experienced a dream or a vision of an old mine, filled with treasure and with a vein of gold three to four feet in width and running the extent of the cavern. He said he felt as if he had been transported to the place in the spirit, and when he looked up, he saw the Angel Moroni standing in the air above him, and Moroni told him the history of the mine.
>
> Moroni said that the mine was worked many years ago by an ancient people who used the gold for decoration and to make gold plates to keep their records and history on. The angel revealed to Uncle Jesse Knight that the plates which Joseph Smith had translated into the Book of Mormon had been made from that same gold source. When Moroni was alive and walked the earth, he obtained the gold for the plates from the cavern and wrote his history on them, carrying them to where Joseph Smith found them in the Hill Cumorah in New York State.
>
> Uncle Jesse Knight said the room or the cavern was filled with gold plates and many kinds of gold artifacts and that the walls had been plated with pounded gold and there were hieroglyphics written on the walls. Uncle Jesse Knight had seen some of the characters from the original plates of the Book of Mormon, and he said these characters were identical in every fashion.
>
> Moroni told Uncle Jesse Knight that sometime in the future, the Church of Jesus Christ of Latter-day Saints would be facing financial ruin, and that when that day came, Uncle Jesse Knight would be called to get gold from the mine and save the credit of the Church.
>
> …When Uncle Jesse Knight awoke from his dream or his vision, he was too weak to move for a long time. Finally he made it back to Salt Lake City and he told members of his family about the experience, and he told them that someday his Dream Mine would help save the credit of the Church…In 1896, about the time that James Twitchell left Beaver [Utah] for northeastern Utah to settle, Uncle Jesse Knight was called to bring gold from the mine to save the Church from going bankrupt, and so his dream was fulfilled. *[The History of James Twitchell, Sr.* unpub. MS.]

This writer's grandmother, Lovina Jones, married William Coleman Boren. Her cousin,

Elizabeth Jones, married Jesse Knight's brother, James Philander Knight (1838-1909), and bore him fourteen children. One of their children, Clara Elizabeth Knight, who died 24 September 1950, at the age of eighty-four, left an account similar to the Twitchell narrative, gleaned from her father, differing only in the following details.

According to this account, Jesse Knight made a trip to his "Dream Mine" as early as 1894, and upon his return told members of his family that he had seen "marvelous things, wonderful things, like the things which the Prophet Joseph Smith had been shown by the angel" many years before. He also told his brother that he had been given a stone, much like Joseph Smith's seer stone, with which he said he could find hidden treasures under the earth. This is in keeping with the Knight family tradition, inasmuch as both Jesse's father, Newell, and his grandfather, Joseph, had been involved heavily with Joseph Smith's "money-digging" ventures. It is said that when Church authorities learned of Jesse's stone, they condemned the use of it. What became of it is uncertain. Some sources state that it was turned over to the Church, while others maintain that the stone still reposes within the ownership of the Knight family.

Isaac Morley possessed such a seer stone, which he had embedded in the altar of the Manti Temple. Brigham Young posssessed at least four such stones, one of which he presented to the trustees of the University of Deseret in about 1853, while two others were part of his estate when he died in 1877. [For more information on such stones, see *The Widow's Son,* by the authors, at Chapter 29, "Seers and Seer Stones."]

Because the details of Jesse Knight's "Dream Mine" are so similar to those known about the

William Coleman Boren and Elizabeth Bromley. Children: (back row) twins Edward (behind his father) Ezra, (front row) Walter, Ellen, Ethel. Photo taken ca. 1902-03. Edward Boren father of author Kerry Ross Boren. (Edward, Ezra and Walter by marriage to Lovina Jones).

Sacred Mine of the Indians, the first thought is to connect the two as being identical. For example, Caleb Rhoades indicated that the mine contained not only gold ore, but "worked gold, bullion, and artifacts of gold of fine workmanship and quality." At another time, Rhoades stated to a reporter for the *Uintah Papoose* newspaper (precursor of the present-day *Vernal Express)* that the Indians not only jealously guarded the mines because of the gold ore, but because they contained "artifacts and other items of religious significance to the Indians."

It is interesting to note that the above statement was made to a female correspondent to the Vernal newspaper in 1896 while Rhoades was in Vernal, protecting his interests on the reservation. This correspondent was none other than Miss Maude Davis, who later that year married the outlaw William Ellsworth "Elzy" Lay, one of the men whom Caleb Rhoades had hired to protect his mining claims from hired guns of the Florence and Raven mining companies.

It nearly appears that Bishop John H. Koyle, who was a close friend of Jesse Knight, obtained his "Dream Mine" story from Knight, inasmuch as they parallel in nearly every detail, including the caverns paved with gold, the presence of gold plates, the hieroglyphics, and the visitation of the Angel Moroni. Jesse Knight, in turn, may have learned his version from Isaac Morley who, many years earlier, stated that the mines were actually mined-out caverns wherein the "Lamanites" had crafted many gold artifacts and that the walls of the caverns were covered with gold leaf and inscribed with hieroglyphics. Morley stated that the Sacred Mine contained "many gold plates written upon and also a Urim and Thummin."

There can be little doubt that the "Dream Mine" of Jesse Knight was the same as the "Sacred Mine" of Caleb Rhoades, and this explains the feud which developed between these two men beginning in 1896.

During 1896 a number of important events were transpiring simultaneously: the Mormon Church was facing bankruptcy; Jesse Knight struck a bonanza in the Humbug Mine at Tintic; Bishop John H. Koyle was developing his Dream Mine; Caleb Rhoades and his new partner, F.W.C. Hathenbruck, were negotiating for a mining lease on the Ute Reservation; and Butch Cassidy, recently released from the Wyoming State Prison, was organizing the Wild Bunch gang of outlaws. All of these events were seminally connected.

On 23 June 1896, the following agreement was entered into between Rhoades and Hathenbruck, on the first part, and W.E. Christiansen on the other part:

> This agreement, made and entered into this 23d day of June in the year one thousand eight hundred and ninety six, by and between F.W.C. Hathenbruck of Provo City, Utah County, and C.B. Rhoades of Price, Carbon County, in the State of Utah, parties of the first part; and W.E. Christiansen of Vernal, Uintah County, in the State of Utah, party of the second part. Witnesseth, That:

> Whereas the parties of the first part have a certain knowledge of the existence and location of certain mines, placer, veins or lodes, bearing precious minerals, on the Uintah Reservation, and desire to enter into a contract or lease, with the tribe of Indians occupying the Uintah Reservation, for the development and working of said placer, veins or lodes, the contract or lease to be on the terms and of the nature and character of the copy which is attached hereto and made a part of the agreement.

> Now Therefor, The parties of the first part, at the request of the party of the second part, and in consideration of the covenants herein expressed to be performed by the party of the second part, do hereby agree to transfer, set over and convey to the party of the second part, a One Twentieth part interest in the aforesaid contract or lease, when the legal title

> in the same shall have been procured and apportioned, as in the said proposed agreement specified.

> And the party of the second part, in consideration of the promises, and for certain expenses paid in hand from time to time as they are merited, hereby agrees to act as guide and liaison (sic) and help to negotiate with the Indians of whom he has particular knowledge and understanding, and to serve in such capacity as is needed to complete the safe and certain consummation of the aforesaid contract or lease between the parties of the first part and the tribe of Indians occupying the Uintah Reservation.

> And it is further mutually covenanted and agree, if, in any manner, the party of the second part to the said proposed agreement shall fail or neglect to procure or help to secure the lease or title to, and the working of said mines, the parties of the first part therein shall be fully and completely exonerated and released from the covenants and provisions of this agreement.

> IN WITNESS WHEREOF, the said parties have hereunto set their hands and seals, the day and year first above written.

> F.W.C. HATHENBRUCK

> CALEB B. RHOADES

> SIGNED, SEALED AND DELIVERED

> IN THE PRESENCE OF

> W.E. CHRISTIANSEN

> ROBERT D. SWIFT

The foregoing document takes on particularly more significance when true identity of W.E. Christiansen is revealed, for he was, in reality, none other than the infamous Matt Warner, gunfighter and outlaw member of Butch Cassidy's Wild Bunch.

Matt Warner was born Willard Erastus Christiansen on 12 April 1864, at Levan, Utah (near Chicken Creek, site of the Mexican massacre which occurred seven years prior to his birth). He left home at the age of fourteen after striking another youth in the head during the mêlée over the attentions of a pretty girl named Alice Sabey. Believing erroneously that he had killed the boy, Christiansen went to the outlaw stronghold of Brown's Park in northeastern Utah where he began his career as a rustler and later as a prolific bank and train robber. He took the alias of Matt Warner and in 1914 had his name legally changed to preserve it.

Matt Warner had joined the McCarty Gang in the northwest (Tom McCarty married Matt's sister, Tene Christiansen) and had only recently returned from a string of bank robberies in Oregon and Washington when he encountered Caleb Rhoades at Vernal, Utah, in the early summer of 1896.

Matt Warner.

Courtesy Utah State Historical Society.

Rhoades hired Warner—as the foregoing document attests—to assure that the signing of the Indian lease was done safely and securely. Opposition had arisen when the promoters of the Florence and Raven mining companies hired gunmen to protect them while on the reservation. Rhoades apparently wanted to ensure his own safety and that of his companions who were in the process of beating the opposition to the mine; and Matt Warner was not only a renowned gunfighter, but had considerable influence with the Ute Indians.

Two opposing forces were converging on the Uintah Reservation, bringing with them all the elements of an impending war. On the one side were gunmen hired by the secret investors of the Florence and Raven companies—one of whom was Jesse Knight—and on the other side were the gunmen hired by Rhoades and Hathenbruck to protect their interests. The force of hired guns running around in the mountains of the reservation country was bound to end in an encounter, and it did so, in August of 1896.

Both Jesse Knight and Caleb Rhoades converged on a location somewhere on the upper reaches of Dry Fork Canyon in the foothills of the high Uintahs, a few miles northwest of Vernal. It is unclear whether both men had prospects in the area, or whether Knight was following Rhoades, hoping to learn the source of gold. Nevertheless, Jesse Knight began running tunnels into the mountain of upper Dry Fork Canyon, and Caleb Rhoades went there to watch developments.

Aaron Daniels was an associate of Caleb Rhoades at this time. Born 1 August 1822, at Dryden, Thompkins County, New York, Daniels had arrived in Utah as a pioneer of 1847 and settled in Utah Valley in 1852. In 1856 he settled at Fort Supply with Dimick B. Huntington and others; a Mormon fort established near Fort Bridger, Fort Supply was a station calculated to thwart the advance of Johnston's Army upon Utah Territory. Daniels would remain at Fort Supply for several years. In about 1858 he moved to Heber Valley and in about 1860 met Thomas Rhoades in nearby Kamas Valley. In 1879 he removed to Vernal, establishing a ranch near the Green River, not far from the crossing-place of Father Escalante in 1776. Eventually he took up a place on the reservation, about halfway between Fort Duchesne and Whiterocks. Aaron Daniels recorded in his journal:

I have prospected many years with Caleb Rhoades and have been privileged to learn the secret location of at least one of his fabulous tunnels Sacred to the Indians and I have often been asked to reveal this knowledge or asked why I don't profit by it, but having taken an oath both for the benefit of Caleb Rhoades and my wife's people (he married an Indian woman) I am not at liberty to divulge the Secret Location or to profit by it. This I owe also in loyalty to the Mormon Church who, as I have personally heard Chief Walker state, the gold in the vein actually belongs.

Aaron Daniels was seventy-four years of age when Jesse Knight began digging his tunnel into the mountain above Dry Fork Canyon, and he went up the mountain to watch the work. On the last page of his journal, he recorded the following:

> I remember when Jesse Knight started his tunnel and Caleb Rhoades came up the mountain to watch them dig and scrape. I asked Cale if he was worried about Knight finding anything and he said, "Oh, not much. He might be the best engineer in the West as some say, but he will lose on this one. All he will strike where he is going is gray soil," and that is exactly what they struck. Cale really knew his geology and mining, but so did Jess Knight. [see *Footprints in the Wilderness*, pp.323,33]

By the middle of summer, 1896, gunfighters from around the region were converging on the town of Vernal, all hoping to be hired by one side or the other in the impending feud, or share in some way in the profits derived from the possible opening of the fabulous gold mine.

The intrigue began seriously when Caleb Rhoades hired one Henry B. Coleman, a mining promoter of dubious character and reputation, to proceed to a location somewhere in the back reaches of upper Dry Fork Canyon northwest of Vernal. Coleman was to meet there with Robert David Swift, another mining promoter, saloon owner, and some-time member of Cassidy's Wild Bunch. Swift, a Missourian, had also ridden at one time with the James and Younger gangs. On 23 June 1896, he had been a witness to the agreement between Rhoades and Hathenbruck with Matt Warner, the latter of whom was his particular friend.

Swift and Coleman made a camp in the mountains and settled down in a tent awaiting the

Aaron Daniels.
Courtesy Uintah County Library, Vernal.

arrival of Matt Warner, whom Rhoades had hired to help them move the camp. Warner had agreed to go up the mountain to protect Rhoades' interest according to their agreement, but was delayed because he demanded $500 in expenses. Rhoades and Hathenbruck wired Salt Lake City to get approval of the money. Warner set out the same day, accompanied by his friend, Bill Wall, a gambler at the Antler Saloon, who went along just "for the ride." They arrived at the camp of Coleman and Swift, which was situated in a grove of trees, just at sunrise. As Warner and Wall rode across a clearing towards the tent, Coleman and Swift were in the process of cooking breakfast.

As Warner and Wall reached the middle of the clearing, gunfire suddenly erupted from behind nearby trees. At the first shot, Warner instinctively pulled his rifle from his saddle boot and leaped from his horse, almost simultaneously firing while he pulled his startled friend Bill Wall to the ground.

The two men took refuge behind some quaking aspen trees where Matt began to return a deadly fire at his ambushers. Protected by a tree, he took a heavy toll on his attackers, even though one of the men kept firing at a single spot on the tree, trying to force a slug through the trunk to kill Warner.

The three ambushers proved to be the Stanton brothers—Ike and Dick—and one Dave Milton. When the gunfight ended a brief few minutes after it began, Dick Stanton and Dave Milton were dead or dying, and Ike Stanton was seriously wounded (he later had his leg amputated). Matt Warner and his companions were untouched.

Warner was arrested for the murders of Stanton and Milton and lodged in the jail at Vernal. Butch Cassidy, Charles Crouse, Elzy Lay and a few other members of the Wild Bunch (including this writer's grandfather, William C. Boren) gathered in the streets and threatened to take Matt out of jail by force, to save him from a lynch mob which had organized to "string him up." Sheriff John T. Pope took Warner and Wall out of the jail secretly at night and transported them over the Uintah Mountains via the old Carter Military Road to the railroad station at Carter Station, Wyoming, and from there by train to the Weber County jail at Ogden, Utah.

Cassidy and his gang converged on Ogden with a force nearly 75 strong, threatening to remove him from that jail too, but Warner talked them out of bloodshed. He said he would rather have a good attorney, and so Cassidy hired Douglas A. Preston of Wyoming. But Preston was expensive, so on 13 August 1896, Butch Cassidy, Elzy Lay and Henry Rhodes "Bub" Meeks held up the bank of Montpelier, Idaho.

Matt Warner was tried in Ogden and sentenced to five years in Utah State Prison on 21 September 1896. He was released in January 1900 by Governor Heber M. Wells, and settled in Price, Utah, on the farm owned by Caleb Rhoades. When Rhoades died in 1905, Matt Warner purchased Rhoades' property.

However, Matt Warner was in jail during the remainder of the year 1896 and Caleb Rhoades was compelled to look elsewhere for someone to defend his claim. On 19 November 1896, Rhoades and Hathenbruck entered into an almost identical agreement with Mathew "Matt" Thomas of Vernal [see *Footprints in the Wilderness*, p. 254.]

J. Mathew Thomas was a gunfighter of some reputation and a close friend and associate of Matt Warner and Butch Cassidy. In addition, Thomas was well acquainted with the Indians and spoke the Ute language fluently.

Thomas chose a carefully selected circle of associates to go with him into the mountains in the late fall, to clean up the camp area that had been vacated by Henry Coleman and Bob Swift. Among those who accompanied Thomas were Mid Nichols (another of Matt Warner's close friends and a renowned gunman in his own right), Bob Swift, George A. Storrs and Elzy Lay. All of these men—with the exception of Storrs—had ridden with Cassidy to Ogden in the month of August in the attempt to break Matt Warner out of jail. By early December they were back in the mountains to retrieve what was left of the campsite and to protect the claims of Caleb Rhoades. Shortly thereafter, Elzy Lay left for his honeymoon at Robbers Roost, having recently married Maude Davis of Vernal. It is not the last we shall hear of Lay in connection with the mines.

Another of the hired guns of Caleb Rhoades who was involved in the Dry Fork campaign of 1896 was George Storrs. George Alfred Storrs was born 5 July 1863, at Springville, Utah, a son of George Storrs and Lydia Mary Kindred. He died 3 May 1937, in Salt Lake City, and was buried in Forest Lawn Cemetery, Glendale, California, very near the grave of Elzy Lay, who had been buried there three years earlier.

Storrs had been a somewhat renowned lawman and one-time warden of the Utah State Prison. At the same time, he was heavily involved in mining and construction.

Storrs remains something of an enigma. In 1896-97, he appears to have been in the employ or partnership of Rhoades and Hathenbruck in securing gold prospects on the reservation. Storrs was one of the "hired guns" which Rhoades and Hathenbruck recruited to protect their interests from the encroachment of the Florence and Raven mining companies. He appears to have been sympathetic to Caleb Rhoades until the time of Rhoades' death in 1905.

On 7 September 1910, F.W.C. Hathenbruck entered into an agreement with George Storrs who then owned a small quarry in Slate Canyon adjacent to certain granite, slate and lime deposits recently purchased by Hathenbruck through the

Timber & Stone Act of 3 June 1878. Storrs and Hathenbruck developed the Provo Slate Company, Inc., which primarily produced purple, green and red roofing slate, and also included a granite quarry. Altercations arose in the company in 1920 and Hathenbruck attempted to bring in other businessmen, but he was unsuccessful.

Shortly thereafter, Storrs switched his allegiance and became involved in mining interests with Rhoades' and Hathenbruck's rival, Jesse Knight. As early as 1912, however, George Storrs was made general manager of Knight's Spring Canyon Coal Company in Carbon County, one of Utah's largest coal producing claims, and, as we have noted elsewhere, the town of Storrs, Utah, was named for him. The townsite belonged to Knight, however, and Matt Warner—also previously employed by Rhoades—worked for Knight and Storrs as a lawman to keep order in the town.

There is no doubt that Butch Cassidy himself had considerable interest in the Rhoades mines. Cassidy was an avid miner and prospector all of his life, when not involved in bank and train robberies. In 1912 he was a partner in a gold mine in Alaska with none other than Wyatt Earp and Walter Knott (founder of Knott's Berry Farm in California). In 1929 he made a major gold discovery in the canyons of the Colorado River not far from Las Vegas, Nevada, but the prospect was never developed due to the proposed construction of Hoover Dam.

As late as 1940, Cassidy was involved in a partnership with his daughter, Thelma Parker Bean, and her husband, a Death Valley prospector known affectionately by all as "Mister," in trying to locate the hidden lode of the old worked-out Johnnie Mine near Pahrump, Nevada. This mine had been developed many years before by Walter Knott and—amazingly—Jesse Knight, who was a major stockholder in the Johnnie Mine when it was controlled by a group of Mormon investors led by the Reynolds brothers of Vernal, Utah. After a major gunfight over ownership of the mine, the Johnnie was closed down.

Cassidy believed that the Johnnie Mine contained a hidden pocket of wealth and he was supervising the search for it when, on 24 March 1944, he was killed at the mine entrance when a cable snapped and an eight-foot wooden pulley wheel toppled over on him. He lies buried in an unmarked grave in the desert near the ghost town of Johnnie, Nevada.

But Cassidy's connection to the Rhoades mines is even more direct, as witnessed by the testimony of one of his henchmen, Joe Walker, who had assisted Cassidy, Lay, and Bub Meeks in the robbery of the Castlegate, Utah, payroll in 1897. Walker was interviewed by James Sharp, onetime assistant to the LDS Church Historian, at a rooming house on 1st Avenue in Salt Lake City in 1947, when Walker was eighty-seven. The complete interview was first printed in *Footprints in the Wilderness* (pp.333-36), but is here reproduced in pertinent part:

> ...shortly after we divided the Castlegate money, me and Butch were riding from the Roost [Robber's Roost] out to Brown's Hole, and not wanting to be too conspicuous, we were trying to avoid seeing too many people. We cut across west to Vernal and when we entered the mountains to the northwest of that town [in the vicinity of upper Dry Fork Canyon] it began to sprinkle.

> Butch spurred his horse and rode up a side canyon and stopped near some thick brush. We left our horses and ran like hell. I followed right behind him and into an old mine tunnel we went, just as the rain came down in bucketfuls.

> Now that tunnel was not over five feet high and three feet wide and was piled about two feet deep with rocks. When we had sat down on some old leather pack bags, Butch told me that the mine was one the Spaniards had worked. The Indians called it "Carre-shin-ob," and the Spaniards called it the "Madre de Oro del Uintah." Butch sure knew his history and he knew a lot the Indians had told him, for he was friendly with them.

> As we sat there I reached under the leather bag and got a rock. Gosh, it was heavy! I took it to the mouth of the tunnel and say, it shined like almost solid gold! Butch called me to come back and told me anyone who took any of that gold would have the curse of God placed upon him...

I slipped a small piece of that gold in my pocket but when we stepped outside, Butch drew his gun and told me to put it back. How the hell did he know I had it? But Butch, he knew everything. Well, I went back and put that piece of rock—about the size of my hand—on top of one of those leather bags, and came back out for I knew Butch was not fooling. When it stopped raining we rode away and Butch made me promise that I would never go there again.

When the "Wild Bunch" broke up—that was what we were called who rode with Butch—it was mighty slim picking for some of us, so one day I got two men who I knew were not afraid of God, man, or devil, or the curse of God, and told them about the gold.

We got eight fine horses and a pack outfit for heavy work, and a light one. Then we rode out and camped about half a mile from the mine for almost a week, just to see if there were any Utes watching. We saw none. Then one night I took one of those men and had a hard time finding it, for you see, the timbers had rotted and it had caved in at the entrance. We had to crawl in on our hands and knees.

Once inside, we let (sic: lit) some matches and there on top of the leather bag was the same piece of gold that I had put there years ago. Then we went back to camp and laid some plans. The next morning I was to take five horses and the heavy pack and go down to the ford at Green River and wait (near present-day Jensen, Utah). They were to wait until night and go to the mine and get not over 100 pounds of that gold ore and make a swift ride to where I was, change horses, and head for Denver, sell the ore and give me my share of the cash. If we made it, then we would make another trip.

I got to the ford and staked my horses around and built a fire and got supper, but did not go to bed for I knew they could make it down there by about three in the morning, as I sat up and kept the fire going so they could not miss me.

Daylight came and no men. Then sun up and along came three Indians! They stopped and talked with me and just then we saw those two men coming, but mighty slow. When they saw the Indians with me, they let go of the rope on the pack horse and lit out for the river, jumped their horses and each grabbed his horse's tail as they started to swim across.

When the horses were about a quarter of the way across, they decided to turn back. The men let go and tried to get hold of the bridle reins, but both went down and we never saw them come up. The horses came out right where we were, and say, those darn fools had about 100 pounds of gold in a sack on each saddle. I'll bet they had at least 50 pounds in their pockets and that was why they could not swim.

The Indians looked at the sacks and opened one and saw it was gold. Then they went over to the pack horse which was too tired to even try to stand up, and say, they must have had at least 250 pounds of gold on that little pack saddle.

Now, the Indians talked for a short time and one got on his horse and rode like the clatter wheels of hell. I thought it was time for me to get going but those two Utes told me to stay there.

About sundown that Indian, an old chief, and two or three more came and examined the gold and asked me a lot of questions, but I lied out of it. Then they searched me and for once in my life I was lucky, for I never had one bit of that gold on me. Just at night fall they reloaded those three horses and the old chief started back alone. The others stayed with me and the next morning let me go to Brown's Hole.

Now, I'm telling you, if those two men had not made damned hogs of themselves, maybe we might have got away with that gold, and if we had, then we would have took more and now I would not be where I am now—with scarcely a thin dime to my name. But I guess Butch was right; he said there was a curse upon anyone who took that gold, and as for me—well, I'll hold on to that thin dime as long as I can, but never again will I go back to where there must be all of a million dollars in almost pure gold, just piled up in an old tunnel!

Chapter Ten

Red Exodus

MY GRANDFATHER, WILLIAM COLEMAN BOREN, was a great friend of the Ute Indians, both in southern Utah and on the Uintah-Ouray Reservation in the Uintah Basin. He also maintained a lifelong association with Butch Cassidy and the Wild Bunch, and with the search for the Lost Rhoades Mines. His entire enigmatic life, it seems, was inextricably connected to the Utes, the Mormons, the outlaws, and the mines.

William C. "Will" Boren was born 17 January 1853, at Provo, Utah, a son of Coleman Boren and Flora Maria Kingsley. Of Irish pioneer stock, his family had explored Kentucky and Tennessee with the redoubtable frontiersman, Daniel Boone; in fact, his own grandmother, Susannah Bryan Boren, was first cousin to Boone's wife, Rebecca Bryan. One of his brothers, Albert Boone Boren, had been named in honor of the illustrious relative.

William's father, Coleman Boren, was born 14 October 1808, on the family plantation on Sulphur Fork of Red River, a few miles north of Nashville, Tennessee. He had grown to manhood in southern Illinois, where he converted to Mormonism and settled at Nauvoo. Following the death of Joseph Smith, he was "called" by Brigham Young to serve as the president of the Mount Pisgah, Iowa, branch of the Church, assisting the Mormon pioneers on their westward trek. Coleman himself arrived in Utah in 1852, setting in Utah Valley (Provo).

William was born not long after the family's arrival. His mother, Flora Maria Kingsley, was his father's second (polygamous) wife, being nearly twenty years his junior. Priorly, she had been one of the plural wives of Joseph Smith. William was only five years old when his father died on 13 May 1858, not yet fifty years of age. The tragedy of his father's untimely death left a lasting scar on his life, for it occurred under the most traumatic and appalling of circumstances.

Coleman Boren was a wealthy and influential man. He owned two large homes, one in Provo City proper, and the other near his peach orchards on the Orem Bench. Coleman fell victim to the events of that fateful year 1857. As a lieutenant of the "Silver Greys" in the Nauvoo Legion (the Mormon militia), he commanded a detachment in Echo Canyon during the "Utah War," when the Mormons resisted the coming of Johnston's Army. Later in the year he led another detachment to the area of Chicken Creek, following the massacre of the Spaniards, to pursue several bands of Indians who had raided Mormon settlements in retaliation for being blamed for the massacre. Still later he became embroiled in the events surrounding the Mountain Meadow Massacre in southern Utah, where Mormons and Indians murdered scores of men, women and children who were part of a wagon train en route to California.

By the time the emigrants reached Provo, some fifty miles south of Salt Lake City, they were suffering severe want. The children were ailing the most, suffering not only from hunger, but dysentery due to lack of fruits and vegetables in their diet.

Coleman Boren was the wealthiest man in Provo. His granaries were full and his peach harvest had been bountiful. By strange coincidence, one of the members of the Fancher party was Isaac Boren, a nephew of Coleman, who had settled in Carroll County, Arkansas. Young Isaac Boren brought two of the starving children to his uncle's home and begged for supplies to alleviate their suffering. Coleman succumbed to the pathetic plea and provided them with several bushels of grain, and some fresh fruit and vegetables. It would prove to be a fatal mistake.

During his youthful years, Coleman's son, Will Boren harbored a deep resentment towards

Brigham Young and the Church, though in later years he underwent a religious conversion.

While still in his twenties, Will secured a contract to freight flour and other staples from the railroad to the Uintah-Ouray Reservation, and thus began his life-long association and friendship with the Ute Indians, though it did not exactly begin on a friendly note. On his first trip to the reservation, the starving Utes surrounded his wagon, demanding that the flour be turned over to them, but he stood his ground, informing them that his contract called for delivery to Indian Agent Pardon Dodds, and to none other.

During the night, several husky young Utes entered his wagon, armed with butcher's knives, in an attempt to take the flour, but Will successfully drove them both away. He sat in the shadows, his Winchester in hand, throughout the rest of the night.

The next morning he harnessed his team and started for the agency at Whiterocks. As he proceeded, Indians by twos and threes began to appear on the hilltops, and soon fell a pace behind him, collecting as they progressed, until by the time he reached the post, there were fifty or more trailing behind the wagon. When Will stopped at the post door and hopped down from the wagon, one of the sub-chiefs, a Ute named Cump-an-nees, approached him with a butcher's knife in hand. Will prepared to defend himself, but Cump-an-nees merely smiled and turned the knife around, handing it to him handle-forward.

"White-eyes is a brave man," Cump-an-nees told him. "You take knife away from young buck and pretty much scare-'em all so. All friend now. You take knife. Cump-an-nees call you 'Witch-i-cook,' all same." In the Ute dialect, "Witch-i-cook" is the word for butcher's knife, and so my grandfather was ever after called by the Utes, and Cump-an-nees became his life-long friend.

During the late seventies, Will turned his freight wagon to the more lucrative business of hauling ore for the newly developed Silver King Mine at Park City; it was here that he met the great Indian prospector, "Pick" Murdock, who first discovered the Silver King lode, before losing it to the machinations of Senator Thomas Kearns.

In March 1880, William C. Boren married pretty Lovina Jones; he was 27 and she was sweet 16. Lovina was born 8 February 1864, at Fairview, in Sanpete County: she was a grand-daughter of Joseph Smith, founder of Mormonism, and a great-granddaughter of Isaac Morley. Lovina's father died when she was only a year old, and as the youngest of a large family, she was "farmed out" to be raised by foster parents — Maximilian and Ann Campbell Gillies Parker. Thus she became the adopted sister of Robert Leroy Parker, a.k.a. Butch Cassidy.

Will Boren was a wanderer, a free spirit, who soon dragged his growing family from one new home to another. He was led by some constant attraction to the Indian county of the Basin and settled briefly in the new town of Ashley, which came to be known as Vernal. He served briefly as a deputy under Uintah County's first sheriff, Sterling D. Colton, but he became swayed by the persuasive fledgling outlaw Cassidy, and estab-lished a ranch in isolated Rainbow Park on the Green River, along what was then known as the "Horsethief Trail." Thereafter, for the next twenty-odd years, Will's life was to be inextri-cably entwined with that of the amiable leader of the Wild Bunch.

During the eighties, Will freighted ore from the mines at Silver Reef, and lived for a time with relatives at Parea, in southern Utah. He took up his own ranch near Cannonville, and operated the Heber Wiley ranch in Bryce Canyon, where young Cassidy and his cohorts boarded rustled livestock. In 1895 he moved his family once again to the Uintah Basin, taking residence in a cabin on the ranch of Lovina's brother, James N. Jones, Jr., in Maeser Ward, near Vernal.

Will's return to the Basin had a definite purpose. In 1896, Butch Cassidy and Elzy Lay moved into an adjoining cabin on the Jones place; Butch was keeping company with the beautiful and enigmatic Etta Place, and Lay had recently married Maude Davis. Then, shortly thereafter, all of them — including my grandfather — removed to Robber's Roost.

Will became the manager of yet another of Cassidy's ranches (a ranch actually belonging to the Meeks family) near Cleveland, in Emery

County. The reason became clear when, on 21 April 1897, Cassidy and Lay, assisted by Bub Meeks and Joe Walker, robbed the payroll of the Castle Gate Coal Company, a few miles west of Price, Utah.

Joe Walker cut the telegraph and telephone lines between Castle Gate and Price, while Bub Meeks waited with the first fresh relay of horses in Spring Canyon. The second relay was kept by gang members "Mizoo" Schultz and Sanford "Sang" Thompson near Cleveland, between Price and Robbers Roost, for the last leg of the escape to the fastness of the latter place.

Shortly thereafter, Schultz and Thompson were captured and interrogated, but were eventually released for lack of evidence. Rumors were rampant, however, and some of these rumors implicated my grandfather. While he was still residing on the ranch (about halfway between Cleveland and Ferron), he wrote a letter to the *Vernal Express*, published under date of 1 September 1898 ("Utah News," page 2), as follows:

> William Boren, of Ferron, Emery County, writes that Butch Cassidy has not been at his ranch—in fact he has no ranch. Neither does he employ Schultz or Thompson who were captured when Joe Walker was killed.

Of course, Joe Walker was not killed; two men had been killed by a posse following the robbery, and erroneously identified as Joe Walker and Butch Cassidy. One of these men, presumed to be Butch, was later identified as Johnny Herring of Wyoming, but the man thought to be Walker was never otherwise identified.

On 11 October 1900, at three o'clock in the afternoon, thirty-six-year-old Lovina Jones Boren died in childbirth, leaving ten children. In 1901, needing a mother to raise his large family, Will Boren married a second wife, Elizabeth Bromley, with Bishop Sterling D. Colton officiating. In an effort to make a new beginning, he moved his family onto the reservation, among his Indian friends.

Will Boren leased a portion of ranch land on the Whiterocks River from Robert Marimon. Marimon had came into the region from Kentucky with the Reed family (see chapter entitled "The Reed Connection)—cousins of Kit Carsons—and had been post trader at Ouray on the Green River since 1896. In October 1902, Marimon became post trader at Whiterocks, and leased his ranch to my grandfather, where Will and his family lived for the next four years.

Will's neighbors included the Reeds, Happy Jack, and Pick Murdock, all of whom lived on Big Tom's Allotment, and Inepegut—the Crazy Indian—who had no home at all. There was a special bond between my grandfather and Inepegut.

Inepegut had been a member of the Timpanogos Utes, who lived in Utah Valley, when President Abraham Lincoln set aside the reservation lands in the Uintah Basin in 1865. He was just a boy then, reluctant to leave his home on the Provo River; he ran away and hid in the ledges on a rocky hillside. His old mother and his brother, Provo John, tried to entice him to come down, to no avail. In a fit of rage, Inepegut threw a stone and killed his mother.

As a result of his mother's murder, Inepegut became an outcast of his tribe. He might have been killed except for the Ute superstition that the spirit of one who is crazy comes back to haunt his killers. Instead, he was taken to Spirit Lake, high in the Uintah Mountains, and tied naked to a tree to die from exposure. He loosed himself and beat his captors home, though they were mounted and he was barefoot. Three times they returned him, and each time he beat them home. It was believed that evil spirits attended him, and so he was thereafter avoided. He lived the rest of his life devoid of clothing, and slept out summer and winter without shelter, exposed to the elements and disdain. He would, in winter, build two fires, sitting on the coals of one while tending the other, then switching places, and so prevented freezing to death.

Inepegut was amazingly accurate at throwing stones, bringing down rabbits and other small game for food, and he was the swiftest runner anyone had seen, frequently out-running the fleet-footed prey. He could often be seen suckling with calves among the milk cows at nearby Fort Duchesne. Often during the winter, Inepegut would fall asleep on his bed of coals and his hair would freeze in the ice. Each morning my grandfather would send one of his sons, including my father, to chop the old man's hair out of the ice so he could rise. The family also left handouts of food and clothing on the back steps of the house, and Inepegut would retrieve the food, but refused the clothing, leaving a freshly killed rabbit or sagehen in repayment—he would never accept charity.

My late uncle, Roy Boren, who was then in his teens, sowed his wild oats by buying liquor from Bill Macginnis' Saloon (Bill Macginnis, a.k.a. Elzy Lay) on "The Strip," a sort of No-Man's Land existing in the middle of the reservation, and bootlegging it to the Indians living at Whiterocks. Because he made these illicit journeys late at night, the Utes called him "Wobanee"—the Night Hawk.

My father also had a nickname, but it came not from the Ute dialect, but because he had an Indian girlfriend living in the little town of Hayden. She bore him a child—and so I have a half-breed, half-brother or half-sister whom I have never met—and the sobriquet "Hayden" stuck with him the remainder of his life.

My grandfather's residence on the reservation during these crucial years put him squarely in the middle of the controversy surrounding the removal of reservation lands in 1905 due to the Rhoades-Hathenbruck lease.

The Ute Indians originally inhabited the area from the Rocky Mountains of Colorado on the east to the deserts of the Great Basin on the west, and from the area of South Pass on the north to the northern regions of Arizona and New Mexico on the south. Their linguistic group, as we have elsewhere noted, is called Ute-Aztecan, indicating they were in some way connected with the Aztec group in history. Then came the Spaniards, and the Utes achieved a brief era of ascendancy by virtue of the horse. They were able to sweep out of their mountains and hunt the buffalo of the Great Plains, and they allied themselves to such nations as the Comanches and Apaches, and became superior in war.

Although the Spaniards subjected the Utes to a certain amount of slavery and abuse, the Indians managed a profitable alliance with them for the most part. Their real problems began with the arrival of the "white-eyes"—the Americans.

The first white Americans encountered by the Utes were fur trappers and traders. These men generally respected the Indian way of life, and many of them intermarried with the Utes. One such man was Thomas L. "Pegleg" Smith, whom we have noted previously. In 1828, when Smith helped the Utes defeat the Shoshones, he was rewarded with as many Ute wives as he wanted. Smith, being as he said, "a modest man," took only three.

In about 1837, Walker became war chief of the Utes, and by his horse raids into California and Mexico became the richest chief in the West. When the Mormons came in 1847, Walker wanted war and led that faction of the tribe who advocated the extermination of these encroachers. His brother, Sowiette used a bullwhip on Walker to convince him of his power over the political affairs of the tribe.

Trouble began in 1849 when the Mormons built Fort Utah (Provo) on the ground that had been used from time immemorial as a campsite of the Ute nation. Some few days before the fort was occupied, five Ute braves were killed by the Mormons for taking cattle. The result was the "Walker War" that ended with a treaty whereby the Utes required Dimick P. Huntington, the negotiator, to swear by the sun that the Mormons would not drive the Indians from their land, nor infringe upon their rights. The Mormons soon broke the treaty in their quest for colonization, and the Utes received their first taste of white treachery.

When Chief Walker died 29 January 1855, his brother Arapeen succeeded him as chief of the Sanpetes; within two years he was completely controlled by the Mormon authorities.

The 1864 Utah Legislature asked Congress for the removal of the Indians, from as far south as central Utah, to the Uintah Basin that had been set apart as a reservation by the executive order of Abraham Lincoln in October 1861. This was a blatant violation of the Mormon treaty with the Utes.

The act itself clearly indicates the attitude of the federal government toward the Utes, stating "that all such reservations shall be selected at points as remote as may be practicable for the present settlements in Utah Territory." In April of 1865, because the Mormons violated their promise not to divest the Utes of their land, and had them removed to the reservation in 1864, in April of 1865 the Sanpete Utes went on the warpath. Led by war chief Black Hawk, the war lasted twenty–one bloody months, killed more than seventy Mormon settlers, and many times that number of Indians.

Nevertheless, by 1867, the Office of Indian Affairs had most of the Indians removed to the reservation in the isolated and arid Uintah Basin. When Black Hawk died in 1870, so did the Utes' hope for future resistance to the Mormons.

For those tribes of Utes who inhabited the western slope of Colorado, the day of disaster was postponed a little longer. One of the reasons for their better condition was the fortunate choice of Kit Carson as the first agent. He served in that capacity from 1853 until 1859.

The great trouble came with the Utes after the discovery of gold near Denver in 1858. That area increased in population so rapidly that a territory was organized in 1861. The following year an agency was set up to serve the northern Utes.

The first band to be removed from their ancestral lands were the Tabeguaches. In return for their lands, the Utes were promised 750 head of cattle and 3,500 head of sheep, $100,000 in ten years, and the government was to furnish them a blacksmith. The government failed to fulfill any of the obligations of the treaty even though the land was surrendered.

The treaty of 1868 gave seven Colorado bands of Utes about one-third of the present state of Colorado, with full assurance of the government that it would remain forever the possession of the tribes. The discovery of mineral deposits in the San Juan Mountains brought an influx of whites into the region, and the Ute chief Ouray protested. At first troops escorted miners off the lands, but public outcry soon put a stop to the practice. The government then "negotiated" and ratified a new treaty without even consulting the Utes. On 29 April 1874, the Utes lost most of their lands in Colorado.

After this time the Colorado Utes were administered through two agencies, one at White River, near the present site of Meeker, Colorado, and the other near Montrose, called the Uncompahgre Agency.

Nathan C. Meeker was appointed agent at the White River Agency in 1878. Meeker had been a successful newspaperman but had failed at virtually everything else he tried. He was a religious fanatic who promoted the government's "Severalty" plan for the Indians, which called for the Indians to be given a plot of ground and be taught to be farmers. Meeker gathered the Indians of northwestern Colorado near the agency and tried to force the horse-loving Utes to take up the plow and the hoe.

The two leading Utes of the region were Douglas and Captain Jack (not to be confused with Happy Jack). Captain Jack had been raised and educated by Brigham Young in Utah, but to the surprise of Meeker, it was this educated Indian who most opposed the beginning of the farms. Douglas was more receptive and convinced a few of the younger braves to help clear the land. Meeker's twenty-year-old daughter, Josephine, just out of Oberlin, came west to serve as teacher.

Meeker was an oppressive taskmaster, withholding rations (goods provided for by the treaty) to force the Indians to help build an irrigation ditch; the Utes went hunting game for food, and Meeker withheld even more because they stopped plowing the fields.

One of the Utes, Johnson by name, became upset when Meeker ordered his horse pasture to be plowed. He confronted Meeker, who told the Indian that he had too many horses and should shoot some of them. Johnson, in anger, dragged the agent from his house and would have thrashed him if agency employees had not intervened.

Meeker, afraid for his life, asked Commissioner Hayt for troops, and Major T.T. Thornburg was dispatched from Fort Steele, Wyoming, with 178 men and 33 wagons. On 26 September 1879, when the detachment was about sixty-five miles north of the agency, Captain Jack and nine other Utes rode into the camp and inquired as to their intentions. By 29 September, three hundred braves had assembled and Captain Jack ambushed the military train. Fifty-three soldiers, including Major Thornburg, were killed.

The same day as the attack on the troops, a group of about 25 Indians led by Douglas attacked the White River Agency. Meeker was killed, as were eight young men who worked at the agency. The three women and two children at the agency were taken captive and were held as hostages for twenty-three days. It was alleged afterwards that all three of the women were raped while in captivity, though it was rare that Indians ever perpetrated this deed historically.

When I was a boy of fourteen (1955), I became a blood-brother to a young Ute named Danny Colorow. Danny's grandfather, an old man of ninety-four, was son of Ute Chief Colorow, and was himself named Colorow. This Colorow had been a youth of eighteen at the time of the so-called "Meeker Massacre." and was present when Meeker was killed. I have often heard the story from the old man's lips, but several things he said stand out clearly in my mind: regarding Meeker, Colorow commented that, "Indian say it is not your guns which kill my people—it is your plow-shares." As for the death of Meeker himself, Colorow stated bluntly, "When white men kill Indians, they say it is a great victory; when Indian kill white man, they say it is a massacre." When I asked him if it was true that the Meeker women had been raped, his reply was very pointed: "White men have amazing minds; they can remember things that never happened."

The Meeker and Thornburg massacres gave the people of Colorado the excuse they needed to remove the Utes from the rich lands of the western slope. The "Treaty of 1880"—which was nothing more than a bill for removal—called for the evacuation of almost all Utes from Colorado to the Uintah Reservation in Utah, already crowded with displaced Utes from that state.

In the spring of 1881 the transfer was made under heavy military guard. Captain James Parker of the Fourth Cavalry has left us this account:

> The next morning, shortly after sunrise, we saw a thrilling and pitiful sight. The whole Ute nation on horseback and on foot was streaming by. As they passed our camp their gait broke into a run. Sheep were abandoned, blankets and personal possessions strewn along the road, women and children were loudly wailing.

It was inevitable that they should move, and better then than after a fruitless and bloody struggle. They should think, too, that the land was lost beyond recovery:

> And as we marched behind the Indians, pushing them out, he (the commander) sent word to all the surrounding whites, who hurried after us taking up the land…in three days the rich lands of the Uncompahgre were all occupied.

By the time the White River and Uncompahgre Utes arrived in Utah, part of the Uintah Basin had already been lost to them. The Mormons had succeeded in establishing the settlement of Ashley (Vernal) in 1878, and Fort Thornburg (named in honor of the late Major) was constructed by the military not long afterwards to protect the settlers, and the surrounding area was never used for the benefit of the Indians as promised. For the next twenty-five or more years the Utes crowded onto reservation lands barely able to sustain their numbers.

Then, in 1905, President Theodore Roosevelt withdrew 1,100,000 acres from the Ute lands to create the Uintah National Forest Reserve. This was followed closely by what proved to be the final straw for the Utes—the reservation was thrown open to white settlement.

It began with a political dispute between certain Mormon Church officials, Mormon Senator Reed Smoot, the Republican Party, and Thomas Kearns and his newspaper, *The Salt Lake Tribune*. In 1901 Kearns—who was Catholic—had been elected to the United States Senate, but in 1905 the Republican Party (composed primarily of Mormons in Utah) withdrew its support from Kearns and elected George Sutherland. Kearns was outraged. When he learned that the Church hierarchy was working on a scheme to secure Uintah Indian Reservation lands for its members, Kearns was convinced that the Church, under the leadership of Joseph F. Smith and Reed Smoot, were working to gain political and economic control of the state.

At the center of the controversy was William H. Smart, president of the Wasatch Stake, which ecclesiastical jurisdiction included the Uintah Indian Reservation. Smart had gone secretly to the reservation prior to its opening to identify suitable land and water resources for homesteading. He organized the Wasatch Development Company to assist Church members in locating Indian lands. Kearns blasted the move, accusing the Mormons of a "most insolent attempt to thwart by underhand means" efforts of the government to open the reservation, blaming "the present odious presidency of Joseph F. Smith."

However much the opposition, the Mormon Church was successful, and nearly 37,000 individuals from all over the country registered for Indian land during the first two weeks of August 1905. Drawing of names took place at the Proctor Academy in Provo on 16 August 1905. During the next few days over 5772 names were drawn from a barrel, each recipient gaining 160 acres of the choicest Indian land.

The Ute Indians were understandably outraged. But they were not alone. Many whites were also opposed to the treatment being accorded these good people, and among these most prominently was my grandfather, William C. Boren. He refused to enter his name in the land lottery and discouraged as many of his white neighbors as he could from participating. Realizing this would not be enough, he raised a delegation of Utes to accompany him to Provo to launch a formal protest prior to the drawing. Notable in this delegation were Happy Jack, Cumpanees, Pick Murdock, Tab-Wash (Tabuache), and Mountain Sheep.

My father, Edward Boren, and his twin brother Ezra, were twelve years of age that fateful year, and they accompanied their father to Provo, riding on the tailgate of the wagon. Happy Jack

Ute Delegation:13 Ohto Blunco, 14 william H. Berry (standing), 15 Tap-uch, 16 Captin Jack, 17 Tim Johnon. Thorn Photo. Coutesy Uintah County Library, Vernal.

rode along behind on his horse, while several of the Ute delegation rode silently in the wagon box. My father recalled that memorable trip vividly; with every jarring bounce of the wagon as it rolled across rocks and ruts, the boys would bruise their butts on the hard tailgate, and Happy Jack, trailing close behind, would grin from ear to ear.

At Provo, the boys took in the excitement of the large bustling crowd gathering in the park in front of the of the Proctor Academy. Rows of benches had been set up near the front for visiting dignitaries and important visitors, while other spectators—and Indians—were forced to stand in the rear. The twins climbed a tree and from a large forking branch, watched the proceedings.

The hearings, intended to give interested parties a forum pro and con, were a mere formality, to assure the propriety of policy and procedure, and were a foregone conclusion. Nevertheless, my grandfather took the podium on the steps of the building and defended his Indian friends (an act of inordinate pride for his descendants) in a fiery and articulate speech about broken promises and broken hearts, and he urged his fellow white men of conscience to withdraw their bids for Indian lands.

But the winning speech of the day, profound in its poignant brevity, was that of Happy Jack. Happy was not invited to speak; he stood with the rest of his people at the rear of the crowd until his friend Will Boren had finished speaking. Then he made his way through the throng to the front row, where the well-dressed dignitaries sat on the long benches.

Happy Jack waited until one of the officials began to speak, advocating the removal of the Utes from their lands. Then he sat down on the end of the bench and began to slide slowly, moving the dignitaries over until the man on the other end fell off the bench. After a minute or two, Happy slid over again, and another white man fell off the end of the bench.

The speaker, irritated by the commotion, asked what was the meaning of the interruption. Happy Jack, considering the question as good as an invitation to speak, stood up boldly, arms folded, and gave the following profound reply: "White man say to Indian, 'Move over, move over." Indian move over. White man say again to Indian, 'Move over, move over.' Indian move over. Indian can no move over more, or he will fall off bench. My people all say, 'We will move no more.'"

But the lottery was approved, and the Indians were once again forced to move over. Many of them, however, determined that rather than move over, they would move on, and they mobilized to leave the reservation. Unable to stem the tide of white invaders, their anger turned to dismay, and the Utes decided to flee. The *Vernal Express*, dated 26 May 1906, observed:

> Indian trouble of gigantic proportions is brewing…a band of the White River Utes, by actual count known to number 321, camped at Dry Fork Wednesday night.

> The Indians were all well armed and had ammunition in abundance, they also had 1,000 head of horses, and about 50 head of cattle…They informed the settlers that they were going to one of the Northern reservations where a great gathering of all the Indians in the West has been arranged for, to council over their supposed grievances. They express freely their determination to fight rather than return…

When, by 9 June, the Indians reached Diamond Mountain, about forty miles north of Vernal the *Express* opined:

> It is hardly possible that, among all the three hundred, there is a single Indian whoever took a scalp; yet these young bucks, sons of the wilder redmen, have slumbering in them the wanton ferocity of the race, which needs but the flaming. And nothing is just suited to awaken all the old spirit of the Indian, more than the war whoop and the war dance.

The *Vernal Express* contacted "Cap" Whitelock, a Uintah Basin resident who had many dealings with the Utes, to gain some insight into their motivations.

> We learned that the evil genius who is in reality the backbone of the present ugly disposition of the natives is no other than Red Cap, a sub-chief of the same stock as the bloody old chiefs Arapene and Walker. That he is a repeat of these bad Indians is emphasized more when it is known that he speaks English well and has twice been a delegate to Washington for his tribesmen and ought, therefore, to counsel peace. On the contrary, he was the first to raise the banner of insurrection. This he did openly on the occasion of the last great Bear Dance at the Indian village on the Duchesne. About once every hour he would get up on a box and deliver himself of a harangue. "The whitemen," said he, "have robbed us of our cattle, our pony grass and our hunting grounds," and then seeing that others approved his words, he grew bolder in his fiery tirade. He called upon all the Indians who were willing to fight for their rights to shave their heads in token. Shortly after, thirty or forty young bucks were seen among the crown with their hair so cut that it stood straight up all over the top of their heads, and with their painted faces looked positively wild.

> Red Cap advocated a trip to the Sioux, the Crows, and all northern Indians for the purpose of forming a league to fight the whites, and it appears that he has prevailed. Other influential Indians told Mr. Whitelock during the festivities, that they did not want to fight. But it seems that the radical element is carrying the band northward, it may be by dint of the enthusiasm aroused and kept alive by war-like demonstrations, together with the novelty of a visit in the distant country. Whichever motive impels them, there is a serious liability of trouble ahead.

The Indians were concerned that the soldiers from Fort Duchesne might pursue them, but legal considerations made it impossible to go after the Utes with an armed force. The agent at Fort Duchesne did, however, follow the Indians as they trekked northward—to keep an eye on them.

My grandfather, William C. Boren, had lived on the reservation for many years with the approbation of the Utes, as their friend. In 1905, when the reservation was opened for settlement, he gathered up a number of relatives and friends, abandoned the reservation, and led a small wagon train over the high Uintahs to settle on Henry's Fork, near the Wyoming border. He knew about the impending storm brewing among the Utes, and his friendship with them compelled him to support them in their exodus by moving himself. That friendship with the Utes may have saved my father's life on a hot day in July of 1906.

In July 1906, my father—not yet thirteen—and his brother-in-law, Will Searle, rode horseback from Diamond Mountain through the timber country of the Uintahs to the Lucerne Valley on the north slope of the mountains.

At Dowd's Hole, a high mountain valley near Flaming Gorge, they came across an Indian burial ground, with at least one fresh internment. Although they both knew better, having been raised among the Indians, their youthful curiosity overcame their good judgment, and they took some blankets, beads, bows and arrows from the burial site.

No sooner had they done so, however, than the surrounding hills come alive with mounted Indians. The two young men leaped upon their own mounts and fled across the valley, closely pursued by the whooping Indians. They managed to keep ahead of the angry Utes until they reached my grandfather's ranch on Henry's Fork.

Red Cap came to the house with two of his braves to speak with my grandfather, whom they knew well. In deference to their friendship, they demanded only the return of the stolen items. Grandfather went a step further, giving the Utes a yearling calf for food. In a gesture of magnanimity, Red Cap gave my father an Indian pony.

"You're damned lucky to be alive," my grandfather told his errant son. "Red Cap is the man who drove a stake through Nathan Meeker's head!"

By August the Utes were in Wyoming, and their numbers had increased from some 300 to more than 700. Citizens of that state took alarm at the size of the caravan moving across the region. A dispatch from Cheyenne on 20 August 1906 stated:

> Seven hundred Utes are slaughtering cattle and sheep, robbing ranches, and committing other depredations in the vicinity of Douglass, on the Platte River 150 miles north of Cheyenne. They are in an ugly mood and refuse to return to their reservation at White Rocks, Utah. Mosisco, a Ute Chief is at the head of the band. Engleston, s Sioux renegade, and Red Cap, who is said to have driven a barrel stave through the head of old man Meeker at the Meeker Massacre, and Red Jacket Jane, the squaw who gave the Indian the alarm when the soldiers came, are also with the party. The three latter are troublemakers, and hate all whites. The Indians have little or no money or provisions. Occasionally they sell a pony and with the proceeds buy flour and ammunition. All are well armed.

> Agent Hall of White Rocks Agency, has been following the redskins ever since they entered Wyoming two weeks ago, but they have reportedly refused to return to their reservation. Tonight agent Hall wired the department for instructions and in all probability troops will be hurried to Douglass from the Crow Creek maneuver camp.

> Ranchmen and townspeople in the vicinity of Douglass are arming and a conflict appears to be inevitable. Should an outbreak occur the Indians could massacre many settlers before troops could reach the scene, although there are 1000 infantry, 1200 cavalry, and 800 artillery in the Crow Creek camp, 130 miles away. [*Cheyenne Leader*, 20 August 1906]

Captain C.G. Hall, Ute agent who followed them to Wyoming, was instructed time and again to try to induce the Indians to return to their reservation with no effect. On 25 August 1906, B.B. Brooks, governor of Wyoming, telegraphed the Commissioner of Indian Affairs, asking the government to remove the Indians from his state. The commissioner replied:

> As long as they (the Indians) are peaceable and do not threaten hostility it does not seem that the Federal Government would be

justified in interfering with them. Moral suasion has been used with little apparent effect in inducing them to return to their homes. It would therefore seem at present that the case is one for the local authorities rather than for this department.

On 17 September the governor protested again through F.W. Mondell, Wyoming Congressman, and the commissioner in desperation sent Inspector James McLaughlin to Casper to attempt to reason with the Utes. He convinced 45 members of the group to return to Utah, and one hundred of the most aggressive said they would go on to the Big Horn Mountains to settle. The rest were bound for Pine Ridge, South Dakota.

But Governor Brooks did not relent in his petitions to the federal government, and at last the War Department sent two detachments of the Tenth Cavalry under Major-General Greely. The commissioner in his annual reports for the year stated: "The purpose of employing so large a military force was to overawe them and persuade them to return quietly to their homes as the alternative of being disarmed and compelled to do so."

As the troops took to the field, newspapers began publishing wild rumors. The agent at Crow, Montana, reported that "the Utes had burned ranch buildings, shot and killed a prominent citizen, raided the cattle of the settlers, etc." In truth, the Utes were very peaceful in their journey. No whites were attacked or killed, and losses to cattle and sheep were extremely small.

When the forces of the U.S. Army converged upon the Utes, they realized the hopelessness of their situation. After a parley with the military, they accepted the escort of the troops to Fort Meade, South Dakota.

The elation of their success at reaching the Sioux nation was short-lived. Not only were the Sioux unwilling to enter into an alliance, but they told the Utes they were not going to share their hunting lands with them. The Sioux had finished their campaigns against the U.S. Army and were facing difficult times.

The Utes' former agent in Utah was sent by President Theodore Roosevelt to help find a suitable place for them. Captain Carter D. Johnson found surplus pasture land on the Cheyenne River Sioux Reservation and negotiated a rental agreement with local members of the Sioux Nation to put the Utes there. Here the Utes sat for some months in idleness.

Now the government began to put economic pressure on the Utes. First they cut off rations. The Honorable Francis E. Leupp, U.S. Commissioner of Indian Affairs, stated:

> But it was no part of the President's purpose, as was explained to the Utes at the time, and has been repeatedly since, to let them live there in idleness; if they wished a change of climate and surroundings, he was willing to give them a change to do as they pleased in these respects, but he did insist that they should, like all other citizens, of every race and color, pay for their own support. ...The Utes were first of all offered an opportunity to work at high wages...on the Santa Fe Railroad. They protested that it was a long distance off and they did not want to go so far; moreover, they had a herd of ponies, and they did not know what to do with those. It was suggested that they should do as white people would under the same circumstances—sell the ponies and use the money for the betterment of their own condition. That did not suit them at all. ...Well, I am sorry to say that I fear this bodes ill for relations of the government and these Utes. I think that later this fall they will be given once more the opportunity of choosing between going to work and doing the other thing...going hungry.... They must either work or go hungry. ...It is possible, as they have carried their arms with them, that they will rise in revolt; if they do, that revolt will be suppressed, and, if necessary, with an iron hand. ...It was not the government's fault that they took the course they did in order to get a place where they could live in idleness and eat the bread of charity. If they persist in that course they will be made to understand what the word "must" means.

When the economic pressure became acute in the fall of 1907, Captain Hall went to their camp and told them that the last limit of leniency had been reached. They became resistant and belligerent but were restrained by the arrival of two troops of cavalry.

After some fifteen months of their sojourn, some of the Utes came to the conclusion that their situation was untenable. At last a council was held and even the most militant felt that there was no other recourse than to return. Federal agencies quickly found $9,920 to help them, and the government had new wagons and harnesses shipped to Rapid City, South Dakota. There they provided horses and mules for dray and rations to sustain them on their return journey. The Utes were escorted by Major Carter P. Johnson and ten soldiers from the Tenth Cavalry. It was a journey of more than 1,000 miles but was made in 101 days.

Following is the report filed by the *Vernal Express* on 16 October 1908:

> The longest distance traveled any one day was 35 miles. Many days the cavalcade did not move at all. The trip was not without its exciting features and death was in the midst. Wherever there is life, death is trying to enter in and he never fails. Three Indians died, it is said from consumption. That is the disease which is carrying most of the redmen off today. While they were housed and kept in confinement in the barracks 126 North, over 40 died, but as soon as they were again given outdoor life they became healthy. This wandering outdoor life agrees with their nature, there were but few accidents...
>
> They have learned to make some quick remarks and witty answers to many questions. One old buck was standing alongside of his wickiup while the squaw was baking bread. To the question as to what his name was he replied that he was too poor to have a name. ...As a rule the Indians all appear to be healthy and in good spirits and glad to get back, although they say they are poor. Capt. Johnson believes in feeding them well and getting them good natured, which he claims will civilize them into the white man's ways quicker than cutting down rations and saying "work or starve." He takes the stand that a hungry Indian is usually a sullen, mean Indian. He makes them get busy, however, and do all the work around camp. ...The wagons and harnesses will be given to the Utes.

So, they were back. Nothing was achieved, unless it was a demonstration of their frustration and desire to be free. The reservation life brought only continued misery for them.

In 1909, the Strawberry Valley Reclamation Project authorized 56,000 acres appropriated from the Indians by "right of eminent domain." In 1931 the ration system was stopped, and in 1934, under the Taylor Grazing Act, 429,000 acres were withdrawn from the Uncompahgre Reservation and placed in the public domain.

Then, in the late thirties, the Utes learned to "fight fire with fire," and meet the white man on his own terms. By this time they had educated some of their people to be lawyers, doctors, and politicians. In 1938, the Utes adopted the Wheeler-Howard Reorganization Act and incorporated themselves as a tribe, and established a Tribal Business Committee.

The following year the Utes of Colorado and Utah brought suits against the government for payment on 4,404,000 acres of land, including the territory embraced within the rich Rangely Oil Field. In 1945, 236,000 acres not claimed by homesteaders was returned to the Utes. In 1947, they won the Judgment Fund which awarded the Utes of Colorado and Utah $32 million. In 1948, the Utes regained the lands claimed from them by the Taylor Grazing Act, and the next year their first oil royalties were awarded. Today the Utes are a very progressive people.

*

When I last visited old Colorow in 1956, there were a total of 6,961 persons identifying themselves as Indians in the State of Utah; only 1,834 being Utes—not much more than double the number who fled the reservation in 1906. They are still beset with numerous problems, among them alcoholism and high rates of infant mortality. The reasons remain basically the same as they were in 1906, when some of them fled the reservation seeking the old way of life.

Old Colorow, who was ninety-five the year he died, sat in front of his wickiup, facing the high Uintah Mountains, where once he had lived and hunted in perfect freedom. He reminisced about the day the renegades returned to the reservation. Red Cap rode forlornly by Colorow's wickiup that sad day in 1908.

"You are home," Colorow stated matter-of-factly.

"No," replied Red Cap. "I am only back. I have no home, for I am an Indian."

Chapter Eleven

Return of the Gunfighters

ON 2 JUNE 1905, CALEB BALDWIN Rhoades passed away at his home in Price, Utah, at the age of sixty-nine. Several years before, the roof of his cabin had caved on top of him, following a heavy snowfall the previous winter, and his health had declined ever since. Following the accident, Caleb had sold his farm to Matt Warner, who had been living on the place since his release from prison in 1900, after serving four years for the Dry Fork shooting.

Caleb's death came just three months prior to the opening of the Uintah-Ouray Indian Reservation, and his partner, F.W.C. Hathenbruck, was left with the task of pursuing their quest to open the mines to exploration. For the next twenty years he would fight injustice, unscrupulous politicians, and constant intrigues, only to die penniless and disillusioned at Provo, Utah, in 1925. Like Caleb Rhoades, he knew the secret location of hundreds of millions of dollars in gold, and could touch none of it, and so like Caleb Rhoades he died with that secret sealed on his lips.

Numerous attempts were being made near the time of the reservation opening to beat Hathenbruck to the prize. But Hathenbruck did not immediately give up the quest. Shortly after the death of Rhoades—apparently in the same month—Hathenbruck allied himself with the Sylvanite Mining Company; he knew that time was of the essence, for the mountains were already filled with anxious prospectors. On 24 September 1905, Hathenbruck wrote the following letter to the President and Board of Directors of the Sylvanite Mining Company:

Gentlemen;

Through unforeseen circumstances not being able to be present at the stockholder meeting, I herewith take pleasure to submit a report of my doings and locating since July 21st, 1905—for the Sylvanite Co—

On August 2nd 1905 I located the Sylvanite #1 and 2 a fissure vein breaking through the country rock—commonly known as Quartzite (but which I term a course Gueis). This mine—the nature and location of which has been described to me, over 20 years ago by Mr. C.B. Rhoades—and at a time before there was only talk over the fabulous Mines on the Reserve—and is what is termed the Rhodes Mine. ...these mines are—in the second left hand fork—going up stream from the narrows of Rock Creek—about 4 miles above the confluence of this fork with the main stream—

Another very important location was made on August 24th for our Company—via the Alice which is situated in the left hand fork of this second left hand fork in which the Sylvanite #1 and 2 are located and shows better values than any—on the surface—and is best approached from the Plateau on the west and can readily be seen from one part of Plateau directly above the mine—but hard of access from the Forks—The A.C. Mine at the mouth of 2nd left hand fork of Rock Creek—going up stream—is a continuation of Sylv: 1 and 2 and a low grate (sic—grade) Gold proposition in contact or Quartzite and Lime shale—located August 3rd—1905...

Respectfully yours,

F.W.C. Hathenbruck

Hathenbruck's directions are somewhat vague, but he seems to be inferring that the Sylvanite #1 and 2 claims are on the second left hand fork of the West Fork of Rock Creek in his statement "about 4 miles above the confluence of this fork with the main stream." This places it in the Lodgepole Lake area, where Rhoades and Hathenbruck had a cabin while working the area earlier. Caleb Rhoades filed a mining claim in 1901 (Wasatch County Recorder's Book O, p.133) in the same area, which he called "Shipwreck #4." Gale Rhoades discovered a rock formation in Red Cliff Lake which resembles a shipwreck, which might well denote the area.

Throughout the year 1906, Hathenbruck, in conjunction with other individuals (M.P. Trotter, E.E. Horn, John Christenson, Mamie C. Singleton), filed on numerous claims in this area: "Castle Rock Mine #1 and 2, " July 9, 1906, "#1—on south side of Hades Canyon and west of what is known as Castle Rock on North Fork of Duchesne River"; and, "#2—easterly of Castle Rock #1." "Little Gulch," July 14, 1906, located "3 miles north of Stockmore on east side of the North Fork of the Duchesne River, in a box canyon running in a easterly direction." "Surprise #1 thru 4," July 17, 1906, located "in Dry Spring Canyon, on the west side, about 5 miles easterly from Stockmore." "Bertram Gold Placer Claim," August 1, 1906, located "1/2 mile easterly of Gran Dad (Granddaddy) Lake, on Little Creek and Little Creek Spring, on Rock Creek Slope." This latter was very near Lodgepole Lake. On 22 September 1906, they filed an annex to this claim following the contour of the nearby high plateau. There is little record of what transpired with these claims of Hathenbruck, et.al., in the ensuing six years.

Then, in 1912, another group descended on the Rock Creek/Granddaddy Lake region and filed several groups of claims. On 14 July 1912, Edward Hartzell, D.C. Miles, L.M. Miles, James Hartzell, W.E. Cox, Parley and Frank Warren, J.C. Fergeson, and a Mr. Summers, filed on a group of claims called the "Eldorado." On 17 July they filed on a second group of claims called the "Klondike #1 and 2."

Their Eldorado claims were located "on the West Fork of Rock Creek at 3 forks, second left-hand fork, 1/4 mile above cabin." It was, in fact, in the meadows adjacent to Lodgepole Lake just east of Granddaddy Lake, one-fourth mile west of the original Rhoades-Hathenbruck cabin. Their two Klondike claims were described as being "2

miles up the West Fork of Rock Creek, 4 miles from the big lake (Granddaddy Lake) in Rock Creek Basin, 8 miles above the (Upper) Stillwaters and 1 mile above the ranger or government cabin (located near the mouth of Cabin Creek), on the Left Hand Fork."

A new cabin with corrugated tin roof was constructed for this group by William Davies, owner of the Rock Creek Ranch, and they began operations on two of the lower grade deposits at Lodgepole Lake. Wooden water troughs and ditches were constructed, and metal sluice boxes installed. But the operation eventually went defunct, and today only the collapsed cabin and some remnants of the sluices bear witness to their attempt. The Rhoades-Hathenbruck cabin, located in the timber one-fourth mile east, has been practically destroyed by a dynamite blast.

This group had worked only the low grade ore mentioned by Hathenbruck in his letters to the Sylvanite Company. The Rhoades Mine was never found by them, though they were extremely close to the site. The reason, according to the Indians, was that this particular mine was situated in a large crack or crevice approachable only by being lowered on ropes. This was probably the mysterious "A.C. Mine" mentioned by Hathenbruck, who was never able to develop it for reasons soon to be made apparent.

Some of the mystery become unraveled when we examine the identity of the Eldorado-Klondike group of 1912. Edward Hartzell, originally from Pennsylvania, had married Sidsie Jensen Rhoades, the widow of Caleb Rhoades, who had provided him with maps left by Caleb, drawn shortly before his death on 2 June 1905. James E. Hartzell was the son of Edward Hartzell by his first wife, Viola, and had been born in Scranton, Pennsylvania, on 15 October 1888. James Hartzell would eventually lose his life by heart attack while searching for the mine in the vicinity of the Bobby Duke Trail in August 1961. Parley and Frank Warren lived at Vernal, Utah, and then at Price, where they had been acquainted with Caleb Rhoades. The history of D.C. and L.M. Miles, J.C. Fergeson and Mr. Summers is vague, but W.E. Cox was none other than W.E. Christiansen, a.k.a. Matt Warner!

Matt Warner, as noted elsewhere, was connected with Caleb Rhoades as early as 1896, and following his release from prison in January 1900, he purchased Caleb Rhoades' old farm near Price and renewed prospecting interests with Caleb until the latter's death in 1905. In the following year we then find him in partnership with Caleb's widow Sidsie and her new husband, Edward Hartzell, and in competition with Caleb's former partner, F.W.C. Hathenbruck.

On his death bed, Caleb Rhoades drew a map on a small piece of paper which appears to have been ripped from a notebook,

Caleb Rhoades and wife Sidsie.

Courtesy Utah State Historical Society.

and gave it to his old Indian friend Happy Jack with instructions to deliver it to Matt Warner. The map details sites in the Granddaddy Lakes region with the notation "This country is dangerous" written on it. Warner recopied this map before his death in 1938 with some additions and notations, both of which maps I obtained from Matt's son, Boyo Warner, in 1971.

By the year 1912 (the year he had his name legally changed), Matt Warner was employed by Jesse Knight and George Storrs to keep the peace in the new town of Storrs, a few miles west of Price. Storrs was involved with Hathenbruck in the slate mining business in the same vicinity, and so Warner joins the curious and convoluted intrigue of competitive relationships. Warner was well known by 1912, and running for political office (thus the name change), and it appears that his use of the alias "W.E. Cox" in his mining partnerships claims was calculated to prevent notoriety.

Matt Warner's association with the locators of the Eldorado and Klondike claims was the product of even deeper associations and intrigues. The story is complex and fraught with twists and turns, and has never before appeared in print. It is recounted here, as near as it can be sorted out, for the first time.

Some years ago, my late good friend Art Davidson of Lyman, Wyoming, discovered a telegram inserted in the pages of an old account book belonging to storekeeper T.C. Hilliard. The account book contained the record of purchasers who maintained accounts of Hilliard's store, including Butch Cassidy, who frequently bought supplies there.

The telegram, dated 3 July 1901, Washington, D.C., was from President Theodore Roosevelt to "Lt. Col. Jack Leroy Dempsey" and signed familiarly "Teddy." It dealt with "Teddy's Terrors" in the Spanish American War, offering amnesty or pardon for their participation in the war. Those to whom President Roosevelt offered amnesty were as follows:

Lt. Col. Jack Leroy Dempsey	Pvt. Harv. J. Cassidy
Capt. Geo. C. Irwin	Pvt. Hiram Benson
Sgt. Richard Angel	Pvt. _____ Jones
Pvt. Jeffery Mereaith	Pvt. William Meeks
Pvt. William Madden	Pvt. George Sullivan

It has been established that Robert Leroy Parker, alias Butch Cassidy, and a number of his gang formed a detachment of Teddy's Rough Riders during the Spanish American War. The telegram from Teddy Roosevelt, offering amnesty to the members of "Teddy's Terrors," seems clearly to allude to Cassidy and his outlaw regiment. The names given are obviously pseudonyms, but they correspond with the identities of the hierarchy of the Wild Bunch. Two prominent names are conspicuous by their absence—Matt Warner and Elzy Lay, both of whom were in prison at the time.

Why is this important? What does the telegram have to do with the mines? The answer is surprising, though convoluted, and poses more questions than solutions.

When the Florence Mining Company was organized, sponsored by Jesse Knight and a group of wealthy and politically-connected easterners bent on beating Caleb Rhoades and F.W.C. Hathenbruck out of their gold sources on the reservation, another group formed a competitive company calling themselves the Raven Mining Company. When the Florence company failed to locate the mines and dissolved itself, the Raven company secured titled to the former firm and thereafter titled themselves the Florence and Raven Mining Company. The stockholders of the newly organized company are the same names which appear on Teddy Roosevelt's 1901 telegram! The Florence and Raven Mining Company stockholders are as follows:

Robert Leroy	Bill Phelps
George Parker	Frank Harris Sullivan
Richard Angell	Bill Meeks
Harv Logan	Harry Parker

Because of the confusion in identification of the men from their aliases, the following chart has been devised for purposes of clarification:

TEDDY'S TERRORS	FLORENCE CO.	WILD BUNCH
	Robert Leroy	Robert Leroy Parker
Jack Leroy Dempsey	Geo. Parker	Geo. Cassidy
Geo. C. Irwin	Richard Angell	Richard Angell
Richard Angel	Jeff Murdoch	Jeff Murdoch
Jeffery Mereaith	Bill Madden	Bill Madden
Wm. Madden	Harv Logan	Harvey Logan
Harv J. Cassidy	(?)	Harry Longabaugh
Hiram Benson	(?)	(?)
_____ Jones	Bill Meeks	Henry Rhodes "Bub"
Wm. Meeks	Frank Harris Sullivan	Meeks
Geo. Sullivan		Frank Harris

Some explanation is required. Robert Leroy Parker and George Cassidy are often confused, inasmuch as "Old Bob" Parker, a near relation of Butch Cassidy, frequently passed himself off as the "real" Butch Cassidy. Jack Leroy Dempsey

appears to have been "Old Bob" Parker, while Geo. C. Irwin was the "real" Butch Cassidy; when Butch Cassidy died at Johnnie, Nevada, on 24 March 1944, he was using the alias Frank M. Ervin. [For more information on these two men and the inter-changing of their names and identities, as well as their mining inter-ests, see the book *Sometimes Cassidy* by Art Davidson].

Frank Harris Sullivan, son of Florence Sullivan and Emily Jane Place, was half-brother of Etta Place, who was married at different times to both Butch Cassidy and the Sundance Kid [see *Wild Irish Rose,* a biography of Etta Place, by Kerry Ross O'Boran and Lisa Lee O'Boran [unpub. mss.]. Etta named one of her daughters "Florence," and there may have been some connection thereby with the naming of the Florence Mining Company. Etta Place's father, George Capel (thus Butch Cassidy's alias, George Capel Irwin), alias George Ingerfield, was a mining partner of the great bonanza king, Senator George Hearst, developer of the fabulous silver mines at Park City, as well as the great Comstock Lode in Nevada.

Harvey Logan was better known to history as Kid Curry. Hiram Benson was one of many aliases known to have been used by Harry A. Longabaugh, a.k.a. The Sundance Kid. Bill Madden participated with Butch Cassidy in several major bank and train robberies in Colorado. Bub Meeks, as noted earlier, partici-pated in the Castle Gate Payroll Robbery in 1897, and the Montpelier (Idaho) Bank Robbery the following year. Richard Angell was a near relation (by some accounts a brother) of Truman O.

Elzy Lay.
Courtesy Utah Historical society.

Angell, architect of the Salt Lake Temple, who utilized the gold from the Rhoades mines as decoration. Jeff Murdoch is an enigma: he was known as a "publicity man," or public relations man for the Wild Bunch. Jones is unknown, but is believed to be one of the Jones family associated with the mines (of which further), and one of the brothers of Lovina Jones Boren, the author's grandmother.

The Raven Mining Company, as we shall see, may have derived its name from some association with the name "Ravencamp," of which further.

In 1951, Amaza Alonzo Davidson, of Bridger Valley, Wyoming, related the following account to Mr. James Sharp, an assistant to the LDS Church Historian, with the stipulation that it not be revealed until after his death.

Arlin Davidson, of Sandy, Utah, eldest son of Amasa Davidson, related the same story to me, adding considerable detail, and providing me with certain documents and other pertinent evidences to support the events. After the death of Arlin Davidson, his brother Art provided even more substantiation and detail.

Gale Rhoades and I withheld the story from the first edition (1971) of *Footprints in the Wilderness*, partly out of respect for the request of Amasa Davidson (who was at that time still living), and partly because not all of the participants were then known. Since that time, however, all of the Davidsons, as well as Mr. Sharp, have passed away. We published an up-dated account in the second revised edition (1980) of *Footprints*; a great deal has been learned since then, and bears recounting here.

Harold Moslander, about 20.
Courtesy Glen M. Walton, nephew.

*

Near the time of the Fourth of July holiday, 1920, a man by the name of Caleb Landreth arrived in Bridger Valley, Wyoming, from Pittsburgh, Pennsylvania. After stepping off the train, Landreth stayed several days at a nearby ranch before setting up his own camp. He was soon joined by a twenty-one-year-old cowboy named Harold Moslander, who had a local reputation as a "fast draw,"—able to draw and shoot either of his pistols with equal speed and accuracy.

A few days later, these two men were joined by another youth, a well-mannered fellow named Ernest Roberts who joined them as a camp-cook. He had a special talent for concocting a delicious Mulligan Stew.

There next appeared two parties consisting of eight-men—a Mr. Warren and his twin sons, Thursday and Friday Warren (so named because they were born before and after midnight on those two days of the week); Matt Warner and Edward Hartzell of Price; and Rock M. Pope, Tom Welch and William Macginnis from Vernal. It was rumored that most of these men were the remnant of Cassidy's Wild Bunch. All of them were well armed and expert marksmen. They brought with them two pack horses loaded with supplies and camp equipment as they made camp with Landreth, Moslander and Roberts. Landreth, who seemed to have plenty of cash, paid for all supplies.

In the meantime, Amasa Alonzo Davidson and his wife arrived at a nearby ranch by buckboard. On the morning following their arrival, the men from the camp rode en masse to the ranch with their horses packed and an extra mount for Davidson. When Davidson saw the group of rough-looking characters, he refused to go with them. Davidson was not a gunman; he was a rancher from nearby Urie, Wyoming, and his only qualification was that he had taught chemistry at a local school, and could assay gold. He was acquainted with young Ernest Roberts, but knew none of the others in the group. Beyond that fact, his only other connection was that he had at one time been a good friend of Butch Cassidy.

The men were sent back to their camp, and Landreth remained at the ranch with Moslander to attempt to convince Davidson to accompany them into the mountains. Landreth, a self-proclaimed prophet, hypnotist and spiritualist, said that he could prove by the "fates" of the cards that there would be no danger if Davidson went along with them.

Landreth produced a new deck of cards and had Davidson break the seal. Without touching the cards himself, Landreth instructed Davidson to shuffle them, as he explained that spades were bad luck cards, clubs signified trouble, hearts represented love, and diamonds meant riches.

Mrs. Davidson then cut the deck and drew one card. The card was the king of hearts and Landreth told her it represented her husband. The cards were again shuffled—Landreth never touching them—and Davidson drew a card, the queen of hearts, which he was told represented his wife. The cards were again shuffled, and Mrs. Davidson was told to draw five cards from any place in the deck and leave them face down. When these cards were turned over, they were found to be the ace, king, queen, jack and ten of diamonds—riches untold, Landreth indicated.

Davidson remained skeptical and even examined the rest of the deck, but found them to be regular cards. Mrs. Davidson, on the other hand, was thoroughly convinced and urged her husband to go. Davidson reluctantly consented, but only on the condition that he leave his rifle with his wife and go unarmed. He borrowed a gentle horse from his brother and rode unarmed into the camp the next morning, bringing along his acids, his blow pipe and camera.

Before proceeding further, perhaps it will elucidate at this place to define the characters of our impending drama. At the time Amasa Davidson first divulged this story, not all of the characters

Harold Moslander 1938 at his ranch.

Courtesy Glen M. Walton, nephew.

were identified or known. Since that time, however, further research has disclosed them, and even added new knowledge to the account.

"Old Man" Warren, father of the twin boys, was either Parley or Frank Warren, both of whom had staked the Klondike mining claims on the West Fork of Rock Creek with Edward Hartzell, Matt Warner and others on 17 July 1912, eight years earlier. Another group of the Warrens—Sara, Ella, W.Z., Hubbard, Dessey, and S.J.—had staked petroleum claims (tar sands) with James E. Hartzell on 23 April 1911. Ernest Roberts, the young camp cook, was the son-in-law of "Old Man" Warren, and thus brother-in-law to the twins, Thursday and Friday Warren.

Harold Maughan Moslander was born 6 November 1898 at Aspen, Uinta County, Wyoming, son of Charles Humes Moslander (1856-1938) and Margaret Ann Maughan (1861-1930). Harold, born too late to participate in the Wild West era, fancied himself nonetheless a gunfighter, and was an avid fan of Butch Cassidy. He hung around remnants of the Wild Bunch and became proficient with his two guns under the expert tutelage of none other than the Sundance Kid. Following the 1920 adventure, Harold Moslander operated a ranch on Bear River, near Evanston, Wyoming, where he died 1 July 1976, at the age of seventy-eight.

Rock M. Pope was the brother of Uintah County Sheriff John T. Pope. On 26 December 1895, Matt Warner, Rock M. Pope and John T. Pope had staked mining claims in Red Creek Canyon in Brown's Park, hoping to discover the Lost Jesse Ewing Mine. Rock Pope was a tough customer who had often served as a deputy under his brother, but just as often favored friendships with members of the Wild Bunch.

Tom Welch was a rancher on Henry's Fork in Sweetwater County, Wyoming, but he had also been a fringe member of the Wild Bunch. Butch Cassidy was his long-time friend. Tom had come West in a wagon train in 1878, when he was twelve, coming from Illinois with his mother and stepfather to the mining camps of South Pass and Atlantic City, Wyoming.

Tom Welch was a tough old cattleman, a veteran of the "Sheep and Cattle Range War" which took place in southwestern Wyoming near the turn of the century. Tom had killed several men in his wilder days, and had even taken a few shots at my maternal grandfather, Willard Schofield, during the range war. I knew Tom Welch well, and interviewed him often in his old age; he died at his home in Green River, Wyoming, in his late nineties, in the 1960s.

William Macginnis (Maginnis, etc.) Was none other than William Ellsworth "Elzy" Lay. Lay was born 25 November 1868, in MacArthur, Vinton County, Ohio, and came West in his teens. His first foray into outlawry took place with Harry A. Longabaugh and Matt Warner, and he eventually became one of the leading members of the Wild Bunch. In 1896, Elzy Lay married Maude Davis of Vernal, and was one of the gunfighters hired by Caleb Rhoades to protect his mining interests on the reservation. On 19 August 1896, Elzy Lay and Bub Meeks assisted Cassidy in the robbery of the Montpelier, Idaho, bank to raise money to hire an attorney to defend Matt Warner following the Dry Fork ambush.

Following a train robbery near Folsom, New Mexico, in 1899, Lay and his companions shot and killed Sheriff Farr and several members of a pursuing posse. He was sentenced to life imprisonment in the New Mexico State Penitentiary for murder and armed robbery on 10 October 1899, under the alias of William McGinnis, #PNM 1348.

Lay was a model prisoner, at one point even helping to quell a prison riot. He became a particular favorite of the warden and during the period of his sentence he was able to influence the warden who had an avid interest in prospecting for gold. Lay intimated that he knew of a fabulous gold source on the Ute Indian Reservation in

Utah, and recounted some of his experiences as a hired gun for Caleb Rhoades. Matt Warner had provided Lay with a copy of Caleb Rhoades' "Mystery Map," which he effectively employed to impress the warden.

The warden became passionately interested in the Rhoades mines and even induced Governor Miguel Otero of New Mexico to become involved. Through Otero's intervention, Lay was pardoned on 10 January 1906 (though he was released before Christmas, 1905), with a promise that he would go immediately to Utah and attempt to locate the mine, with the warden and governor as his financial backers and silent partners. Lay teamed up in 1906 with his old cronies to form the Florence and Raven Mining Companies.

Elzy Lay became a renowned, self-educated geologist, entering the field of mining and oil field exploration. He discovered the vast Hiawatha Oil Fields in Wyoming, and natural gas deposits near Ogden, Utah, among others. Lay died in Los Angeles in 1934; but in 1920 he joined his old friend Matt Warner to renew the search for the Lost Rhoades Mines.

Shortly before the group left for the mountains, they were joined by Jim Chrisman, a Wyoming gunman and some-time friend of Tom Welch. James Sharp, that ever-astute interviewer, recorded the following information from an interview with Tom Welch:

> For over 20 years I was livestock appraiser for one of the largest banks in Salt Lake. It seemed to me that whenever there was a bad storm, some bank official would get a bright idea in his head and send me out to look after some loan or another. It was in that capacity about 1928 that one night I rode very hard on a tired horse into Burnt Fork, Wyoming. The snow was deep and it was bitter cold. There was no hotel in the town so one Tom Welch took me to his home for the night.

> After supper we sat around a large fireplace and told stories of men who had made and lost fortunes in the cattle business almost over night. I was enjoying the heat from the fire as well as his stories.

> One I remember him telling concerning a young cow puncher who used to ride to

Sublette Range along about 1900, and one day one of the cowboys took a pack horse and rode away somewhere in the mountains, and when he came back he went up into northeastern Wyoming and purchased 2,000 head of cattle which he turned on that range. He said some of the ranchers got mad at him because he did not own a foot of ground—so he took another trip. When he came back he purchased two ranches—both large ones—which he paid for with cash. One was down on Ham's Fork, the other up above Cokeville. I asked where he got the money and he said some of the other riders supposed he had found a cache of gold that some outlaw had buried. Someone said his name was Jim Chrisman....[See *Footprints*, p.366]

The most startling information dealing with the group of gunfighters involves Caleb Landreth. When I interviewed Tom Welch in the early 1960s, he readily admitted his part in the expedition, and identified their leader, Caleb Landreth, as none other than Harry Longabaugh, a.k.a. the Sundance Kid!

There is no reason to question this identification; in fact, there is ample evidence to verify the presence of Longabaugh. Despite the many adherents to the wholly unsubstantiated account of the death of Butch Cassidy and the Sundance Kid at San Vicente, Bolivia, in 1908, the evidence of their return is overwhelming and too lengthy to discuss here [we refer the reader to the 1995 PBS documentary by *NOVA* wherein DNA tests proved the bodies buried at San Vicente were not those of Butch and Sundance—more especially the latter].

Harry Alonzo Longabaugh was born 19 April 1868 in Pennsylvania, a son of Josiah Longabaugh and Mary Ann Place. Inspired by dime novels, he left home and headed West at the age of fourteen. After spending time in southern Colorado, southern Utah and New Mexico, he served 18 months in the Crook County jail at Sundance, Wyoming (thus his sobriquet, the Sundance Kid) He rode into infamy with Butch Cassidy and the Wild Bunch, and married a Mormon girl—Annie Marie Thayne, of Wellington, Utah—before leaving for South America in 1901.

Following a string of robberies in Argentina, Chile, and Bolivia, Longabaugh returned to the United States, then toured Europe and the Orient.

In the latter place he picked up a strong Eastern religious influence, especially the writings of Omar Khayam. Returning to America, he organized a group of disciples in Ohio and came with them to California. He operated a burglary ring in San Francisco, and served four years in San Quentin, afterwards bringing his "family" to Utah. In 1945, at the age of 77, he killed the town marshal of Mount Pleasant, Utah, and spent the next decade in the Utah State Prison where he died in 1955, at the age of 87, under the alias Hiram Bebee.

Longabaugh appeared—as Caleb Landreth—in Bridger Valley, Wyoming, in 1920, shortly after his release from San Quentin, and organized a search for the Lost Rhoades Mine. Longabaugh (a.k.a. Hiram Benson, Hiram Bennion, Hiram Beebee, Caleb Landreth, etc.) possessed a very dominant personality, and it was inferred by those who knew him that he "mesmerized" people. He was a voracious reader and frequently quoted passages from the writings of Omar Khayam. He was a health food advocate, lauding Ralston products as superior to most other foods, and he professed to have dreams and visions and was adept in the occult sciences. It must be remembered that Longabaugh, under the name Hiram Benson or Bennion, was one of the stockholders of the Florence and Raven Mining Company.

Thus, it is clear that at least half of the 1920 group were former members of the Wild Bunch, or in some way associated. All were proficient gunmen, even Davidson, though he was unarmed.

Before the group left Bridger Valley, Landreth had himself blindfolded, then went into a trance and drew a rough map on a piece of paper. Drawing an "x" on the makeshift map, he indicated that this would be their camp, and pointed out certain landmarks, saying that just below the camp there would be a small lake or pond, and that the stream flowing into it would be filled with trout. There would be lush meadows on all sides, he predicted, providing ample feed for the horses, and, "Just above us is what appears to me to be some ancient castles." Some of these landmarks and locations were familiar to some of the more experienced men present, and they were amazed at the precision of his knowledge, but Landreth attributed it to "the spirit of the departed Indian Princess Ravencamp."

The group of thirteen men at last set out on their mysterious quest for the Lost Rhoades Mine. They camped the first night on Stillwater Fork of the Bear River and caught pan trout for supper. The next morning Landreth again asked to be blindfolded and charted out the course for the day ahead. He predicted that they would come to an old cabin with plenty of wood and water. "The spirit of the Princess assures me of this," he told them. At least several of the men must have known that Landreth's accuracy was enhanced by a secret map in his possession.

Just before reaching the place, Landreth left Old Man Warren and his two sons to watch their back trail, to make certain they were not being followed, and to watch for Indians. Warren was chosen for this mission because he spoke the Ute language fluently, having been an interpreter at Whiterocks for many years. Rock M. Pope took Landreth's "inspired" hand-written map and went ahead in search of the cabin.

Near sunset they arrived in the vicinity of Mirror Lake and found the cabin, just as Landreth had predicted. It was a dilapidated old structure situated on the edge of present-day Scout Lake (near the Boy Scout summer camp called Camp Steiner). A well-defined trail led from the cabin up the mountainside, and some of the men were anxious to follow it right then, but Landreth encouraged them to wait until morning when he would seek directions from the spirit.

After supper all of the men went off by themselves for about an hour, leaving Davidson, Moslander and Roberts alone at the cabin. Moslander watched the men closely as they returned and silently went to bed. He expressed an uneasiness to Davidson and Roberts about the strange behavior of their companions, but Roberts put their minds at ease by saying that Old Man Warren was his father-in-law, and the twins were his brothers-in-law, and would never conspire against him. The other man from Price (i.e. Matt Warner) had been a close friend of Butch Cassidy, but was a man of good character, and one of the other men was a retired cattleman and widower. The Vernal group, however, consisting of four hard men, had never been introduced—not even to Moslander and

Roberts—and it was this group, headed by the surly Rock M. Pope, that Davidson feared most.

The next morning after breakfast, all of the men were anxious to go to the gold mine, but Landreth called them around him and delivered a sort of sermon. He informed them that he had had a dream or a vision in which the Lord had showed him the location of the famous lost mine, and had told him that he would be the instrument by which it would be brought forth, and that one-half of the money obtained from the discovery was to go toward organizing a new church, of which Landreth had been chosen as prophet and leader.

The men murmured their protest at these claims, for they had assumed they would all share equally in the mine. Landreth confused the issue by having himself blind folded again and tried to draw a map to the mine, but the spirit of the Princess Ravencamp had forsaken him, he said, so he would have to find the mine without her help, or without the help of God.

Rock Pope, seeing the confusion of the men, took command of the situation. He placed Matt Warner in charge of Davidson and Moslander, instructing him to not let them leave the camp that day, and ordered young Roberts to have a meal ready for their return about sunset. The men then paired off, Landreth accompanying Pope.

After the men departed, Matt Warner sat down with the three men and took them into his confidence, saying that during the conference of the night before, Rock Pope had made it plain that Moslander, Roberts and Davidson were to be killed as soon as the mine was found. He instructed Davidson to declare whatever kind of rock that was found by Landreth to be worthless and this might save their lives. He informed them that their horses had been un-hobbled and started off down the back-trail the night before. There had been a discussion about shooting the horses, he said, but it was decided the shots might attract the attention of the Indians. Warner handed Davidson one of his pistols and told him not to hesitate to use it if it became necessary.

Near sunset, Landreth and Pope returned, and were soon joined by the others, all of them somber and silent as they ate their supper. Just as darkness fell, the last two men returned.

"What did you find?" Pope asked them.

"Nothing," came the reply.

"It's a lie!" cried Landreth. "Search them!"

One of the men reached for his gun and Pope shot him in the back. The critically wounded man was dragged to the firelight and Landreth searched his pockets. They were crammed full with high-grade gold-bearing ore. Pope asked the dying man where he had found it, and was promptly told to go to hell; in a fit of rage Pope shot the man in the head and killed him instantly.

Pope then turned to Davidson and ordered him to get his acids and test the ore for gold. Davidson tested the samples with his chemicals, then glanced briefly at Matt Warner before saying, "This is nothing but iron pyrites, sometimes called 'fool's gold'—it's worthless."

Pope looked at Davidson with scorn, knowing that he was lying. He started to draw his pistol, but before he could clear leather, a shot rang out; Matt Warner had shot the man dead. Instantly, all of the men began shooting at one another in mass pandemonium. Davidson and Moslander fired as they ran away from the firelight. They ran along their back trail all night and by morning caught up to their horses somewhere near Hilliard Flat about 14 miles southeast of Evanston, Wyoming (where Moslander later established his ranch).

Ernest Roberts was shot in the groin, and it took him more than a week to make it out of the mountains. His wounds ended his marriage to his wife, Violet Warren Roberts, and caused his untimely death two years later. The official records state that he died from the effects of a ruptured appendix—his close friends knew better.

Of the thirteen men who participated in the ill-fated 1920 expedition, only five were known positively to have survived the gun battle—one dying as a result of wounds two years later. The known survivors were Amasa Davidson, Harold Moslander, Ernest Roberts, Matt Warner, Edward Hartzel. Landreth (i.e. Longabaugh), Macginnis (i.e. Lay), and Tom Welch on the other side can be accounted as survivors, but all the rest—five in number—were either killed or disappeared. The Warrens were never seen again.

When I interviewed Tom Welch in 1963, at his home in Green River, Wyoming, he was 97 years of age, but still alert and powerful. He was a huge man physically, with a brusque and forceful personality—a man who was used to being in control—and even in his nineties, a man to be feared. Fortunately, we were friends, and he spoke freely with me about many things. Nevertheless, in 1963, when the following interview was conducted, I was unaware of the connection to the Lost Rhoades Mines, and in retrospect I now realize that I should have asked more questions. Still, Tom's responses are revealing:

KRB: How many gunfights have you been in...besides the one with my grandfather at Sawmill Springs?

TW: (laughs) Oh, more than I like to remember. Them was rough times, you know, and everybody packed guns.

KRB: Can you tell me about one of the gunfights you remember best?

TW: Well, I remember one particular time, when I lived over on Burnt Fork...you know, just before you get to Lonetree? ...a bunch of us got together for a prospecting trip up into the mountains above Evanston. There was some pretty rough men in that group, don't you know. Some of them was pretty good friends of mine, but some of them I only met for the first time on that trip.

KRB: What year was this?

TW: Hell—I don't know! It was before the Depression hit, 'cause I was still on my ranch at Burnt Fork. Anyway, we ended up at the headwaters of Burnt Fork, up near Granddaddy Lakes, and there was a falling out over something or other...somebody went for a gun, and before you knew it, all hell broke loose. When the smoke cleared, near a half a dozen was killed and two or three wounded—even me. I was shot in the forearm...see—I still have the scar. But I wasn't the worst. Kid Roberts, who lived over near Hilliard, was shot the worst. He had a bullet in the groin. He showed up at my place about a week after the fight and was about on his last legs. I put him in the bed of my wagon and drove him over to Carter Station and we took a train to Green River (Wyo.). Doctor Hawks, who was a friend of mine, removed the bullet and patched him up, but he only lived a year or so after that. He wasn't very old when he died...This all happened over looking for gold. I never did much prospecting after that...

Dr. Hawks was a prominent Wyoming physician, known to have frequently patched up members of the Wild Bunch near the turn of the century. Interestingly enough, shortly after the gunfight in 1920, Tom Welch and Dr. Hawks, suddenly flushed with money, bought a hotel and bar in Green River, Wyoming. The hotel was called the Tomahawk Hotel (an anagram on both their names—Tom and Hawks), and the bar was called the Red Feather.

Arlin Davidson summed up his father's participation in the event in the following words, first published in the revised edition (1980) of our book, *Footprints in the Wilderness*, repeated here only in pertinent part:

Dad would never talk about this trip at all back then, but hurriedly moved his family a thousand miles away (sic: to northern Wyoming and southern Idaho), and dad never went back to Bridger or to Utah until after World War II. One time I asked dad about the deal. He told me he would never tell us about it and to please not ask him about it, ever again.

Now I say I never heard what happened when I was just a kid, but little mice have big ears,...I'm not sure who did the killing or just who was killed. ...But none of the Warrens were ever seen in Wyoming again—they never even came back to help Violet Warren Roberts (Ernest Roberts' wife) put up all that hay, and nobody seems to know what happened to this spiritualist Landreth.

...And, as I pointed out before, Harold Moslander (sic) was in the party. He was the young son of a neighboring rancher who married a girl named Annie or June Gill. He was a real good kid and was fairly well-to-do, having inherited the family ranch at a very early age. I believe he was about 18 years of age (sic: 22) at the time of the gun battle. Landreth could never manipulate this

boy or my father like he could the others and perhaps, because of it, he made the decision to have them killed. In fact, everyone in the group knew Landreth and had great faith in his ability to lead them to the gold, that is, all except dad and Moslander.

It seems that he had some unusual power or hold over his men. He'd make them line up before him and force them to admit to horrid crimes which they had done in the past. One man, dad said, actually admitted to having killed a small child, chopped her body into small pieces and then dropped the pieces down into an old well. That sort of thing. And Landreth seemed to hold a strange contempt for dad and Moslander because he could not manipulate them as he could the others....

You see, dad had kept that pistol which had been given him by their guard, in hopes of someday returning it to its rightful owner if he ever saw him again— a sort of gesture to show his thanks for saving his life. Dad kept that pistol for the purpose for 16 or 17 years...

It was about this time, in 1937 (sic: 1938), when Matt Warner of Price, Utah, died. At that time there was a large write up in the papers about him and, lo and behold, there was also a photograph of him. When dad saw the photograph of old Matt Warner, he said, "Why, that's the man who gave me the gun—the man who probably saved my life!" It was shortly after that the gun just disappeared. I don't know, to this day, what dad did with it.

The identity of the old cattleman, of course, was not known until 1976, just a few weeks before dad passed away. Now, I got your book on the Rhoades Mines [*Footprints in the Wilderness*] just a few weeks before dad died and he was real ill, one might say he was dying then. He wanted to know what it said, so I told him what I could. Along with your book I had a magazine article that had a picture of the man who married Caleb Rhoades' widow (Edward Hartzell). Dad looked at the picture for quite a while and then wanted to know who it was. Then dad told me that the particular man was on the trip for the Rhoades gold, but that he had never known or realized who the man was.

He said the man was older than the rest of them, that he only sat, looked and listened and never said anything. He was the retired cattleman and widower that was in the group that came from Price, Utah.

Following the death of Caleb Rhoades in 1905, his widow, Sidsie Adams Rhoades, searched for the mines for several years with the aid of Dr. Andrew Dowd and Joseph Sharp. Then she met and began courting Edward Hartzell whom she married in 1911. Hartzell had a life-long obsession with locating the Lost Rhoades Mine. It is certainly no coincidence that Edward Hartzell is also known to have been a cousin of Harry A. Longabaugh on the Place side of the family.

When Amasa Davidson had tested the gold ore at the campsite, he had slipped a piece of it into his pocket. That sample is now said to be in the University of Mines at Laramie, Wyoming.

Davidson had also taken a photograph of the old Rhoades cabin on the ill-fated trip of 1920. On Saturday, 28 July 1951, Amasa Davidson, accompanied by an attorney named Day, returned to the site of the old cabin at Scout Lake. Even after 31 years the old cabin was still standing, and Davidson found that it compared exactly to the old 1920 photograph. After exploring the area in search of the mine with no success, they returned home by way of Bear River.

In 1975, just a year before his death, Amasa Davidson, accompanied by two of his sons, made one last attempt to locate the elusive mine. The cabin was still standing, though the roof had caved in. Later, the cabin was burned to the ground by the U.S. Forest Service to prevent it being a danger to the many Boy and Girl Scouts who camp nearby during the summer months.

Matt Warner, who was eventually elected Justice of the Peace, town marshal and deputy sheriff at Price, returned to the Mirror Lake region several times before his death in 1938 to search for the mine. He brought out numerous gunny sacks of ore samples which, according to his son Boyo Warner, he stacked in his garage; but he never found the elusive mine. He named two small lakes in the area after his son and daughter, which still bear their names—Boyo Lake and Joyce Lake.

In about the year 1972, I went to the vicinity of Scout Lake accompanied by Tab-Wash, the grandson of old Chief Tabby. Tab-Wash (Tabuache—usually called simply Wash) was then in his mid-eighties (he was born, as near as he could recall, about 1885), but remarkably agile for his years. As we followed an old trail leading southwest from the cabin (which was then still standing, though roofless), Wash informed me that we were being followed. I became a little nervous at hearing this, but he merely smiled and said, "It's okay, they are Utes. No bother if you stay with Wash." Needless to say, I followed his advice.

As we climbed an incline where the trail entered sliderock, Wash pointed out where smaller rocks had been thrown between larger ones to fill in holes: "Make trail for horses so horses no break legs," Wash explained, with an economy of words typical of the native race.

Between two of the larger slide-rocks, both as large as an automobile, we came across a skeleton. Wash picked up the skull and turned it towards me. Above the left eye was a bullet hole, and the back of the skull, where the bullet had emerged, had been blown away. "White man," Wash said, without further explanation. I presumed it was one of the men killed during the 1920 gun battle. We laid the skull on a ledge near the trail as we proceeded farther up the ridge. When we returned an hour later, the skull was gone.

Afterwards, we had a picnic lunch beneath some pines near the old cabin. I rustled up the courage to ask Wash how he knew so much about the battle. He stopped chewing the bite he had taken from his sandwich and looked at me with no discernible expression on his face. Finally I noticed the hint of a smile curling the corners of his mouth.

"Wash was about your age when white men come up to look for mines," he said. "Set in trees over there, small way off, with mebbe four or five Utes. We watch, mebbe three days. See whole thing." He smiled widely as he added, "White men shoot each other up pretty good. All go home same day. Utes clean up all mess. Cover dead white men with rocks up there, on mountain. Spirits of dead white men guard the mine now. Scare away other whites."

"But I was up there just now, and nothing happened to me," I said.

"Sure, okay," replied Wash. "You not bothered by spirits because you were with Wash; and Wash have powerful medicine. No go there alone."

I never did.

Chapter Twelve

The Golden Legacy

ON THE 3RD OF JULY (1835), Michael H. Chandler came to Kirtland (Ohio) to exhibit some Egyptian mummies. There were four human figures, together with some two or more rolls of papyrus covered with hieroglyphic figures and devices. ...He was immediately told, while yet in the custom house, that there was no man in that city (New York City) who could translate his roll; but was referred, by the same gentleman, (a stranger,) to Mr. Joseph Smith, Jun., who, continued he, possesses some kind of power or gifts, by which he had previously translated similar characters. [*Comprehensive History of the Church,* Joseph Smith, Jun., 2:351]

Thus wrote Joseph Smith of his purchase of a collection of Egyptian mummies and papyri from which he purportedly translated the *Book of Abraham,* one of the doctrinal scriptures of the Mormon Church. The "stranger" mentioned by Smith—who was certainly no stranger to the Mormon Prophet—was Benjamin Bullock III, son of Benjamin Bullock II and Sybil Drake, born 30 March 1792 at Grafton, New Hampshire, and who died 27 July 1852 on the North Platte River, Nebraska, en route to Utah. He married, 24 January 1808, at Grafton, Dorothy Kimball, daughter of John Kimball and Polly Hoyt. The Bullocks resided at Moirie, New York, and according to the Bullock family history [*Bullock Family History,* Clara Fullmer Bullock, Taber, Alberta, Canada, 1917], Benjamin Bullock happened to be at the customs house when Chandler arrived to collect his mummies.

According to this account, it was Bullock who instructed Chandler to take the artifacts to Joseph Smith and, indeed, personally drove Chandler the 250 miles to Kirtland, Ohio, to meet the Prophet, with the mummies and papyri in the back of his wagon.

The same source informs us that it was a Mormon missionary, Dr. J.R. Riggs, who converted the Bullock family to Mormonism. On 8 October 1853, Dr. Riggs married Bullock's daughter, Jane Kilton Bullock (1819-1910).

John Riggs was born 20 December 1812 at Oxford, New Haven, Connecticut, son of Major Gideon Riggs and Susan Pitcher. The Riggs family came from Connecticut in 1817 with Isaac Morley and settled at Kirtland, Ohio. He converted to Mormonism in November 1830, but his father forbade him to join the Church. He was eventually baptized 1 August 1839 at Nauvoo, Illinois, by Parley P. Pratt, and was blessed by Patriarch Isaac Morley at Lima, Illinois, on 8 October 1840. Riggs studied medicine in 1838 under Dr. Frederick G. Williams, Joseph Smith's personal physician, and finished at Quincy, Illinois in 1847. Migrating with the pioneer exodus he arrived in Utah on 5 September 1851 and settled at Provo to practice medicine.

Benjamin Bullock himself never joined the Mormon Church, although he moved to Kirtland, Ohio, and endured all the persecutions of the Saints in Missouri and Illinois, giving as his reason that he could "do more good for the Church by staying out of the Church," a strange statement indeed.

Bullock joined the pioneer wagon company of Coleman Boren, the author's great grandfather, but died of cholera on the North Platte River while crossing the plains. Coleman Boren took Bullock's widow, Dorothy Kimball, into his own home at Provo, Utah, where she died 23 September 1853. Benjamin Bullock's son, Benjamin Kimball Bullock (27 January 1821-22 March 1901), brother-in-law of Dr. John Riggs, married Martha Elizabeth Hart, whose mother was Mary Riggs, aunt of the good doctor. Benjamin Bullock IV, who was for many years mayor of Provo, married Martha Hart on 26 January 1851. Their son was Benjamin Hart Bullock (Benjamin V), born 27 October 1878 at Provo, and who died, at the same place, on 12 July 1962. It is with Benjamin Hart Bullock that we note the first connection with the Rhoades mines.

Ben H. Bullock was—like Bishop Koyle—a man who professed to possess gifts of the spirit. Indeed, Bullock claimed to have had a dream wherein he too was visited by a heavenly messenger who revealed the location of a lost Nephite gold mine. Bullock worked his secret mine for many years and during this time he formed a close friendship with Bishop John Koyle. Koyle himself openly stated that Bullock was his closest personal friend, and Bullock often claimed that Koyle's Dream Mine was a "twin" to his own Nephite mine.

During the period when the Mormon Church threatened excommunication to anyone who worked Koyle's Dream Mine, that mine was closed down, and the assessment work that was necessary to be done in order to retain legal ownership to the property was neglected. When the deadline for the assessment work arrived, Ben H. Bullock was sitting in the lobby of the Kenyon Hotel in Salt Lake City, dazing in the early morning hours of the day. He later claimed that a clear voice spoke to him, interrupting his sleep, informing him to go immediately to the Dream Mine and take up the claims to save them for the stockholders of Koyle's company.

Bullock proceeded immediately to Spanish Fork where he obtained a horse and headed for Water Canyon. The deep January snow hindered his progress and he was forced to abandon the horse and proceed on foot, but even this was impossible, for he continually broke through the drifts up to his hips.

Bullock fell to his knees and prayed to the Lord to make the snow firm enough to support his weight so he could complete his mission. When he arose and tried again, the snow supported him easily, and he proceeded to place notices on the main series of eight claims. Within three days he had recorded the claims and signed quit-claim deeds back to the Koyle Mining Company stock-

holders, thus securing it without losing their Church membership.

Then, in the summer of 1958, Ben H. Bullock reported that he had discovered the Lost Rhoades Mines! *The Daily Record* newspaper of Salt Lake City, dated 23 June 1958, reported as follows:

LOST RHOADES GOLD MINE DISCOVERED RECENTLY BY BULLOCK MINES—METALS

Discovery of the lost Rhoades Gold Mine west of Moon Lake in Duchesne County, Utah, was announced this week by Mr. Ben H. Bullock of the Bullock Mine, Metals and Oil Corporation of Utah. Mr. Bullock stated that the mine was located by instrument test and through use of an old buckskin map drawn by Caleb Rhoades. The map is owned by Mrs. Mary Steele of Goshen, Utah. The mine was discovered by Mr. Bullock and his son, Vern Bullock, 100 W. 960 N., Provo.

In an interview with Mr. Bullock, he stated that the mine was originally discovered by Indians living in that area. "Caleb Rhoades," he continued, "was liaison between the Indians and Brigham Young who was believed to have used the gold to mint money used by the settlers in the Salt Lake Valley."

"The gold vein," said Mr. Bullock, "is 600 feet in width by 2,000 feet in length in a contact vein between porphyry and quartzite. Operation of the mine will begin soon," he continued.

Though Bullock reported that he had found the mine with the aid of the buckskin map and by instrument test, it would appear that the story of the discovery is not so simple.

As early as 1940, Clark Powell, Sr., a relation of Caleb Rhoades through Caleb's marriage to his first wife, Melinda Powell, struck up a friendship with a young lady named Sadie who lived in Carbonville, a suburb of Price, Utah. As it happened, Sadie was the younger sister of Sidsie Adams Rhoades, Caleb's second wife.

Sadie supplied Clark Powell with a copy of a map showing the location of three rich gold mines, which map she said she had obtained from Sidsie Rhoades before her death, and that it was a copy of the original which Thomas Rhoades had taken from the massacred Spaniards at Chicken Creek in 1857. By the use of the map, Caleb Rhoades had discovered at least two of the mines by 1859.

Sometime during the early 1950s, Powell came into contact with Carlos Foote who had discovered a vertical mineshaft in the area of one of the mines listed on the map. The two men decided to go to the mine and perhaps, by the use of the map, then discover the location of the other two. They set out on the expedition in the company of one other man, Roy Powell. On the way to the mine, however, an argument ensued between the parties, and Foote became concerned for his life, and he silently departed from the camp one night and left the Powells on their own.

On his way off the mountains, Foote encountered Ben H. Bullock whom he told about the shaft. He also described a large pine tree which stood near the shaft of the mine, and that had "Gold-1856" carved into the trunk. Foote had seen such a tree clearly marked on Powell's Spanish map, and he was convinced that this was an authentic Spanish mine. He and Bullock thereby entered into some sort of agreement for Foote to show him the location of the shaft.

Foote placed three "x's" on Bullock's map which he had obtained from Mrs. Steele, but unfortunately his memory did not serve him correctly and the marks were not in the correct location, causing much confusion to this day for those who still search for the mines.

Though Bullock Mines, Metals and Oil Corporation did not find the other two mines, there is no doubt that what Ben H. Bullock did discover was Caleb Rhoades' famous "Pine Mine," clearly mentioned in Rhoades' mineral leases and other documents.

Bullock's exploration of the mine revealed some interesting circumstances. The shaft was barely large enough to permit a man to enter, and Bullock improvised a "lift" by cutting a 55 gallon barrel in half and making a sling out of it by which he could be lowered into the vertical shaft.

At a depth of about 60 feet the vertical shaft ended and the tunnel continued horizontally into the bowels of the mountain. At this point the tunnel had been filled with fallen rock and all efforts to remove it from the confines of the barrel lift failed.

While Bullock returned out of the mountains to devise a new approach, claim jumpers entered the area with a bulldozer, hoping to scrape away the top layers and expose the vein, taking as much gold as they could and departing before Bullock returned. All they succeeded in doing, however, was to push the shaft full of rock and debris and to make it even more inaccessible.

A tragic side-note to this invasion was that the historic old pine tree with the inscription "Gold-1856" was pushed over the side of the mountain and permanently buried. Ben Bullock was blamed for this destruction, but the following letter, written by his son, Benjamin Vern Bullock (Benjamin VI), of Provo, to Gale Rhoades and Kerry Ross Boren (see *Footprints*, p.396), dated 25 October 1971, indicates that Bullock had nothing to do with it.

> We hired a man by the name of John Munz, who lived on a ranch easterly of Duchesne, to haul two horses to our base camp site in his cattle truck. These we were unable to ride because of wind-fallen trees, so we tied them up, and I pulled my father up the mountain by him holding on to my belt—he was 80 years old at the time and crippled from a broken back and hip from a car wreck in 1950.

> He and I found the location we wanted and when I located the claims (I) found an old logging road which made it possible for me to ride into the area on a tote gote; a little repair at the base of the mountain would (have) enabled me to drive all the way in my pickup...

> We did not push over the tree with date & inscription on it. We did not have a bulldozer in the area and fill up No. 1 shaft, or any other shaft. At about the same time, an outfit from California operated out of Hanna with a bulldozer but...no heavy equipment was ever taken in by us. ...The heaviest piece of equipment we had, or caused to

have, on the mountain was the 25th Tote Gote built by the Borham Co. of Provo. I rode and hauled out surveying equipment on it when staking our claims...

Ben H. Bullock died 12 July 1962 at his home in Provo in his 84th year. He never opened the Pine Mine, although his son Vern maintained the claims on it. Before his death, Bullock intimated that the reason for his abandoning the project was not so much lack of accessibility or financing, but because of something he had either seen or experienced at that place.

Vern Bullock related in an interview in 1971 that after the article appeared on the discovery of the Pine Mine, his father received numerous letters, phone calls and visits from people interested in promoting the discovery of the mine.

"I could have told great tales," Vern Bullock said, "but what we learned was our business."

Ben H. Bullock left a golden legacy. He may well have been one of the greatest prospectors in the West, even though his productivity may have been minimal. It is quite probable that Ben Bullock knew a great deal more about the lost mines than he was ever willing to reveal publicly.

Ben Bullock's heritage was deeply rooted in the Mormon Church. His family boasted names closely connected with the Prophet Joseph Smith and Brigham Young, including Thomas Bullock (personal secretary to both Joseph Smith and Brigham Young, as well as founder and manager of the Deseret Mint, and thus in charge of the gold from the mines), Seth Bullock, Isaac Bullock, and other prominent early Church leaders.

Ben Bullock considered himself to be a prophet, seer, and a diviner of earthly treasures — just as Joseph Smith, John H. Koyle, Caleb Landreth, Caleb Rhoades, and Jesse Knight claimed to be.

Is it coincidental that all of these men claimed to have had a dream about this mysterious mine? Did they all just "happen" to describe the contents of this "sacred mine" in exactly the same fashion — including the caverns, the walls of which were plated in gold leaf with inscribed hieroglyphics, and containing golden relics and treasure?

Was Koyle's Dream Mine in reality the Sacred Mine of the Indians? Was it therefore the Lost Rhoades Mine which was worked for the benefit of the Mormon Church? If so, this might explain the pressure put upon Koyle by the general authorities of the Church to cease operation of the mine. But if this is the case, why did Koyle mine the mountain at Water Canyon?

Perhaps the answer lies with Ben H. Bullock's statement to *The Mining Review*, published at Carson City, Nevada. Under date of 21 June 1959, Bullock stated to a *Review* reporter:

> ...Bishop Koyle's fifty year charter ended in the early spring of this year. I don't know whether or not any of his stockholders will pick up the lease, but it is my guess that they will, because they still see great potential in the claim.

> I personally knew John Koyle for many years and I can verify that he knew what he was talking about and that a gold source did exist. On the other hand, I have always been of the belief that it was not at the location where so much attention is being given, but in a place which I discovered many years ago when in my youth when I had a dream similar to that of John Koyle's dream.

> The Nephite mine — which is what I call the mine I discovered through a dream when I was in my youth — is located in the Uintah Mountains in Utah, *northwest of the present-day town of Vernal*...and there are at least a dozen other gold sources along those mountains just as rich in ore, but none which contain the relics I saw in my dream except the Nephite mine...and this I believe was the same mine that was shown to John Koyle in his dream...

> ...Koyle's interest in the Dream Mine near the present town of Salem in Utah was, I believe, brought about as a speculation, and had nothing directly to do with the true location of the Nephite mine...

> ...Some forty years ago Uncle Jesse Knight approached me and wanted to invest in my Nephite mine, but I didn't then, nor do I now, wish to reveal the location of it. I am negotiating instead to open up several other mines which belonged to Caleb Rhoades,

and which do not have the curse upon them that is contained with the Nephite mine. I sincerely believe that John Koyle failed to open his mine because of the curse of the Nephites, and if I were to reveal the Nephite mine to the world at this time, it would be taken from me, too.

The same article, while devoted to other locations in Nevada and elsewhere, also gives several other references to Koyle's Dream Mine that are worth noting here:

> John Koyle saw the Nephite mine, all right, but not the one they are now speculating on near Salem in Utah. ...The Dream Mine, that hasn't produced enough ore to pay for exploration, would not be worth mentioning beside the real Dream Mine, or the Nephite mine.

> ...I believe Koyle was accurate in his description of the Nephite mine, but somehow it was placed near Water Canyon, and that source is yet another, having little to do with the mine of Koyle's dream...

It is apparent from Bullock's statements that he did not claim the "Gold-1856" mine, or Pine Mine, to be the same as his Lost Nephite Mine, but equated the latter with a source northwest of Vernal. He also professed to believe that Koyle's Dream Mine near Salem was not the actual mine of Koyle's dream, and he equated the latter with his own Nephite mine. Obviously, Bullock knew more than he was willing to tell.

One fact of all this information emerges as being certain, that somewhere in the Uintah Mountains of northeastern Utah lies the real "Dream Mine." According to legend, the mine contains fabulous gold wealth, with caverns of gold leaf and marvelous relics of ancient civilization.

Some men have found the "Dream Mine," and lost it again. Others have been fortunate enough to bring gold out of it for the benefit of "the Lord's work," but have been sworn to an oath of secrecy which, because of strong religious proclivities, they have maintained to their graves. For some, the Sacred Mine holds the hope of dreams fulfilled; for others, it has been a nightmare.

In retrospect, the Sacred Mine of Caleb Rhoades was undoubtedly the Dream Mine of Jesse Knight, the Nephite Mine of Ben H. Bullock, and perhaps even the original source of Bishop Koyle's Relief Mine or Dream Mine.

It seems apparent that the lost "Nephite" relics are synonymous with the treasure of the Aztecs, a theme we will develop in later chapters. The reader must be the final judge of the evidence and determine whether or not these men, whose lives were so intertwined, all knew of the same mine, or whether their claims were based on religious aberrations. What is certain is that all of them—and many others connected with them who knew of the existence of the mine—had shared a common dream. Chief Walker had seen the mine in a dream or vision of the great Towats, and Caleb Rhoades often inferred that his knowledge of the sacred relics within the mine were revealed to him in a dream. Jesse Knight—descended from a family of gifted dreamers—saw the location of the mine in a dream, and with gold from the mine, allegedly saved the credit of the Mormon Church. Ben H. Bullock was renowned as a prophetic dreamer and diviner, and his description of the Nephite Mine matched in every detail with that of the Sacred Mine of the Indians. Even Caleb Landreth (Longabaugh) claimed to have seen the mine in a dream. Finally, Bishop Koyle's dream carried him away into the nine caverns and began a legend in Utah history that has prevailed to the present day in the amazing story of the Dream Mine of Salem, which has cost millions to maintain, but in nearly 100 years has not produced a single ounce of gold!

Dry Fork Canyon

BENJAMIN HART BULLOCK STATED that his Lost Nephite Mine was located northwest of Vernal, which would place it somewhere in the area of Dry Fork Canyon. Jesse Knight also claimed this location for his Dream Mine, and Caleb Rhoades himself hired Matt Warner and other gunfighters to protect his own interests in that same area. This focused interest on this section of the Uintah Mountains merits a further investigation of Dry Fork Canyon in connection with the Rhoades mines.

The canyon runs in a westerly direction along the base of the northern slopes of Lake Mountain and Middle Mountain to the eastern slope of Mosby Mountain and proceeds northward into the Horseshoe Park area at the southern base of Marsh Peak.

Dry Fork Canyon has long been associated with lost Spanish mines, both gold and silver, and while it is one of the more accessible locations in the rugged Uintah Mountains, it is generally overlooked by all but the most serious treasure hunters for some unexplained reason. This is probably a serious oversight on their part, inasmuch as the vicinity is replete with evidences of genuine lost mines and veins, and is one of the major sites considered as a possible location of at least one of the Rhoades mines.

Butch Cassidy.

Courtesy Utah State Historical Society.

Nearly thirty years ago I was exploring Dry Fork Canyon, in search of an inscription on the ledges which an old-timer had informed me was carved there in 1896 by Butch Cassidy, when I discovered an inscription of a different kind. In the vicinity of "Doughnut Rock Arch," just west of the mouth of North Fork, high on a cliff face, large bold letters deeply etched into the rock face displayed the name and date: ALVAREZ DE LEON—ANNO DOMINI 1669.

I was not the first or only discoverer of the inscription: Shirl Atwood found the inscription many years ago as a boy playing along the ledges in the main canyon, but he reports that it was not far from the "Remember the Maine" flag painted on the cliff side near the mouth of Dry Fork Canyon. Perhaps there is more than one inscription—Stephen Shaffer, author of *The Lost Josephine Mine* (1987), states that "On a ledge in Dry Fork Canyon northeast (sic) of Vernal, Utah, we found this inscription: ALVAREZ DE LEON ANNO DOMINI 1669."

During the 1970s I had considerable research done in the Spanish archives of Madrid and Seville, Spain. I was searching for evidence of Spanish gold shipments from the region of the Uintah Mountains, but the search uncovered instead a surprising document. In the Archives de España, Archivo de Madrid, was found a document dated 1671, entitled: "Relación de la jornada de la Provincias Internas de la tierra de las Yutas la cual fue el año de

1669" ("Relative to the journey to the Internal Provinces of the land of the Utes in the year 1669"). This document is a report by the officers of an expedition sent out by the Council of the Indies to determine the extent of damages done by the "revolt of the Yutas in the years 1648-1651" and the possibility of recovering strategic outposts in that region. The third signature on this report is, notably, "Alvarez de Leon."

It appears that part of Alvarez de Leon's mission, in addition to exploring the possibility of recovering strategic outposts in the region following the Indian revolt of 1648-1651, was to re-open some of the Spanish mines in the Uintah Mountains. His name is associated with at least one mine in this area, a silver mine by most accounts, which has achieved local fame as the "Lost Souls Mine."

The legend persists that a party of Spaniards, including a grandfather, father, and son (by other accounts a girl, or a woman and her husband) were working at the mine in Dry Fork Canyon. The miners had cast many silver ingots which they buried in a pit beneath the floor of their cabin.

The Utes began to steal their pack animals and attacked anyone who wandered too far from the protection of the camp. One day when the miners were working at the mine and the smelter, the boy and his grandfather went out to pick chokecherries. When they returned in the evening they discovered that the camp had been attacked by Indians in their absence, the cabin burned, and every member of the party killed. Fearing for their own lives, the old man and his grandson lingered only long enough to drag the dead bodies of their comrades into the mine tunnel, and to pull out the supporting portal timber, caving the mine over the entrance. Covering the remains of the entrance with rocks and brush, the old man knelt and prayed, lamenting that there was no priest present to administer the last rites of the church to save the souls of his son and the other miners who had been killed.

The old man and his grandson fled the mountains, subsisting on roots and berries, until they reached Sante Fe. The grandfather died soon after their arrival, but not before drawing a map for his grandson which was passed down through his family and became the focus of later searches.

One day in 1967 I visited the Uintah County Courthouse at Vernal, Utah, to collect some documented information for our book, *Footprints in the Wilderness*, and became engaged in conversation with Mr. Morris Cook, the Uintah County Clerk. Mr. Cook proved to be a veritable fount of information on local history, and from his lips I gleaned the following story:

Sam Reynolds was an old sheepherder; since that time he has been a game warden, rancher and several other things locally. He owns a big spread way up on the other (west) end of Dry Fork Canyon.

Well, back here some time ago, I don't know just how long, an old man of Mexican descent came into town (Vernal) and he had a map. He said that it showed there was a silver mine somewhere in this area. He said the map had belonged to his mother and that his family had at one time helped mine this silver. The silver was mined and taken by pack train to New Mexico or somewhere further south to be made into jewelry and things of that sort. The old fellow got Sam Reynolds to help him look for it because Sam had an honorary degree from some geology school or another and really knew his ores.

According to Sam, the map led them up Dry Fork Canyon to a small natural arch or rock bridge (the "Doughnut Rock Arch"), and he was able to find this all right. But, up near the head of the canyon the map showed where there was a cave, and search as they might, they never could find it. Nobody had ever heard of there being a cave in that area, so the old Mexican finally gave up and went home. Sam searched around once in awhile but never came up with anything.

Then, some years later, Sam's kids were playing on a hill near the top of Dry Fork Canyon when their little dog fell down a "prairie dog hole." The kids came running to the ranch and begged Sam to rescue the dog, so Sam took a shovel and went up and began to dig the dog out. As he was digging, he opened up the entrance of this cave which went back at least a half-mile into the hill.

Now that Sam had found the cave, he didn't know what to do. As near as he could remember, the silver mine was supposed to be "just around the hill" from the cave, but he couldn't find it. He didn't know how to get in touch with the old Mexican who was probably dead by that time anyway. This lost mine still intrigues a great many people today.

It should perhaps be pointed out that Sam Reynolds was the son of one of the Reynolds brothers who had formed a mining corporation with Jesse Knight to work the old Johnnie Mine near Pahrump, Nevada, where Butch Cassidy later lost his life.

In February 1982, Dale Rex Bascom of Santaquin, Utah, who was raised in the Dry Fork area, related the following account to Gale Rhoades:

> The sister of Max Harrison (of Vernal) was up in Dry Fork Canyon some years ago hiking around with a couple of other girls and some boys when they came across a small cave. They went back into this cave to snoop around and back inside a short way it dropped off into a shaft-like hole. Having a flashlight, they lowered one of the boys down into the hole with a rope. The cave was spooky to them anyway and they had mixed feelings about being there in the first place, but they were not ready for what was about to be discovered. When they lowered the boy down into the hole, he took one look around and screamed for them to pull him back out. When they pulled him from the hole, he described in graphic detail what he had seen; a room-like chamber where 15 or 20 human skeletons were sitting or lying around in the form of a circle against the walls, most of which were still wearing old Spanish armor. They ran from the cave and returned to their homes, swearing to one another an oath never to tell where this place was at.

My late friend George A. Thompson located the remains of an old Spanish smelter just north of Dry Fork Canyon near the Red Cloud Loop road. By the use of a metal detector, George discovered an old iron midden laden inside with nearly a half-inch of molten gold, strong testimony of the Spanish mining activity in the Dry Fork Canyon area.

Some years ago I obtained a copy of a journal which had belonged to Aaron Daniels, an early pioneer and prospector, as well as friend and partner of Caleb Rhoades in several mining ventures [see *Footprints*, 1980 edition]. Daniels had dictated his journal to his daughter, Caroline Amelia Mills, on 26 July 1895, shortly before his death, in the hopes that his family might profit from his knowledge of the mines. Among his many notes and reminiscences is the following:

> Dry Fork Canyon branches up near the Indian writing (petroglyphs), and back up the North Branch is where I found the tunnel which caved in just big enough for a man to crawl into, dropping straight down and on the floor was a lot of old Indian Pottery filled with ore and back farther was some bones of dead men and two kids it looked like. There was strange marks all over the wall which I think was Spanish signs because they looked like the ones on the trees, but when I went back two years later, there was nothing to be found. You should someday search for it. I still have the name written down here that I found on the ledge of Dry Fork. It was *Alvarez De Leon,* and the date says Anno Domini 1669.

Caleb Rhoades and Jesse Knight fought to secure possession of a gold source somewhere on the upper reaches of Dry Fork Canyon northwest of Vernal. Jesse Knight referred to the Dry Fork Canyon site as his "Dream Mine," which would tend to identify it with the Sacred Mine, but Caleb Rhoades himself tried to secure the Dry Fork mine, which seems to indicate that it was not the Sacred Mine, inasmuch as he had taken a blood oath that he would never work the Sacred Mine.

In about 1903 Uncle Jesse Knight formed a limited partnership with my grandfather, William C. Boren, who had recently moved from Maeser Ward, near the mouth of Dry Fork Canyon, to the Marimon ranch on the reservation near Whiterocks. As such, my late uncle, Roy Boren, gained some personal knowledge of the mine in Dry Fork Canyon:

I was only a little tyke when the Dry Fork ambush happened (1896), but I remember it. It was the big news in the Uintah Basin at that time. I remember my father talking about it for years after that, because he knew all of the people involved. Later, I became good friends with both old Bob Swift and Uncle Jesse Knight.

Bob Swift married one of the daughters of old Joe Duncombe, and he lived in Vernal for a long time and over at Linwood (Utah) and eventually moved to Price where he lived not far from Matt Warner. They was good friends all their lives. I've heard him tell the story about the gunfight a hundred times…

I worked for Uncle Jesse Knight out on the reservation. I helped him build a flume for the irrigation project on Blue Bench, and I helped him drive a tunnel for a coal mine just above Neola. He also had something to do with the round-up of wild horses which we sold to Cudahy Meat Packing Company not long after the reservation boundaries was changed…

What I knew about Jesse Knight's Dream Mine is this; he come to our place one day in an old buckboard and wanted to talk to my dad. We lived at that time just below the old Marimon Ranch at the mouth of Whiterocks Canyon, not far from the Indian trading post. He asked my dad if he would not take him up to the ridge between Whiterocks Canyon and Dry Fork Canyon where he knew of a mining prospect. He asked dad to keep it a secret because there was guys who would do anything to know about the mine. Dad agreed to go, and they set out early one morning from the ranch and they was gone for nearly two weeks. I remember that Uncle Jesse Knight was getting up in years at that time, but he was pretty tough, you know, and he could hold his own pretty good.

When they came back, I asked dad what they had done up there, and he wouldn't tell me. He said, "We seen some things and I was told not to talk about them and you are better off never to know about it." I don't remember dad ever breaking his word about what he seen there, but I knew it was something strange because of the way he acted about it.

One day I was moving sacks of grain in the granary and lifted up one of the sacks and it had a hole in the bottom of it, and some of the grain spilled out. I guess the mice had chewed through it, so I got down on my hands and knees and started to scoop the grain back into another sack when I seen some rocks in the grain. I picked them up and took them to a window and looked at them in the light, and it was almost pure gold!

I didn't know what to do with the stuff. I didn't dare tell dad, but I knew he would find out anyway, because I had moved the sacks, so I eventually got up enough courage to talk to him about it. He listened without saying anything and then told me to follow him to the granary., He took out some of the gold and turned it over a few times in his hand. "Do you know where this comes from?" he asked me. I told him I didn't, but I had my suspicions it had something to do with what he had done with Uncle Jesse Knight.

Dad didn't tell me any more than he had to, but he said that the gold came from a mine shaft which Jesse Knight had seen in a dream. When they had gone to that mine to take out some samples of the gold, Uncle Jesse Knight gave some to my dad, telling him that he could keep it, but not to ever exchange it for money, because it had a curse on it.

Dad kept that gold for years and I remember seeing it several times when I visited at his place, even after I moved away. Then my dad moved over to Maeser and started a ranch there in about 1922 or 1923; he nearly lost the place because he couldn't keep up the payments. He took some of the gold and exchanged it for cash to pay off the debts. The next spring (1924) he was driving his Model T Ford along the canal bank between Vernal and Maeser in a rain storm and the car slid off the road and into the canal, killing him. I often wondered if Uncle Jesse Knight's curse had anything to do with it.

Jesse Knight had drawn a crude map to indicate to my grandfather approximately where the mine was located when he first attempted to convince him to go there. That map, obtained from my uncle before his death (he died 2 October 1979, at age 90), is reproduced in this book for the first time.

According to the best information available from Jesse Knight's map, and from Knight himself, as related to my grandfather, the following clues emerge:

1. Knight's mine lies somewhere to the northwest of the Dry Fork Canyon upper reaches, where the canyon forks, perhaps on the dividing ridge between Whiterocks Canyon and Dry Fork Canyon.

2. There is a mountain peak to the northwest of the Dry Fork Canyon mine. The line on the Knight map indicates either snow line or timber line, which means the peak is bald (Marsh Peak?).

3. There are trees with Spanish symbols carved on them near the entrance to the mine.

4. The mine is within a day's horseback ride from Whiterocks.

Dry Fork Canyon emerges time after time in early accounts of the Rhoades mines, enough to convince even the most skeptical treasure hunters that *something* is there to be found.

Chapter Fourteen

Guns, Ghosts & Gold

OUTLAWS HAVE, IN ONE WAY OR another, long been associated with the Lost Rhoades Mines. Butch Cassidy is the most notable example. In 1897 he took refuge in one of the mines near Dry Fork Canyon with his outlaw companion, Joe Walker. Walker later returned with several companions to remove some of the gold, only to be curtailed by the Indians and his companions drowned in the Green River. Harry Longabaugh shows up in 1920 as "Caleb Landreth" to lead an expedition that included Matt Warner and Elzy Lay, both of whom searched for the mines most of their lives. Henry Rhodes "Bub" Meeks and his brother Bill searched for the mines many years, and the latter was a long-time friend of Amasa Alonzo Davidson.

A young school teacher from Wellington, Utah, near Price, became an unwitting catalyst in this intrigue. Annie Marie Thayne was attracted to the wild outlaws of the Robbers Roost country. She had "sparked" Joe Walker and Bub Meeks and would later become the lover of Harvey Logan, alias Kid Curry. In 1900 she became the wife of Harry Longabaugh, alias the Sundance Kid (a.k.a. Caleb Landreth), and on 4 January (by other accounts 2 February) 1901, bore him a son.

When Joe Walker fled the country following the Castle Gate Payroll Robbery in 1897, Annie turned her attentions upon Sanford "Sang" Thompson, who was at that time working for my grandfather, William C. Boren, on his ranch near Cleveland, in Emery County. Tom Dilly, a wild Texas cowboy, decided to stake his claim on her, and so he laid up in the rocks of Thompson Canyon and killed Sang as he rode by. To avoid detection, Dilly decapitated the body and buried it in a box, where it was not discovered until some time later. Dilly then found work with Dan Kinney, foreman of the Webster Cattle Company.

When a man named Fullerton took over management of the Webster company, on his first day on the job he took it upon himself to give Dilly advice on how to shoe a horse, and Tom commenced to pistol-whip him. When another cowboy, Sam Jenkins, tried to interfere, Dilly gave him the same treatment, and they ever after hated each other.

In 1899 the Webster company was taken over by Dr. Andrew Dowd and a man named Forrester, and they took Dilly in as a partner, contingent upon his promise to rustle livestock to build up their herd. They reorganized as the Patmos Head Land and Cattle Company. During the winter of 1899-1900, Dilly was joined in his rustling enterprise by Flatnose George Currie.

In May, Sheriff Tyler returned to the Book Cliffs, accompanied by Billy's old enemy Sam Jenkins, whom Tyler had deputized in the hopes of bringing Dilly in. Instead they encountered three men sitting by a fire, wrapped in Indian blankets. Not knowing who they were, Tyler commenced to boast about having killed Flatnose Currie. The men proved to be Kid Curry and two companions. The Kid, a close friend of and namesake of Flatnose George, fired from beneath his blanket and killed both Tyler and Jenkins.

Tom Dilly was believed responsible for the murders, but was eventually cleared at a preliminary hearing at Provo. Nevertheless, it cost the Patmos Head Land and Cattle Company $40,000 to get an acquittal. Tom promised to work something out to pay them back.

That fall Dowd and Forrester shipped a trainload of cattle to Kansas City in Dilly's care. Tom promised to ship some registered Hereford bulls to Dowd and Forrester, but instead absconded with the proceeds of the cattle sale and hastily fled to South America. He proposed to buy a ranch there, but soon joined Butch Cassidy and the Sundance Kid in robberies, only to be shot to death a few years later, in August 1911, at Villa Mercedes, Argentina.

In an attempt to recoup his losses, Dr. Andrew Dowd solicited a partnership with a man named Ketchum and Joseph R. Sharp to obtain possession of the Big Spring Ranch near Sunnyside, Utah.

In the fall of 1905, only a few months after the death of Caleb Rhoades, his widow, Sidsie, approached Dr. Andrew Dowd and Joseph Sharp with a proposition. She had been referred to them by Matt Warner, who had bought the Rhoades farm. She offered a limited partnership to Dowd and Sharp if they would help her find the Rhoades mine indicated on a map left to her by her late husband. This is confirmed by the journal entries of Mr. Lester Eklund.

The map, drawn by Caleb Rhoades on his death bed in 1905, was sketched on a small piece of paper apparently ripped from a notebook. It is reportedly a map of the mine to which he directed his brother Enoch Rhoades, who was killed by the Indians in September 1884.

Sidsie and her partners, Dowd and Sharp, searched for the mine for more than two years, from 1906 until 1907, with no success. On his death bed, Caleb had told her that "the mine was located below Low Pass," but Low Pass could never be located, and without that starting place, the mine could not be found.

Matt Warner in wagon. Man on horse—Mayor of Price. Matt and the Mayor were out on one of the prospecting journeys.

While associated with Dowd and Sharp, Sidsie met Edward Hartzell, the manager of Big Spring Ranch, whom she married in 1911. In July of 1912, Edward Hartzell, his son James, Matt Warner, the Warrens and others filed on the Eldorado and Klondike claims in the Rock Creek/Granddaddy Lake region.

Frank Noyes was foreman at Big Spring Ranch from 19 June 1922 until the early summer of 1928, at which time he was approached by Joseph Sharp to search for the lost mine. He produced a copy of the map he had obtained from Sidsie Rhoades and gave it to Noyes, who spent the next two years (1928-30) searching diligently for the lost mine.

Then one day near evening in 1930, Noyes came upon a small vertical shaft which had a pine tree "ladder" protruding above the entrance. Although the tree had notches for access down the shaft, Noyes decided not to enter, being alone, and returned home that night. He brought Sharp back with him the next day. The only clue to location that we have today is the fact that Noyes and Sharp passed through the town of Duchesne and headed northwest on an old road which they later stated took them within 200 yards of the old mine.

The shaft was very near the reservation boundary and this fact made them very nervous. Noyes walked to the mine shaft with Sharp to point it out, then returned to the automobile to keep watch for Indians. Sharp descended the tree-ladder equipped with two empty bank deposit bags.

The shaft ended at a depth of 12 to 13 feet, at which point a small tunnel continued into the mountain to a point where a large boulder blocked the path. Sharp scooped up enough ore to fill both bags and made his way back to the old tree-ladder.

Just as he was about to climb out of the shaft, Sharp was confronted by two Indians standing at the entrance and staring sternly down at him. One was a chief, wearing full headdress, and the other was a brave. The chief spoke with a voice of authority and conviction and in perfect English, saying, "Put the gold back. Leave here and never return or you will surely die!"

Joseph Sharp always maintained that the two Indians then disappeared into thin air! He was so frightened he dropped the bags of ore and ran hell-bent for the car, and they left the mountain in a cloud of dust.

Lester Eklund gives a somewhat different account. He relates that:

> Joe Sharp made several trips out here; I am told that the reason he quit coming is because old Mountain Sheep told him that if he thought anything of his life to make that trip his last one.

> He seemed to believe what the chief said, and took him at his word. Old Joe was probably pretty close to something.

Frank Noyes verified Sharp's version of the story. He stated that from the car where he waited, the view was clear for hundreds of yards in every direction, and he did not see the Indians until they stood at the shaft of the mine itself. Though he was 200 yards from the mine, he related that he heard the voice and the words of the chief very clearly, and that the Indians literally disappeared before his eyes. He swore ever after that they were ghosts.

Noyes applied to the Secretary of the Interior for permission to mine the shaft, but was denied access since it was on the reservation and he needed Indian permission, just as Caleb Rhoades had done thirty years earlier. Noyes then contracted with the Carter Oil Company in the hopes that they would be able to effect the lease on the property as a part of their already secured reservation rights, but they too failed to obtain Indian approbation. Carter Oil Company went to great lengths and expense to influence the government officials, even sponsoring a celebrated barbecue and picnic for them, to no avail, because the Indians withheld their consent.

Florence Mining Company. Matt Warner, second from left, Elzy Lay far right. Other two unidentified.

Courtesy the late George Thompson.

What emerged was the startling information that Jesse Knight already knew about the mine, and that just prior to his death in 1921, he had made an attempt to recover it. Knight, ever resourceful, bypassed all legal transactions with the Indians by driving a tunnel through the off-reservation side of the hill. But his expensive effort was doomed to fail, for he struck nothing, and as soon as the Indians discovered it, they put a stop to it. William Henry Wells related that "Jesse was in the right place all right, but his tunnel was too low, and he missed it."

Following his failure to gain legal access to the mine, Frank Noyes moved to his old farm at Victor, Utah, where lived his brother-in-law, William Henry Wells, and his good friend, John J. Petitti.

For the next several years Noyes worked his farm, but the lure of the gold worked on him. It was ever on his mind. One day in 1934, John Petitti drove over to the Noyes place for a casual visit, and when Frank Noyes came out on the porch to greet him, he said, "John, why don't you bring your truck over and we'll go out to the reservation and fill it with gold." It was said in jest, but a seed had been planted. According to Petitti, it was the first time Noyes had discussed the mine with him, although he frequently spoke to Wells about it. Now the three of them began to seriously consider a trip to the mine.

In the following year (1935) the three men set out on a secret trip to the mine. So hasty was their departure that Petitti neglected to inform his wife that he was leaving, and she worried for three days as to his whereabouts.

They took Petitti's 1928 Chevrolet touring car, and Wells did all the driving. Their route took them through Indian Canyon to Duchesne, but when they tried to enter the mountains below the mine, they were turned back by Indians. Determined to succeed, they retreated down Currant Creek, doubled around through Heber City and came in above the mine, taking the Highland Drive out of Charleston to the headwaters of Currant Creek. From there they drove to the base of the ledges of Tabby Mountain, to a place where the road became impassible due to recent flooding, and walked the rest of the way up the mountainside to the mine.

As they approached the mine, Noyes saw an Indian standing on a large rock near the entrance to the shaft, and he turned to his companions, his face ashen with fear, and whispered hoarsely, "Oh, oh! Let's get out of here—they know me!" They ran back to the car and hastily left the area, retreating by way of an old pioneer road "shortcut" which dropped off into Hanna. They became stuck in loose dirt between two steep grades, and there they remained two days before a farmer from Hanna could come with a team of horses to extract them. They had been away three days when they finally returned home.

Florence Mining Company. Matt Warner and Elzy Lay are part of the group.

Courtesy the late George Thompson.

None of the men ever returned to the mine, primarily due to their fear of the Indians. Their fear was very real and protracted. When Gale Rhoades interviewed Wells and Petitti in 1967, less than a year before their deaths, he noted that when Wells recounted the Indians, his voice faltered and his hands shook; Mrs. Petitti cautioned against going there, pointing out that her husband had not been the same since his return.

I visited with Noyes at his home in Hanksville, Utah, in 1967. Noyes was a relation of mine by marriage, though I had never met him prior to that occasion. I wanted to glean some family history from him, as well as hear his story of the search for the mine.

Noyes' fear of the Indians was as real as that of Wells and Petitti. He recounted for me the story of two other men who had gone to this same mine in 1925, about five years before his visit there with Joe Sharp. These men returned late one night to a local tavern and began to boast that they had just discovered the Lost Rhoades Mine.

Later that night these men began to argue about their discovery and one of the men stabbed his partner to death. Remanded to the local jail (Duchesne), the murderer was himself discovered stabbed to death by a fellow inmate—a full-blood Ute Indian!

In recounting this story, Noyes became visibly shaken. With great emphasis, he said: "There are things there that I don't dare talk about, and I won't ever go back! It's worth a man's life to visit that place, and the feeling that a person gets when he is there is something you never forget. My advice is to leave it alone. It belongs to God and the Indians."

Noyes admitted to having made one more secret trip to the area in 1956 or 1957, but only under cover of darkness, and not to the mine proper. "I only gathered samples from the creek below the mine," he confessed, "and even that was too close! I was scared ever minute I was there, expecting an arrow or a bullet in the back." Assays later revealed even these random float samples contained a considerable percentage of gold.

Noyes, Wells and Petitti all died in 1968. Wells died on 8 May and Petitti in September. Only Noyes survived when in November he called Gale Rhoades and asked him to come see him because he didn't have long to live. Because of other commitments, Gale couldn't go, but sent Leland Stevenson of Altamount, Utah, to visit Noyes in the hospital. After soliciting a promise that his wife would be taken care of financially if the Indians ever permitted them to work the mine,

Noyes revealed details of its location to Stevenson. In a few days, he was dead.

Frank Noyes' instructions were these: "Go up Currant Creek 10 or 12 miles to what they call the Red Narrows. The mine is at the base of the Red Ledges to the northeast of there. There's a road that goes up near the ledges and you can see the ledges from the Red Narrows."

After Noyes' death, Gale Rhoades and his wife Beverly, accompanied by Leland Stevenson and Edwin J. Larsen of Roosevelt, Utah, proceeded to the area. They found the remains of a very old cabin and three ancient mine dumps, as well as a large quaking aspen with the date "1850" carved into the trunk—but they never found the mine shaft with the tree-ladder protruding from it.

Gale Rhoades subsequently (1971) negotiated with Rex Curry, a Tribal Administration official, to meet with tribal attorneys at the Kennecott Building in Salt Lake City for the possibility of obtaining a mining lease on the area. After haggling for more than five years with no success, Gale gave up and turned his efforts elsewhere.

In about 1976 I drove to the upper Currant Creek area with my old Ute Indian friend Tab-Wash. Wash had waited for me at the Currant Creek Lodge on Highway 40, and promised to show me some of the sites in the vicinity of the Red Ledges.

As we reached the Red Narrows we were stopped by several Indians who ominously approached our vehicle on either side. As soon as they saw Wash, their stern countenance at once changed to respect, and after a few words in Ute passed between Wash and the men, they allowed us to proceed.

By this time a make-shift road had been made down into the basin where the remains of the old cabin—a few logs of the walls—were situated, and we were able to drive right to the Red Ledges. We walked through the whole area that day and Wash pointed out a number of old mines that had, for the most part collapsed. There were mining relics strewn here and there: the remains of a wooden rail-track and a wooden cartwheel, a few old iron buckets and the like. We walked along the base of the Red Ledges and circled a ridge, returning to our vehicle late in the day.

Wash had told me many things about the history of the area, and even some information relating to the various mines in the basin. At last I managed the courage to ask about the open shaft with the pine tree ladder. Wash grinned wryly. "You walked right by it today," he said. "You were very close." I asked him if he would take me back there and show me exactly where it was, to which he replied simply, in the Indian way, "No."

When I left Wash back at the Currant Creek Lodge later that day, he said to me in parting, "You no go back up there alone anytime. I like you pretty much. Hope you live a long time." I got the message.

We cannot leave the topic of this particular mine without mentioning James E. Hartzell, whose search for the elusive shaft cost him his life. James Hartzell was born in Scranton, Pennsylvania, on 15 October 1888, to Edward and Viola Hartzell, some years before Edward married Caleb Rhoades' widow, Sidsie. James Hartzell had been one of the claimants of the Eldorado and Klondike claims near Granddaddy Lake in 1912, and had often accompanied his father on prospecting ventures.

But James Hartzell's particular quest was the old Rhoades Mine at the Red Ledge on Currant Creek. For years he had eliminated one area at a time, moving his search pattern carefully along a planned course that would have placed him at the location within a few days of his death.

John Hartzell, of Price, Utah, a nephew of James, related the following information to Gale Rhoades:

> Yes, my uncle did die looking for that one thing. He was somewhat of a loner. I can remember once when he left (Price) on foot, with no gun and walked over the mountain at night alone and back again. He was, himself, somewhat a woodsman and like Caleb he grew a bushy beard.

> I remember well that last trip of his, when he died. At that time, he said he was going into the mountains and asked my step-brother, Charley Williams, to take him up there, leave him for two weeks and then go back in and pick him up.

James had been complaining about his health so Charley told him that he'd rather not take him in, especially to leave him alone because of his age and his poor health, but James said he'd get up there one way or another even if it meant doing it without Charley's help. So, Charley took him in, left him with his pet dog, and returned to work—planning to return fourteen days later to get him.

Subsequent events are best recounted in the following article, published in the *Salt Lake Tribune* of August 1961:

SEARCH DISCLOSES BODY OF PRICE PROSPECTOR

Fruitland, Duchesne County.—A growling fox terrier puppy Sunday morning brought searchers to the side of his dead master in the mountains 18 miles northwest of here.

The decomposed body of James E. Hartzell, 71, Price, last seen by a sheepherder August 7th, was discovered by George A. Sorenson, Tribune Staff Writer and member of Salt Lake County Sheriff's Jeep Patrol, off Bobby Duke Trail on Red Creek, Wasatch County...

A 40-man search was started Saturday when a nephew returned to the man's camp to take him home and could not find him. Mr. Sorenson said he stumbled on the body when the seven-month-old puppy growled at him.

Hiram Beebe, a.k.a. The Sundance Kid. Photograph taken at Utah State Prison.

Courtesy George Sorenson Photograph, Salt Lake Tribune photo.

The man's diary and testimony of a sheepherder led authorities to believe Mr. Hartzell died on or about August 7th. The prospector's last entry in his diary on August

6th read: "Tomorrow I'll work in the southeast direction toward Bear Hollow area."

A sheepherder, Steven Hamilton, said he saw Mr. Hartzell August 7th when Mr. Hartzell complained of feeling ill. The man's nephew took him into the area August 5th. When he could not find his uncle on his return Saturday, he notified Sheriff Witt.

I was acquainted with George A. Sorenson, discoverer of Hartzell's body. I was introduced to him because of his ironic association with another participant in the 1920 gunfight. In 1945, Harry Longabaugh, a.k.a. Hiram Bebee, shot and killed Mt Pleasant, Utah, town marshal Lon T. Larsen, and barely escaped the death penalty. He was sentenced to life imprisonment at Utah State Prison, where he died in 1955, aged 85. While in prison, "Hiram Bebee" gained considerable notoriety as an eccentric, and a young George A. Sorenson, who was then a photographer for the *Salt Lake Tribune*, was sent to get the old man's photograph. He got the picture, but Bebee also covered him with honey when he threw a jar of the sticky stuff at him against the bars of his cell. I interviewed Sorenson to glean information about Bebee, and learned the story of Hartzell and many others; Mr. Sorenson had led an extraordinary life in his own right.

According to Sorenson, James Hartzell's body was hidden in dense brush at the bottom of a hollow, where he had apparently crawled under his own power. Had it not been for the crying puppy, Sorenson said, the body might never have been found.

John Hartzell added the following information concerning his uncle:

When Charley took James in there, they ate breakfast together before Charley came back home for work. Charley knew how much grub James had and when he went back after him only a few eggs and etc. had been eaten, and he said that there were spider webs across the top of his water bucket. Charley figured from that, that James had died the day after he had left on August 6th — not August 7th as the newspaper article pointed out.

A sheepherder gave James a lift toward camp and when he got near his camp, James told him that he could make it on in on foot, so the sheepherder left him there. His body was found in high brush and had it not been for the pup, which had lain by his body for about 13 days, the searchers may not have found him, which by the way was only about 400 to 500 yards away from the camp.

I helped in that search for James. As near as anyone could figure out, when he left the sheepherder, he started to walk to camp but he soon started to suffer a heart attack and began to drag his feet with every step. Inside the brush he laid down and placed his pack under the back of his head. He died there and in that position, with his faithful dog at his side.

James Hartzell's camp was near the Bobby Duke Trail just east of Low Pass near the divide between the headwaters of Currant Creek and Red Creek. Low Pass was the same area searched by Sidsie Rhoades, with Dr. Andrew Dowd and Joseph Sharp in 1906-07. Sidsie was unable to locate the mine because she had searched too high; the mine was south of Low Pass, at the Red Ledges. It seems ironic that both Sidsie Rhoades and her step-son, James Hartzell, came within two miles of one of Caleb Rhoades' rich mines.

Locating this mine, with the accurate clues available, is no particular problem. Gale Rhoades located it before his death, but covered it up again, unable to work it. The reason is simple: in 1934 this portion of the land was removed from the reservation and made part of Forest Service domain. However, as a trade-off with the Ute Indians, the U.S. government returned all mineral rights to this land (10 square miles) to the Utes by Public Law 717 — 84th Congress, Chapter 603 — 2nd Session, H.R. 7663, in 1956. In order to work the mine, one must still obtain permission of the Indians — and they will not grant it.

Chapter Fifteen

Henry Boren's Lost Spanish Mine

AARON G. DANIELS FIRST ENTERED Heber Valley in the spring of 1858, in the company of George Bean, William Meeks, William M. Wall and a few others, coming up from Utah Valley seeking pasturage for their livestock. George Bean was an Indian interpreter and deputy sheriff who had lost an arm during the discharge of a cannon at the Indian battle at Fort Utah (Provo) in 1849; William Meeks had been one of the founders (with Daniels) of Fort Supply, near Fort Bridger, in 1856-57, and was, moreover, father of the outlaw Henry Rhodes "Bub" Meeks; and William Madison Wall had married a daughter of my great-grandfather, Coleman Boren.

Daniels so liked the Heber Valley that he took up a homestead about one mile north of the mouth of Daniels Creek where it enters the Provo River. In the fall of 1858, when his companions returned home with their cattle to Utah Valley, Daniels remained behind to trap and to explore the new valley during the winter.

It was at this time that Daniels accidentally discovered several old Spanish mines near the head of Center Creek while out rounding up his cattle to protect them from marauding wolves. He first noticed the mines by Spanish symbols carved on ledges nearby, but having a cabin and barn to build at his new homestead before winter, he had no time to explore them immediately.

During the spring of 1859, William Jasper Boren, Moses Meacham, Ed Stokes, Dixon Greer, and Asa C. Bethers came into the valley and established the towns of Heber and Charleston. William Jasper Boren—my grandfather's half-brother—was only 22 at the time, having been born in Illinois in 1837. His father, Coleman Boren, as related elsewhere, had died tragically the previous year, and young William Jasper Boren had recently married Lucina, daughter of Moses Meacham, who accompanied him to Heber Valley that spring.

William Madison Wall had married William Jasper Boren's sister, and with his family established the town of Wallsburg. Formerly, Wall had been prosecuting attorney at Provo. Asa C. Bethers settled at the head of Daniels Canyon on the Strawberry Summit some 18 miles southeast of Heber, where he operated a food and supply store, a sort of way-station for travelers between Heber Valley and the Uintah Basin.

In 1859, Aaron Daniels revealed his discovery of the Spanish mines to William Jasper Boren and Asa C. Bethers, and the three men attempted, in their spare time, to excavate the rubble from the entrances which had been placed there by the Indians. When Aaron Daniels moved from Heber Valley to Wanship in Summit County in 1860, the mining project was more or less abandoned.

Coleman Boren, a polygamist, had two families and fourteen children when he died in 1858. His second wife (my great-grandmother), Flora Maria Kingsley, was left a young widow of 31 with a young family to raise alone, her husband having signed over all of his estate to Brigham Young prior to his death. She remarried thereafter to Robert Broadhead and moved to Heber Valley where she died in 1879. Among her children who grew to manhood in Heber Valley were her sons, William Coleman Boren, Albert Boone Boren, and Henry Kingsley Boren.

In 1896, some 38 years after Aaron Daniels' initial discovery of the old Spanish mines, Henry Kingsley Boren joined with William Bethers, son of Asa C. Bethers, in a joint effort to re-open the old mines on Center Creek. Rumors soon spread about their discoveries, and the *Wasatch Wave,* Heber City's only newspaper, sent an investigator to get the story. The findings were reported on 12 February 1897, as follows:

After finding Messrs, Bethers and Boren at their homes on Daniels Creek, the writer took up a long and tedious march under their guidance to the spot in question. Just one hour and twenty minutes were taken up in the ascent from Boren's ranch up the dividing ridge between

Daniels and Center Creeks, at an angle of what seemed forty-five degrees, to the newly discovered mine and about two miles distance and almost on top of the Wasatch range. Here we found a tunnel which had been driven about twenty-five feet into the solid rock following a vein of ore from the surface, which is reported to return very good assays in gold. This tunnel is the result of labor at odd times during the past year of the two men. Northwest of this prospect is another which has only recently been known to exist there, although it has every appearance of being there for many years past. How far this tunnel enters through the solid rock into the side of the lofty mountain remains yet to be found out, as the work of cleaning out the dirt and rock that now fills it up has only been completed far enough to enable the prospectors to determine its course and dimensions.

A short time ago there was still another mouth of a tunnel accidentally stumbled onto, lying southeast about 75 yards of the other two, and on a direct line. This also was filled up with loose dirt and rock but very easy digging. The work of cleaning this tunnel out is being given the most attention at present, about twenty feet of which had been accomplished when the reporter was a visitor there, leaving a hole through solid rock from three to four feet wide and from five to six feet high, so far as exposed. As stated above, the work of cleaning out the tunnel is done mostly with shovels, laying bare the top and sides of solid stone, which plainly demonstrates that the implements of man have been used in the first excavation.

The foregoing are some of the reasons advanced for thinking that these tunnels might at one time have been the source from which the Mexicans in former days replenished their larders. Another circumstance which is also used in this connection, is a large granite rock which stands perpendic-

ular in the ground about half a mile distant down the ridge from the prospect. It is covered with peculiar looking hieroglyphics cut into it with apparently an instrument after the style of an ordinary punch. The rock is a wedge shape being about a foot thick on one side and tapers down to about two inches thickness on the other; it stands about five feet high and is about four feet wide. The characters upon it can only be translated by those accustomed to such signs. One of the figures is of a man with hands thrown up as though suddenly surprised; another is what we would call that of a burro or pack mule; another of half moon, and there are a number of others, while perfectly visible, we were not able to decipher their meaning.

Messrs. Bethers and Boren, the owners of the find, argue that these hieroglyphics have been put on this rock as a guide for the persons who formerly worked the mines to go by in returning to them after several months (or years) absence, as would of necessity been the case if the Mexican theory is true. A careful watch is constantly kept by the men engaged in cleaning out the tunnel for bones of the murdered Mexicans who were thrown therein, but none have been discovered as yet. Whether or not the gentlemen have found any lost mine is a matter that will unravel, but they have found prospect holes of some description, made by human hands, is a positive certainty, and we hope that development will open up to them a bonanza, whether Spaniards first discovered it or not.

Until recent years, little was known about the outcome of the Boren and Bethers excavations. I went to the site myself in 1972, having first located the site of Henry Boren's old ranch on Daniels Creek, not far from Aaron Daniels' original homestead. About a mile-and-a-half south of the old Boren ranch, an old trail leads up Center Creek Canyon, marked by trees with Spanish symbols carved into the trunks. A trek of nearly two hours up to the crest of the ridge brought me to the old stone with "hieroglyphics" on it; someone had toppled it onto its face, hiding the symbols. With considerable effort I managed to turn it over, clean its surface, and take several photos. It was later removed by someone and is said to be in the possession of a valley resident.

Several old tunnels exists at the crest of the dividing ridge between Daniels and Center Creek, but the main tunnel which was the focus of Borens' and Bethers' efforts is located about half a mile directly above the hieroglyphic rock. When I visited the site in 1972, the tunnel had been cleaned out to a depth of nearly 150 feet, but at that point was clogged with rock and debris. The tunnel is barely wide and high enough to stand in, at places being so narrow that it becomes necessary to turn sideways, and is not high enough for a tall man—such as myself—to stand without stooping slightly. This is, of course, typical of old Spanish mines, for the Spaniards were a head shorter than his American counterpart.

Henry Kingsley Boren was called on a mission to southern Utah in 1898, and the excavation was abandoned. In more recent years a letter emerged, written by Henry Boren to his brother (my grandfather), William Coleman Boren, part of which sheds some light on the story of the mines.

Cannonville, Garfield County

William Boren

Cleveland, Emery County, Utah

June 12, 1899

Dear Brother,

I have finally settled in with time enough to write since arriving from Silver Reef three days ago. The old place here is much as you left it, and everyone at Cannonville remembers you fondly...

I left Heber is such haste last fall that I neglected to tell you about all the doings with my prospects... Bethers had about given up on the mining business to go into merchandising, and I found myself the sole proprietor of the hole which had taken so much of my time and work since we discovered it about five years ago (1894). Bill and me had cleaned out more than 100 feet of tunnel when he gave out on me and left for Wanship. I worked another year by myself, and cleaned out another 50 feet or 75 feet when I was called by the Bishop to take my

mission, but before I left, I struck something which made me convinced that I was on the right track. Just where I left off cleaning out the rocks, at about 130 feet or so, I uncovered a niche in the sidewall of the tunnel, which I first thought must be a secondary tunnel, but when I uncovered the opening of it, it was instead a kind of room or little chamber. On the floor and against the back wall was pieces of old Spanish armor, all perfectly preserved, and two old Spanish swords, and beneath the rubble I found three human skulls and some bones... I only took out one sword, which I left at Mina's place, and will get when I go back next summer and show you. It is in mint condition, with a beautifully carved hilt in the shape of an eagle and the initials S.V.R. scratched on the guard. I covered everything back up just as I found it, hoping nobody finds it until I can get back up there...

It seems certain now that the Spaniards once mined the tunnel, and they must of been killed by the Indians who filled up the tunnel after burying them up inside. They (i.e. the Indians) wouldn't of gone to so much work unless the mine was valuable and they didn't want anybody to find it. Bill and me had samples assayed from the side veins and it showed both gold and silver in high content, and farther in must be the main vein or lode. But how much deeper the tunnel goes I don't know, because it showed no signs of ending where I last stopped...

I have copied the hieroglyphics from the stone and showed them to a Mexican geologist working at Silver Reef. He says they are old Spanish treasure signs, just as I always said they was, but he can't read them. Do you remember the old Summit Park and Center Creek trees with the signs on them which we found when we was boys? Well, these signs are just like those. I can't help but think there must be dozens of old Spanish mines in that area. Maybe you remember, too, the stories that our step-dad (Robert Broadhead) used to tell about the Mexican miners who came down out of the mountains through Heber to Provo by way of the canyon (Provo Canyon) before Heber was settled by the Mormons. I think it was from these mines that they took all their gold in those days...

When you stand on the ridge where the mine is and look off towards Park City, you can see where the same vein might of once run across the valley (Heber Valley) and cropped up where the Silver King and Ontario (mines) struck it rich. If I can finish cleaning out the tunnel, maybe one day I'll be as rich as old Tom Kearns…

Your loving brother,

Henry Boren

Henry Kingsley Boren never returned to clean out his tunnel. He either died or left the state sometime before 1900, for nothing further is known about him. In my own exploration of the tunnel I could not find the "niche" or side-room, but there were numerous places where such a room might have been covered with rubble (Henry Boren's letter states that he covered it up again "just as I found it"). Moreover, Henry does not make it exactly clear which of the several tunnels he is talking about, for there are at least five on the ridge itself. We may only assume that it was the tunnel on which he spent so much time and effort. Since Henry Boren's time, no one has made a concerted effort to clear any of the old tunnels. Some of them have partially collapsed; all of them are now dangerous to enter.

There is other evidence of early Spanish activity in that general area. In about 1924 or 1925 an old man rode his horse from the Uintah Basin through the Strawberry Valley to Heber. He had just crossed the Strawberry River near Daniels Pass when he came upon a very old road or trail, which appeared not to have been used in many years. Trees had long since grown up through its tracks in places, but its route was still discernible. Out of curiosity, he began to follow the trail, inasmuch as it proceeded northward in the same direction as his travel.

About nine or ten miles north of Daniels Pass the old road stopped at an old rock fortress, situated on the top of a small shelf of rock which was no more than 15 feet high. Inside the stone fort the old man found three brass canons, "one four-man and two smaller two-man cannons engraved with Spanish inscriptions on the barrels."

The old man discovered three cone-shaped depressions in the side of a hill to the east of the stone fort, which he recognized as old collapsed mine shafts. After poking about the area for awhile, the old man continued on his way to Heber.

In 1927, the old man told his story to John Patterson. Patterson was a half-blood Ute; in fact, his father, John H. Patterson, was a full tribal member and was signer of #82 on the Rhoades-Hathenbruck mining lease on 18 December 1897 (see *Footprints*, p.263). The two men decided to return to the site of the old stone fort and explore more thoroughly.

According to Patterson, everything at the site was just as the old man had described, except that the three brass cannons were no longer within the confines of the old stone fort. Upon closer examination it was discovered that someone had pushed out the south wall of the fort and attempted to remove the cannons. They were able to push them into some heavy brush nearby where they had been abandoned.

According to Patterson, "the small ledge, on which the fort had been built, had some sort of brown-colored stringers or veins running all through it…from the old fort, you could see all of the Strawberry Valley to the east, and to the west (towards Heber) there's a jagged ridge of rock that looks like a dinosaur's back protruding from the mountain."

Patterson and his friend (whom Patterson never identified) found no mines in the near vicinity, other than the caved-in shafts, and so they never returned. However, for the curious, Patterson gives the following directions to the site of the old Spanish Fort:

> Drive east about one and one-half or maybe two miles from the top of Daniels Pass on Highway 40 to where a finger-like ridge comes out toward the road there, on the east side of the ridge and on the north side of the road, you'll see a jeep road. Follow this jeep road three-quarters of a mile or maybe a mile up the small canyon to its end. The old wagon road takes off from here, but walk up in and look closer because it isn't always easy to see it. The old fort and cannons are about nine miles to the north up this old trail.

It should perhaps be mentioned that Robert Broadhead, stepfather of Henry Boren, was himself a renowned prospector and long-time friend of Caleb Rhoades. Broadhead Meadow in Murdock Basin, south of Mirror Lake, is named for him.

Chapter Sixteen

The Mystery of the Nephite Temples

ONE OF THE MOST PERSISTENT AND intriguing legends pertaining to the sacred gold of the Ute Indians concerns the existence of ancient Indian temples in the Uintah Mountain region. In most instances the discoverers of these sites describe similar structures and treasure characteristic of the Aztec or Mayan civilizations. Because of the predominantly Mormon culture in this region, the ancient temple sites are most often reported to be of Nephite origin.

Nephi was, according to the Book of Mormon, a character who lived at Jerusalem circa 600 B.C. When Jerusalem was destroyed, Nephi sailed with his family to the New World. Eventually the descendants of Nephi (called Nephites) and his elder brother Laman (called Lamanites) became numerous and spread throughout the Americas. The Book of Mormon tells us that:

> ...the people of Nephi had waxed strong in the land...And they were scattered upon much of the face of the land, and the Lamanites also. And they (the Lamanites, i.e. the Indians) were exceedingly more numerous than were they of the Nephites; and they loved murder and would drink the blood of beasts. [Jarom 1:5-6]

Of the Nephites we are told:

> And we multiplied exceedingly, and spread upon the face of the land, and became exceedingly rich in gold, and in silver, and in precious things, and in fine workmanship of wood, in buildings, and in machinery, and also in iron and copper, and brass and steel... [Jarom 1:8]

Nephi himself allegedly wrote:

> And I did teach my people to build buildings, and to work in all manner of wood, and of iron, and of copper, and of brass, and of steel, and of gold, and of silver, and of precious ores, which were in great abundance. And I, Nephi, did build a temple; and I did construct it after the manner of the temple of Solomon...and the workmanship thereof was exceedingly fine. [2 Nephi 5:15-16]

Throughout the Book of Mormon there are frequent references to the Nephite and Lamanite temples and their abundance of gold and silver, of records written upon plates of gold, silver, brass, and copper. There is even a complete account of the measure of Nephite coins [Alma 11:1-20]

The nature of the alleged curse on the sacred Indian gold also comes from the Book of Mormon:

> And behold, if a man hide up a treasure in the earth, and the Lord shall say—Let it be accursed, because of the iniquity of him who hath hid it up—behold, it shall be accursed. And if the Lord shall say—Be thou accursed, that no man shall find thee from this time henceforth and forever—behold, no man getteth it henceforth and forever. [Helaman 12:18-19]

Whether or not you believe the writings of the Book of Mormon, most of the discoverers of the temple sites that have been found have been Mormons, and *they* believe it, and have perpetuated the legends by associating the locations with the Nephites. Even if the temple sites are Aztec or Mayan in origin, these people claim, the Aztecs and Mayans were Lamanites, and the Book of Mormon clearly indicates that the Lamanites, too, had temples.

The Mormon Church, however, while officially refusing comment on the subject, unofficially frowns on associating religious doctrine with lost treasure sites. Due to this fact, most of the discoverers of ancient temple sites are reticent to have their names published or even to come forth with information about what they have seen or found. Those few who have dared to reveal their finds have been ridiculed and even threatened with dire consequences should they continue to publicize their claims. Keeping that in mind, let us examine a few accounts.

First of all, it should be pointed out that the accounts of such men as Jesse Knight, Ben H. Bullock, John H. Koyle and other contain descriptions of what might well be considered temple sites: caverns or rooms of gold with ancient artifacts in abundance.

The most notable mention of a temple site is that of Temple Hill at Manti, Utah, which both Brigham Young and Isaac Morley declared was the site of an ancient Nephite temple mentioned in the Book of Mormon [Alma 1:15]. It was alleged and still believed by many that the hill beneath the present Manti Temple is honeycombed with ancient secret passages and sacred caverns.

But most accounts come from less religious sources who merely stumble upon sites by chance while prospecting or casually tramping the hills. One such story was given to Gale Rhoades by a man who, for obvious reasons, asked to remain anonymous.

In 1960, this man and his black friend were out in the hills hunting for Indian arrowheads when they came upon the entrance of a small cave which had very strange symbols chiseled into the rock above its portal. His first inclination was that the symbols were Egyptian hieroglyphics, but he soon discounted this as a possibility.

With some trepidation they entered the cave and made their way into an interior room where they were aghast at what they beheld. Before their eyes were statues of various sizes, in the forms of strange animals, all of solid silver and gold. The walls of the room were adorned with large gold and copper plaques with strange symbols carved on them, which reminded him of sunbursts. There were chests of unusual artifacts, made primarily of precious metals and adorned with gems, and there were numerous stacks of 10 x 12 inch stone boxes sealed with pine gum and wrapped with cedar bark. The cave also contained two mummified

bodies of a man and a woman. The man appeared to have been near 7 feet tall, and the hair of each was still visible, the man having red hair and the woman's hair was blonde. The bodies reposed in stone caskets each weighing about one ton.

The men were astonished by their discovery and more than just a little frightened. Before hastily retreating, the man picked up eight small copper plates and wrapped them in a coarse cloth found nearby. They swore each other to secrecy until they could decide what to do about it.

The discoverer was a member of the Mormon Church who didn't want the Church involved, so he took the copper plates and details of his discovery to anthropologists and archaeologists at the University of Utah at Salt Lake City.

According to this man, the professors literally laughed at him and implied that he had likely fashioned the plates himself. Nevertheless, one of the professors, whom he identified as Jesse Jennings (renowned as the "Father of Utah Archaeology"), kept four of the small plates, promising to return them to him following certain tests. The plates were never seen again.

This event occurred late in 1960. Gale Rhoades discovered information which indicated that two of the plates had been spray painted with gold by the professor and sent to an eastern museum. The museum returned the plates along with a letter declaring them as fakes. Gale located Dr. Jennings, who had retired to another state, and contacted him by telephone, asking him about the plates. Jennings denied that any plates had ever been brought to the university. Moreover, he stated blatantly that anyone who thinks the American Indians had any metal records is in great error and that anyone professing to have found metal plates in Utah should be considered a fraud.

After hearing Gale Rhoades' account, I did some research of my own. I had contacts at the University of Utah Special Collections Department who permitted me to go through acquisition accounts for the year 1960. There, plainly written, under date of 12 October 1960, was the acquisition receipt of "four small plates of pounded copper bearing inscriptions of unknown origin." It was signed by none other than Dr. Jesse Jennings! More importantly, another reference indicated that two of these plates had been subsequently (1962) donated to the Church of Jesus Christ of Latter-day Saints!

I placed my own telephone call to Dr. Jennings to confront him with my discoveries. It was obvious that he had not told the whole truth when he informed my cousin that no such plates had ever been submitted to the University. When I confronted Dr. Jennings with the existence of the signed receipt and asked him to explain, I was met with silence. I then asked if he could at least tell me why two of the plates were subsequently donated to the Mormon Church. His only reply was that "The Mormon Church exerts a tremendous amount of influence in Utah."

The story does not end here for the man who discovered the "temple" cave. He brought the plates to the elderly parents of an acquaintance of Gale Rhoades—people he trusted—and they were laid out on a table and photographed. He described the plates left behind in the cave in the stone boxes as being round in shape, six or seven inches across with a 3/4 inch round hole in the center, and of the thickness of a manila folder. The plates were inscribed on one side with strange hieroglyphics.

A week later, the man took the plates to Provo and showed them to a BYU professor, who is currently retired from the Archaeology Department. When he returned home shortly thereafter, his problems began to escalate rapidly. His black friend, who had been part of the initial discovery, was killed in an unexplained accident, and shortly thereafter his own life began to be threatened if he continued to publicize his find. When he ignored the threats, his eldest son was killed under mysterious circumstances. The man blames his incredible misfortunes on his discovery of the "Nephite" temple.

Whether or not this is true, it seems apparent that someone in high places is covering up something, and whatever the plates represent, it is sufficient to cause university officials to misrepresent institutional involvement.

While it is necessary that we should protect the identity of the man involved, we can safely reveal that the location of his discovery was in the vicinity of the head of Minnie Maud Canyon, a branch of Nine Mile Canyon northwest of Price, Utah, at a place called Sand Wash. The canyon ledges are here covered with Indian petroglyphs, and the surrounding area is renowned for Indian arrowheads, artifacts, and even mummified remains. [For more information and illustrations of metal plates connected with this topic, the authors recommend *Treasures of the Ancients,* by Stephen B. Shaffer, Cedar Fort, Inc., Springville, Utah (1996).]

The above account does not represent the first discovery in this area. An old timer who lived in the Uintah Basin for many years revealed the following story to Jim Nebeker of Roosevelt, Utah.

The old man reported that when he was a young boy he was taken out to the Sand Wash area by an old neighbor who had prospected that area prior to the turn of the century. The old prospector showed him where gold nuggets could be dug from the clay banks of a small ravine. More importantly, however, the old prospector showed him some...

> ...old and ancient ruins which he referred to as an Indian Temple. It was just above the ravine where the gold was located. There were rooms and stairways cut through solid rock and upon the walls inside were large disk-like metal plates which all had strange pictures or symbols carved or stamped into them. But what scared me most of all was this one large room where there was this skeleton of a man, sitting and kind'a leaning back against the wall, still wearing a hat and boots.

There are obvious similarities between the two accounts. One day the old man agreed to take Nebeker to Sand Wash and show him the Indian temple. They were stopped just short of the site by a large chain-link fence with signs attached which read:

KEEP OUT. NO TRESPASSING. PROPERTY UNIVERSITY OF UTAH.

Another temple site is to be found just west of the Uintah River and north of present-day Cedar View Reservoir. Here there is a plateau known as Jefferson Park, on the western edge of which are a series of red ledges which can be seen for many miles from the south and the west.

Somewhere in these red ledges is a concealed cave filled with artifacts of gold and silver, in a room or rooms described in much the same fashion as other temple sites, with statues, gold-leafed walls inscribed with strange writing, and stacks of gold plates and bullion.

It was discovered by a man from Salt Lake City (whose family, as in most instances with these cases, has asked that he remain anonymous) who brought some of the gold back to that city, but found himself faced with a dilemma. At that time gold was illegal to possess, except in jewelry or coin, and the only sale that could be made of it was on the black market. He called an associate of his and asked for advice, knowing the man to have "connections." His associate assured him that there were ways to dispose of the treasure, but that he would have to see it for himself in order to convince the people he had in mind. The Salt Lake City man agreed, but only on the condition that his associate be blindfolded both coming and going, and when these terms were accepted, they set out for the site.

As soon as they arrived on the reservation, the man was blindfolded, and they walked to the site. Inside the cave, the blindfold was removed, and the man saw the tremendous treasure of gold and silver and was awestruck. After reveling in the sight and handling some of the artifacts, the man moved towards the cave entrance in hopes of viewing some landmark, but was stopped short by the discoverer of the treasure who pulled a pistol from his pocket and demanded that he replace the blindfold. Protesting his treatment, the man did as he was told and they returned to the car and drove back to Salt Lake City.

Everything began to fall apart at this point. Disgruntled over his treatment by the Salt Lake man, the associate turned the matter over to his friends, who happened to be the principals of a local crime syndicate. These toughs strong-armed the Salt Lake man in an effort to get him to reveal the location, but to no effect. "If you kill me," he told them, "then you will never find it." The syndicate then turned their threats upon his family, and launched a campaign of terror, with threatening phone calls in the middle of the night and a series of arranged accidents. The pressure

became so intense the Salt Lake man fell into a deep depression and eventually took his own life. His secret died with him.

While a great deal of the above account is based on unverifiable information, one thing is certain—the family of this man still retains in their possession two small statuettes of solid silver in the shape of cats, and three gold ingots each weighing about half-a-pound. I have personally handled these items and can verify their existence.

There are numerous old mines and prospects in the vicinity of the red ledges. Southeast of the ledges, in Jefferson Draw, is an old cabin built with the back wall against the ledges, covering an open tunnel, but this mine is on Indian land and is not open to investigation.

Not far away, on the Uintah Reservation (most maps show the spelling as "Uinta," but in the Ute dialect, the "h" is more correct), is the old Zokerite Mine (gold and silver) which was claimed on 7 October 1905 by Pickett (Pick) Murdock, J.B. (Jimmie) Reed, Joseph Helm and Cecil Calvert. The Zokerite Mine yielded its owners a substantial profit, the ores consisting of an iron pyrite bearing gold and silver, in rock containing an unusual oily base. The old mine tunnels can still be seen about one-half mile south of the remains of an old sawmill which once stood in the sagebrush flat just west of the Uintah River bridge and just south of the reservation boundary.

In February of 1982, Dale Rex Bascom, of Santaquin, Utah, revealed the following information to Gale Rhoades:

> Brent Rich, of Vernal, found what appeared to be an "Alter" (altar) up in Dry Fork Canyon just above the settlement of Dry Fork. It's located up on a bench south of the road where there are three campgrounds and before you get to the first big canyon on the right. The rock and marks cut into it may have been some sort of direction indicator, but it really looked like some kind of sacrificial alter (sic). It was made of white stone and was about chest high when kneeling at it—about 2 feet wide, with a notch cut into it as if where the head might be laid during human sacrifice before the head was cut off. A trough had been cut into it from the area of the notch to the bottom of the rock, as if

it were a place for the blood to flow after the sacrifice was over... If it was a direction indicator, the trough in the alter pointed northeast across the canyon and up three small canyons.

The Ute people have their own traditions about an Indian temple somewhere on Rock Creek. This story has been told to me by very many Indians over a period of many years, without much variation, indicating a common source. I was first told about the place by old Cump Murray who said he thought it was somewhere near Farm Creek Pass. He said that the old temple was near one of the Rhoades mines, and that the place was guarded by "two bears."

At first I thought that Cump Murray was speaking literally, or that he meant to say the bears were spirits that guarded the temple, because to the Utes the bear is a sacred animal, able to change its form from bear to spirit at will. But he soon assured me that the bears were life-size stone carvings near the old temple entrance.

Another old Ute, Waubin Q. Wanzitz (born 1 May 1902, now deceased), confirmed this account independently, adding that "just below" the two carved bears was a "white horse," also carved in stone. In fact, according to Waubin, there are carved bears "on both sides of the mountain." In that peculiar way Indians have, he would never elaborate. "You will see, when you find them," he would say.

Waubin left the reservation because of a tribal dispute over a piece of land he wanted to own, and for many years lived in California. He was an old man by the time I first met him. "If I was younger, I would take you there," he told me. "I know right where it is. Mountain Sheep showed it to me when I was just a boy. Too damned old now."

I know that Waubin could have told me much more, but I became wary of associating with him too much because of his connections with a very disreputable character who, for a brief time, was my business partner. I regretted that decision somewhat after Wash told me, laughing as he did so, "Waubin never tell that man all the truth. Little bit, sometimes. Keep him happy, that's all." So, the bears were real, but Waubin never gave accurate directions to locate them.

Another Indian made a concerted search for the bears from Farm Creek Pass, and reportedly found one of them. He described it as being life-size, of intricately carved detail, standing erect with its front paws forward, looking over the edge of a mountain ridge. So life-like was it that he was initially startled by it, thinking it was real.

Several other Indian friends have told me that the statue of the white horse was also life-size and in perfect likeness. This statue stood for many years on a sagebrush flat facing towards the mountain, supposedly a direction indicator to the mine or temple.

Old Wash took me to this area at the base of Rhoades Canyon on lower Rock Creek about 1972. He showed me where the horse statue had once stood, in a rather protected part of the flat, hard to find without direction. Wash said that the statue had stood at that place until 1969 when one of its legs had been shot off by deer hunters, and it had fallen over in the sagebrush. Later, he said, the Indians had dug a shallow pit and covered it over with rocks.

A mixed-blood friend of Gale Rhoades once told me of another similar but smaller statue, called the "little pony," farther up the canyon on the opposite side of Rock Creek. He said it was "somewhere near the ancient underground Indian Temple in the vicinity of the Lower Stillwaters of Rock Creek."

The question remains unanswered as to who built the temple, and who carved the statues. Indians, for the most part, seldom indulged in such endeavors, and while the most obvious choice would be the Aztecs, they were unfamiliar with horses until after the arrival of the Spaniards—so far as is known. The Book of Mormon, however, clearly indicates that the ancient inhabitants of this continent, i.e. the Nephites, "as we journeyed in the wilderness, that there were beasts in the forests of every kind, both the cow and the ox, and the ass and the *horse*,... [1 Nephi 18:25]

I asked Wash if there was not an Indian tradition for the origin of the temple and the horse statue. The following is his account of an old Ute legend concerning the site:

> Many years ago, when the Utes were a free
> people, and roamed the mountains which

they loved, they had much gold and fine things made by their ancestors—the Ancient Ones. The Utes had never seen a white man. Then, in the year of the great trembling of the earth (earthquake), there came a white man on a white horse. He was a great teacher. He told the Utes that many white people would be coming, more numerous than the trees on the mountains, and he said they should hide up the temples of the Ancient Ones, for these men would be greedy, and would not honor the sacred things. In the year of the trembling earth, Towats spoke to the medicine men and told them to cover up the temples of the Ancient Ones. All the sacred places were covered. In that year the white horses made of stone were carved by the great white medicine man on the white horse, so that the Utes would never forget.

I asked Wash if he knew how long ago the great trembling of the earth had taken place. "Oh, maybe ten Wash," he replied, meaning ten of his lifetimes. Wash was then over ninety—no one knew how much over (his father lived to be 108)—so it must have been between 800 and 1,000 years ago, or not long after the Aztecs (Ancient Ones) abandoned the region on their epic southern migration.

As we have noted elsewhere, the Welsh prince Madoc ap Owain Gwynedd landed in the New World in 1170 A.D., establishing a colony at Mobile Bay, Alabama. Returning to Wales the following year, he brought a second sailing expedition to the New World in 1171 A.D., but his ships were blown off course by a tempest in the Gulf of Mexico, and he landed somewhere in the Yucatan, where he established his second colony.

The existence of Madoc and the history of his several voyages has been quite firmly established [see *The Widow's Son: The Esoteric History of the Prophet Joseph Smith and the Origin of Mormonism,* Kerry Ross O'Boran with Lisa Lee O'Boran, chaps. 50-57, privately printed, Salt Lake City (1997)]. Dr. David Powel, in his landmark book, *The Historie of Cambria, Now Called Wales* (1584), allows that Mexico was the probable landing place of Madoc because of:

A common report of the inhabitants of that countrie, which affirme that theyr rulers descended from a strange nation that came thither from a farre countrie: which thing is confessed by Montezuma, king of that countrie, in an oration made for quieting his people, as his submission to the king of Castille, Hernando Curteis (Cortes) being present, which is laid downe in the Spanish chronicles of the conquest of the West Indies.

The reports of Cortes in fact do clearly show that he supported the accounts of Mexico having been settled by a strange race from across the ocean, and he further mentioned in his reports the speech by Montezuma. A copy of the speech by Montezuma was discovered in an ancient Spanish manuscript found in Mexico in 1748, and was, in pertinent part, as follows:

Kinsmen, friends and fellow-countrymen, you must know that I have reigned as a King over you for eighteen years, as a lawful descendant of my ancestors, who reigned before me. We came from a generation very far, in a little island in the north; the language and religion continue here to this day. I have been an affectionate Father and Prince, and you have been my faithful subjects and willing servants. Let it be remembered that you have a claim to illustrious blood and that you are worthy of your kindred, because you are a free, manly race.

[Spanish Chronicles of Cortes, as quoted in *Madoc* and the *Discovery of America,* Richard Deacon, George Braziller pub., New York (1966)]

The history of Madoc is patent: he became King of the Aztecs, and every king after him, down to and including Montezuma, were his descendants. Madoc became a great teacher and benefactor of the Indian people, teaching them the arts of building, writing, planting and many other things in the European fashion. The Aztecs came to revere him as a god and, according to author John P. Brown, they may have equated him with their greatest god, Quetzalcoatl:

The god was white and he had a beard. He was certainly no Indian. How would the Indians have known of such a person unless he existed? The legend contributed largely to the comparative ease with which Cortez conquered Mexico... The god really existed and he may have been Madoc, who arrived in Mexico on the second of his voyages, earned the affection of the Indians, taught them, and eventually left them, but promising to return...The Indians thought that the Fair God, Quetzalcoatl, had returned to them when Cortez came. [*Old Frontiers*, John P. Brown, as cited in *Madoc*, Richard Deacon, op.cit.]

Madoc and his fellow Welshmen, by their intermarriage with the native race, both north and south, became the progenitors of the "white Indians" or "Welsh Indians," so frequently mentioned in early chronicles. These Indians were distinguished by red hair, blue eyes, and beards. True Indians, or course, have no facial hair.

Was the mysterious white man on a white horse, who carved the statues in the high Uintahs of Utah, really Madoc or one of his fellow Welshman? It seems likely. The date "ten Wash" corresponds with the year 1170, the year of the arrival of Madoc, and also corresponds with the date of the Aztec migration south to Mexico. There is other strong evidence. For example, F.W. Hodge wrote that:

> ...the myth of a tribe of Welsh Indians...placed them first on the Atlantic coast, where they were identified with the Tuscarora, and then farther and farther west until about 1776 we find "Welsh" or "white" Indians on the Missouri, where they appeared as the Mandan, and later on Red River. Later still they were identified with the Hopi of Arizona, and finally with the
>
> Modoc of Oregon, after which they vanish. [*Handbook of American Indians North of Mexico*, F.W. Hodge, Bureau of American Ethnology, Smithsonian Institution (1910), vol.2, p.282]

Can this Welsh strain be connected to the Utes? In fact it can. The Utes are among the few tribes which have bearded men among their number, and writer Richard Deacon adds an even more significant connection:

There are extravagant accounts that Madoc and his companions reached Mexico and established the Aztec Empire, and then traveled on their all-conquering way to found the Mayan civilization and the Empire of the Incas in Peru. It has been suggested that because there are red-haired people in the Galapagos group that they eventually sailed on there. For good measure there is the legend that one of them named Mormon lived to write their story which was duly handed down to Joseph Smith, who founded the Mormon religion. This may have originated in the fact that many Welshmen were among the Mormon pioneers. Brigham Young told Captain (Daniel) Jones, one of his lieutenants, of a Welsh settlement on the Rio Colorado and that he believed that the Moquis were descendants of Madoc. [*Madoc*, Deacon, op.cit., pp.151-152]

Moreover, Madoc is said to have recorded his own history and the history of the Indian people on brass and gold plates, with strange hieroglyphic writing that was a combination of the Welsh language and symbols familiar to the Aztecs (for more information see *The Widow's Son*, O'Boran, op.cit.). Even if Madoc himself did not visit the Uintah Mountain region, this would still explain the stacks of brass and gold plates said to be a part of Montezuma's treasure.

But there are evidences that quite early, as much as a hundred years before the advent of the Mormons to Utah, certain explorers were aware of the connection between the "Welsh Indians" and Spanish mines in the Uintah Mountain region. Space permits only one example, but it is a prime one.

Lord Edward Fitzgerald (1763-1798), Irish rebel, was one of the most remarkable men of his age. He was one of seventeen children of James Fitzgerald, Viscount and first Duke of Leinster, in Ireland, by Emilia Mary, daughter of Charles, Duke of Richmond. His father died in 1773 and his mother married William Ogilvie. The Duke of Richmond lent his house at Aubigny in France to the family, who resided there until 1779, and Ogilvie undertook Edward's education.

Primarily interested in the military, upon returning to England he joined the Sussex militia, of which his uncle, the Duke of Richmond, was colonel. He then entered the 96th infantry as lieutenant, served in Ireland, changed to the 19th infantry in order to get foreign service, and in 1781 was sent to Charleston, South Carolina, where he participated in the American Revolution. At the battle of Eutaw Springs, August 1781, he was wounded in the thigh and left unconscious on the field. He might have died had not a Negro boy, Tony, discovered him there, carried him to his hut, and nursed him to health. Tony was thenceforth, to the end of Lord Edward's life, his devoted friend and servant.

After a decade of political service in parliament and a course of professional study, a disappointment in love sent him to New Brunswick to join his regiment, the 54th of which he was by then major. Infected by the fashionable Rousseau admiration for savage life, Fitzgerald made his way by compass through the woods from Frederickton to Quebec, and at Detroit was formally admitted into the Bear tribe.

Afterwards, Lord Edward Fitzgerald went down the Mississippi River to New Orleans to seek permission from the Spanish governor, Miro, to visit the "Mexican mines"—i.e. the mines in what was then Mexico, but that became Utah Territory. In a letter from Governor Miro to the King of Spain, dated 3 October 1790, which speaks of the visit of Lord Edward Fitzgerald "but three months since this last year past," Miro wrote: "I have denied his request for escort to the Mexican mines, where the Lieutenant (i.e. Fitzgerald) wished to parley with the Indians who labor there, believing as he does they are related to the Foreign Indians he met on the upper Missouri." By "Foreign Indians," Miro meant the Mandan or "Welsh Indians," descendants of Madoc. Thus Fitzgerald obviously believed that the Indians who worked the Mexico mines (i.e. the Utes) were of this same race.

Obviously, Lord Edward Fitzgerald never made it to the Mexican mines, though his attempt gives us a record of their existence and importance. In 1792 Lord Edward was back in France where he married Pamela, sister of the "Citizen King," Louis Philippe. Lord Edward Fitzgerald was subsequently murdered by the English for his participation in the great Irish Rebellion in 1798.

Therefore, once again we find connections between Madoc, the Aztecs, and the mines of the Utes. If we interpret the facts correctly, the following story emerges. Madoc, the Welsh prince, arrived in America in 1170 A.D. and established at least two colonies among the Native Americans, in both North and Central America. He became nominal King of the Aztecs, and taught them the rudiments of a new and lasting civilization. He also invented a hieroglyphic language and with it recorded his own and the Native American history on metal plates, the most part of them being gold from the Aztec mines in the Uintah Mountains. These records are apparently the source of the Book of Mormon (see *The Widow's Son*) and thus the connection is made by many with the "Nephites."

Chapter Seventeen

The Lost Nephite Horde

ON THE NORTH SLOPE OF THE UINTAH Mountains, at Linwood, Utah (now under the waters of Flaming Gorge Reservoir), there lived an old prospector named Pete Miller. Miller had come into the region during the 1870s to prospect, and had spent considerable time and effort searching for the Lost Ewing Mine in the Brown's Park-Goslin Mountain area.

Near the turn of the century old Pete briefly became deputy sheriff at Linwood, where one of his closest friends was Bob Swift, owner of the "Bucket O'Blood" saloon. Swift, it may be recalled, was one of the men involved with Matt Warner in the Dry Fork ambush in 1896, while in the employ of Caleb Rhoades.

Pete's tenure as deputy was short-lived. Being a member of the law in the vicinity of one of the Wild Bunch strongholds was not a popular choice of occupations. On one occasion, when he tried to quiet two young ruffians, Clarence and Stanley Crouse, who were firing off their guns on horseback in the street, they roped him and commenced to drag him behind a horse. He might have been killed had not my maternal grandfather, Willard Schofield, a bartender at Swift's saloon, jumped in and cut the rope with his pocket-knife.

In time, old Pete became disenchanted with man's company and retired as a recluse to an isolated cabin on the upper headwaters of Carter Creek to spend the rest of his life prospecting the north slope of the Uintahs. For more than thirty-five years he wandered the hills, returning occasionally to his cabin to feed and care for a menagerie of animals he had domesticated for company—a deer, a beaver, a porcupine, a magpie, and a small brown bear, among others.

Twice a year my father, Edward Boren, brought supplies up on the mountain to old Pete Miller. Pete had an account at the Smith & Larsen Mercantile at Linwood, and his credit there was

good because he paid annually in gold—sometimes in dust, other times with nuggets. There was nothing unusual about it, George Rasmussen, clerk at the mercantile told me in later years; it was generally assumed that this gold was the result of Pete's yearly wages from panning the mountain streams.

One day in the late 1920s, my father took the usual load of supplies to the clapboard cabin on Carter Creek, but this time the usually reclusive old Pete came hobbling up the rocky road, seemingly anxious for company, which for him was very much out of character. My father could see that he was bursting at the seams with the urge to tell him something. After they had unloaded the supplies and sat down to supper, old Pete could contain it no longer.

"Ed," he began, "if I was to tell you something, will you promise never to tell anybody else as long as I'm alive?" My father, who had known old Pete most of his life, and whose word was inviolate, gave his word. Pete then recounted to him the following story.

He had been hunting new lakes for fishing, he said, on the upper headwaters of Carter Creek, about two miles due south of Hickerson Park, when he came upon a strange rock cairn in the midst of heavy timber. It seemed very much out of place in the middle of nowhere as it was, but even more unusual was the careful way it had been constructed. Someone had gone to great pains to fit the rocks together so uniformly that "you can't even insert a knife blade between them," Pete told my father. The rocks surrounded and held upright a stone pillar, taller than a man, on which were strange hieroglyphics the likes of which he had never seen before.

The rock cairn seemed to be aligned with a bold mountain a little to the south, so Pete began a summer's effort of wandering the area south of the cairn towards the baldy. At one point he found an old Indian village in the midst of heavy timber almost halfway between Red Lake and Potter Lake, and about a mile from the rock cairn. The village was very old and seemed to have been hastily abandoned, for though the tepees still stood in place, the hide covers were mostly rotted away. Around the camp were implements left as though they had been in use when suddenly the Indians evacuated. Pete did not presume the village had anything to do with the strange rock cairn, however, for Indians seldom engaged in such activities and had no propensity for writing.

South of the village, however, on a slide-rock shelf near the baldy, he found another rock cairn, somewhat smaller and less crafted than the former, but containing another small pillar at its center with only one or two of the hieroglyphics carved on it.

Pete was now convinced that the cairns were some kind of trail marker, and sure enough he soon found an ancient trail in the slide-rock which had been made by building up with small stones within the larger spaces—a sort of elevated trail. Following this trail he discovered that it wound its way to the crest of a mountain, near the 13,000 foot elevation, and then veered westward along the summit, with small rock cairns every half-mile or so. The trail led westward for more than ten miles until, "somewhere a little bit west of Spirit Lake" (where Chief Walker had his vision of Towats and the sacred mine), the trail suddenly descended back down the north slope and disappeared at the base of a towering cliff.

Fearing he had lost the trail completely, he began a systematic search around the base of the cliff until at last he found where more of the hieroglyphics had been carved into the solid cliff face. High on the cliff wall above the writing was a crevice, and protruding from the crevice was a piece of a tree trunk. Since the place was far above the tree-line, he knew it had to have been placed there by someone a long time ago, and who ever went to so much effort must have had a good reason.

Pete returned to his cabin on Carter Creek and retrieved ropes and other equipment, then made a second trip to the site. At the top of the cliff he drilled a core-hole with a hand-chisel and wedged

a railroad spike in it. Securing the rope to the spike, Pete lowered himself over the edge of the cliff (with some effort, one supposes, inasmuch as he was a large man) and down to the pole protruding from the crevice. As he stood as last on the tree-pole, he saw that the crevice was, in fact, the opening to a cave or tunnel, literally carved out of the face of the solid rock cliff.

Proceeding cautiously inside, he found that the tunnel was barely wide enough to walk in without turning sideways, and he had to stoop to avoid bumping his head. The tunnel made a near 90-degree turn at a point some 30 feet inside the cliff, and after another 20 feet or so, it turned back again towards the interior of the mountain. At this point, Pete was confronted by a solid wall of paved rocks, against the base of which rats had constructed a twisted nest. His heart was pounding with excitement; anyone who went to so much effort to hide something must have had something incredible to hide.

It took Pete nearly a week to clean out the entrance. He encountered three separate rock walls, one in front of the other, which, in the confined space, he could only remove one rock at a time. He carried them to the protruding tree one at a time and tossed them down to the slide-rock more than 100 feet below.

When the last wall was removed, the tunnel continued another 20 or so feet, then opened into a massive cavern. In fact, the tunnel ended abruptly and dropped away into an abyss. In the darkness, he nearly walked over the edge. He returned with a supply of pine knots (called "pitch" by old timers) and lighted them to make long-burning torches. In the flickering glow he could see that the cavern was about 30 feet deep and another 10 or so above his head. There were old pegs driven into holes like steps below him, but he didn't trust them to hold his heavy weight, so lowered himself down by rope.

What Pete Miller claimed to have seen on that occasion is like something out of *A Thousand-and-One Arabian Nights*. On the floor of the cavern were numerous skeletons, apparently tossed from the tunnel shelf 30 feet above; some of these still wore Spanish armor, and other pieces of armor were scattered among the bones. Around the walls of the massive room were stacks of bullion—gold and silver bars—and statuettes of unusual looking creatures which, said Pete, resembled dragons or alligators (or perhaps the Aztecan winged serpent: John P. Brown has written, "The winged serpent of Mexico also has never been explained. It may have derived from the Griffin of Wales."), and others were of cats and snakes and a few resembled human form. All were of gold or silver and magnificent to behold. On the walls were huge disks of gold with "spokes" of hieroglyphic writing. There were, said Pete, "wagon-loads" of treasure within the great room.

At several locations other tunnels continued into the mountain. He dare not enter these with the little light he had and so contented himself with looking around the great room. He found stone boxes, some sealed, some not; some of these contained flattened gold and silver plates, mostly round or oblong, with more of the strange writing on them. Some of the stone boxes were filled with precious stones. Putting a handful of the gems in his pocket and taking one of the gold bars with him to examine in the sunlight outside, he climbed the rope and emerged to discover that it was nearly dark. He had spent the better part of a day inside the chamber.

Old Pete wasted no detail in explaining all of this to my father, but he ended with a most unusual postscript to his story. "I've lost it, Ed," he said. "I've lost the whole damn thing." He explained that he had brought the gold bar and the few gems home with him, gathered up a bit more equipment with which to retrieve more, and hurried back to the location. Part way, he said, he had become disoriented, dizzy, and somewhat ill. He laid down under a pine tree and slept all one day and night, and when he continued the next day, he could no longer find the cavern. Nothing looked familiar to him any longer. He believed that some supernatural force had altered his mind, but my father was more of the opinion that old Pete had suffered a mild stroke, destroying much of his memory.

One thing was certain, though: Pete Miller had found something substantial, because he had a gold bar and a cigar box full of precious gems to prove it. He convinced my father to go with him and help him retrace the route. They started at the aban-doned Indian village, the only landmark Pete could remember, which they readily found (my father showed this village to me, still standing in the late fifties), but they could never find the rock cairn nearby, or the subsequent smaller ones. After one entire summer of searching, my father returned to his ranch, convinced that even though a treasure must certainly exist somewhere in the mountains, his own immediate fortune lay in the harvest.

Pete Miller never stopped searching for his elusive temple of treasure. It became an obsession with him, that drove him to tramp the mountains for the last twenty years of his life. While he obviously discovered something, most people were skeptical of his story about a treasure room in the mountains. Nevertheless, he was driven to search relentlessly.

In the end, his health began to fail him. In the fall of a certain year in the 1940s, my father took the usual load of supplies to the old cabin on Carter Creek as he had done, off and on, for many years. Pete failed to respond to shouted greetings, and the door of his cabin was ajar. My father found him inside on his old spring bed, dead for many weeks. He had taken coyote poison, unable to further bear the old age and infirmity which kept him from his search. His pet animals had nearly devoured his body. The place where he lived and died is still shown on Forest Service maps as "Pete's Miller's Cabin."

There is one other unusual discovery which, though not directly associated with the Uintah Mountains, is supported by considerable documentation and involves eye-witnesses of impeccable reputation.

J.H. Martineau was a respected resident of central Utah, a local businessman, a prominent civic leader, a devout and active member of the LDS Church, and an amateur historian with enough expertise to become an assistant to the LDS Church Historian. In his spare time, Martineau tramped the hills, documenting historic sites, petroglyphs, cabins, trails and the like.

During the thirties and forties, Martineau took on the ambitious project of mapping the old Spanish Trail, a branch of the Sante Fe Trail, which was the major route of the Spaniards who visited Utah from Sante Fe for nearly 300 years. Roughly speaking, the old trail entered Utah near present-day Moab, angled northwestward across the San Rafael Swell, up Grand Wash past the Henry Mountains, thence westward to the Wasatch Range via the Sanpete Valley. There were, however, numerous branches of this trail extending outward from the main stem into outlying regions.

Part of this route, specifically the stretch across the San Rafael country, followed the legendary "Trail of the Old Ones" or Ancient Ones, presumably the Aztecs, which led to and from the Uintah Basin to Mexico City. The Utes maintain that the Old Ones were their ancestors, and there is little doubt that the Old Ones were synonymous with the Aztecs.

Martineau spent many years following and charting this route, which he carefully recorded in a journal with very precise maps and detailed descriptions. Then one day he returned home extremely excited about something. He went directly to the home of his bishop and stated breathlessly: "Bishop, I need your advice on something. I have found something on the San Rafael which could very well affect the Church. What should I do?"

"Well, Brother Martineau," the bishop replied, "unless I knew what it is you have found, I don't know what advice to offer you."

Martineau dug into his pocket and produced a handful of large coins, of solid gold, with strange characters and inscriptions carved or stamped onto them. The bishop examined them at length.

"They are most peculiar and probably of immense value," said the bishop at last, "but how does this affect the Church?"

"You don't understand," retorted Martineau excitedly. "Those are Nephite coins! I've found the Lost Nephite Hoard!" The Lost Nephite Hoard was a famous local legend in southern Utah.

The bishop advised Martineau to take his discovery directly to the Church headquarters at Salt Lake City, and gave him a written "recommend" to see the First Presidency personally. The general authorities listened intently, then spoke of the serious repercussions such a discovery might have on the Church at large, and called upon Martineau to turn over the coins and all of his

records and maps to the Church Historian. They further urged him to speak of his discovery to no one.

Martineau returned home and gathered up his maps and journals, having already left the coins with the Church authorities. At the last minute, however, Martineau began to have second thoughts. He told his son, J.H. Martineau, Jr., that he was afraid that Church officials had plans to suppress the find, and he had hoped that his discovery might benefit his family and further the knowledge of history.

In the end, Martineau turned over only the coins, general area maps, and his journals, having first carefully removed the pages establishing the location of his find. He retained in his possession two of the coins, the accurate map, and the important journal pages.

Martineau died not long thereafter, having had no further opportunity to develop his discovery or even return to it. Using his father's map and journal descriptions, J.H. Martineau, Jr. took up the quest and hunted for the Lost Nephite Hoard for many years, with no success.

During the late 1960s I was assistant to LDS Church Historian A. William Lund, and then had access to a great many of the Church's early acquisitions. I was approached one day by J.H. Martineau, Jr., who offered to reveal his father's maps and papers to me in return for my help. He had reached an impasse in his own search, and was in hopes that the information his father had given to the Church many years earlier might offer new clues.

I subsequently located the Martineau donation in the Church vault. It consisted of eight "Nephite" coins of curious design, several area maps of the San Rafael Swell showing only general detail, and two handwritten ledger-type journals of day-to-day accounts of searches covering a period of many years.

I was able to provide Mr. Martineau only with descriptions of what I saw and read in the Church vault, of which only a small amount was helpful. In return, I was permitted to photograph the two coins in Mr. Martineau's possession, and to make a copy of the map—the journal pages were withheld from me.

According to the Martineau account, he first discovered a large carved thunderbird or "angel's wings" on a ledge somewhere in Grand Wash or one of its many side canyons. At a point some 75 feet above this carving, or about three-fourths of the way up the cliff, was a cave, approachable only by rope from above. It was necessary, he said, to go up the canyon more than a mile in order to gain access to the top of the cliff.

The cave itself was man-made, extending into the cliff side about 20 feet before entering into a room about 10 x 12 in measure, the roof being so low as to cause an average-height man to stoop slightly.

The coins were abundant, being contained in stone boxes, earthen jars, and leather pouches, some of the latter still having animal hair on the surface of the hides. There were "other things" in the cave which Martineau nowhere describes. He intimates at one point in his journals that whatever it was, it was too heavy to carry up the scaling ropes on his initial visit, and he took only a pocketful of the coins.

The coins are real and are fashioned of pure gold. If they are a hoax, they are an expensive one, for the ten coins known to exist, at today's value in gold alone, are worth more than $2,000 apiece; in historical value, they may be priceless. The LDS Church, as usual, will neither admit nor deny possession of the Martineau discovery.

Somewhere in the San Rafael Swell lies a treasure worth millions. There may be other relics in the cave relating to lost Indian temples. The greatest treasure, however, if it could be proved, would be the immense contribution the "Nephite" writing might provide to a better understanding of an ancient civilization.

On the surface, the story of Nephite coins sounds incredible. There is no evidence historically that Native Americans ever minted coins or used them as a means of exchange. On the other hand, the introduction of Madoc to the equation lends credence to the claim. Madoc, a European prince who became King of the Aztecs, might well have introduced his subjects to coinage. The Aztecs had a form of coinage, using sea shells and beads as currency for exchange; it would have been a minor step for them to accept and adopt the European form of exchange.

It seems equally plausible to assume that the Book of Mormon is based upon the history of Madoc, who is equated with Nephi by substantial evidence [see *The Widow's Son,* O'Boran, op.cit]; and the Book of Mormon explicitly states that the Nephites minted gold coins, and even records their weight and size. [Alma 11:1-9]

my Family connection!

The Reed Connection

JIMMIE REED WAS A CLOSE FRIEND, associate and sometime partner of Caleb Rhoades, and one of a handful of men who was early acquainted with the locations of Spanish and Indian mines in the Uintah Mountains. Reed left both maps and written clues to some of these mines, and therefore his personal history is important to any account of the mines.

Bill Reed, grandson of Jimmie Reed (Sr.), was my uncle by marriage to my father's sister. Bill Reed was also three-quarter Ute by blood, with a portion of Shoshone, and lived on the Uintah-Ouray Reservation. He was an interesting and colorful man, dark-skinned, quite heavy (especially in his older years), with long braids of black hair which turned salt-and-pepper color as the years advanced.

When I was a boy growing up on the north slope of the Uintah Mountains during the forties and fifties, my father took wheat and barley over the mountain to Vernal to have it ground into flour following the fall harvest. The entire family would go along for a holiday, and while the grain was being milled, we visited with seldom-seen relatives. Often we stayed with my uncle and aunt at their home on Big Tom's Allotment on the reservation near Whiterocks.

Bill and his wife were foster-parents to young Ute Indian children, and there were always half a dozen living at their place. I peeled off my shirt and played games with them, and my Uncle Bill would fashion a bow from birchwood, and a few willow arrows, and would take me over to the foothills northeast of Whiterocks to teach me how to hunt rabbits. I became a proficient archer under his tutelage.

This was my earliest personal acquaintance with the Ute Indians, a people I came to respect and admire to a high degree. But it was not my only knowledge of them. My grandfather,

William Coleman Boren, was a lifelong friend of the Utes, among whom he lived most of his life. He resided on the reservation until the land allotment of 1905 opened it up to white settlement, at which time he left the reservation in disgust, crossing over the mountain to settle on the north slope. My father, Edward Boren (1893-1975), was delivered into the world by an Indian midwife—a grand-niece of Chief Walker, whom the whites called "Queen Victoria"—and most of the older generation of my family had Indian names and spoke the Ute language fluently. In his wild youth, my father sired a child by a Ute girl, giving me a half-blood, half-brother or half-sister I have never met. In time, I had two Indian blood-brothers—a Ute named Colorow and a Nevada Shoshone named Bob Sargent; I am privileged to be godfather and namesake of the latter's son, Samuel Kerry "Little Bear" Sargent.

During the 1960s, being an accredited genealogist, I had the opportunity of researching Bill Reed's family genealogy, and when I began researching for the book *Footprints in the Wilderness*, my uncle became a primary source for the detailed history of his grandfather, Jimmie Reed, and for the Ute Indian connection to the mines. Not only was he a font of information, but through his influence I made the acquaintance of many Ute elders familiar with the mines, including my old friend Wash. For the purpose of this chapter, however, we will concern ourselves with the history of Jimmie Reed.

According to Indian sources (among them being Nauhnan, son of Chief Tabby) and the Reed family, in about the year 1828 four white men whom they identify as William "Toopeechee" Reed, his young nephew James Scott "Jimmie" Reed, Denis Julien, and Augustus (Auguste Pierre) Archambeau, established a trading post in the Uintah Basin.

Toopeechee Reed was part French and part Scotsman; he and his nephew were from Kentucky. Denis Julien was a veteran French-Canadian trader from St. Louis. Auguste Archambeau had run away from his St. Louis home at the age of twelve or thirteen and went west "to live with the Indians in the mountains." Jimmie Reed and Archambeau were both about the same age whey they came West. Reed himself stated: "I came out West with my uncle, William Reed, when he set up the trading post. I was about twelve years old, I guess, and we come all the way from Kentucky."

When Major John Wesley Powell made his famous voyages down the Green and Colorado River in 1869 and 1872, he discovered that a "D. Julien" had preceded him and left his inscriptions on the canyon walls some forty-three years earlier. Julien remained a man of mystery for many years; a search was even made at the Vatican in Rome in the belief that he might possibly have been an early Catholic missionary.

However, the records of the St. Louis Cathedral bear witness to the fact that the Indian account was correct:

> Julien, Marie Jos, born May 5, 1793, daughter of Denis Julien and Cath. (Indian), baptized April 15, 1798. Julien, Pierre Paschal, 18 mos. Old, same parents, baptized October 25, 1801. Julien, Etienne, 5 years old, same parents, baptized October 21, 1804. Julien, Paschal, 9 years old, son of Denis Julien and Cath. (Indian), buried Feb. 3, 1809.

In 1800 Denis Julien and his brother Etienne volunteered "for service in Louisiana," in an artillery company organized by Gov. William Clark and captained by Benjamin O'Fallon. In old papers on file in the St. Louis library is found an order for "358 barrels of lead" belonging to Denis Julien, which was being shipped by Antoine Busebois to William Clark, on Mr. Wilson's barge. Denis Julien may have come west with the Reed party as early as 1826.

On Inscription Rock, east of the Uintah River, and just east of the old Aaron and Rose Daniels place, about halfway between Fort Duchesne and Whiterocks (near the site of old Fort Robidoux), is the inscription "Denis Julien, 1831." Nothing more is heard of Denis Julien after he left his name carved in five different places along the Colorado River canyons, the last dated "16 Mai, 1836." It is generally believed that he lost his life attempting to navigate those waters, but in recent years his inscription has been found in Arches National Park with the date 1841 or 1844 (the last number being uncertain).

William Reed—whom the Utes called Toopeechee—was a Kentuckian who, like many of his contemporaries, migrated to Missouri just prior to 1800. His family had long been associated with wilderness exploration, having come through the Cumberland Gap into Kentucky with Daniel Boone as early as 1775. In fact, William Reed was a cousin of both Boone and Kit Carson, as well as the renowned trapper-trader John Robertson, better known as Uncle Jack Robinson. It was this kinship which brought the Reeds, Carson and Robinson to Missouri with Daniel Boone in 1799.

In 1826 William Reed organized an expedition to Santa Fe and Taos, New Mexico, which included, beside himself, his eleven-year-old nephew, Jimmie Reed, Uncle Jack Robinson, Denis Julien, Auguste Archambeau, Shadrach "Shade" Large, and a number of others. Young Kit Carson followed the expedition independently, to join them later in the West.

In 1828, after some time around Sante Fe and Taos and a trip to California, William Reed, Jimmie Reed, Julien and Archambeau, came to the Uintah Basin to establish a trading post among the Ute Indians. According to the Indians, the Reeds brought in the first butcher knives, coffee beans and other articles ever traded to the Utes for furs and buffalo robes. This is confirmed by Jimmie Reed, Jr., who recalled in CWA interview at Moffat County, Colorado, in 1933-34:

> My father was the first man to trade iron to the Utes; traded butcher knives, needles, guns. The Indians used to pile beaver pelts as tall as a gun to get it. That's why they made the old guns so long. It was to get more beaver.

From an interview with Henry Harris, Jr., grandson of Jimmie Reed and son of Henry Harris, Sr., former interpreter for the Uintah-Ouray Agency, we learn:

[asked which trappers had preceded Antoine Robidoux:]

Only one that I've heard my mother (Mary Reed Harris) say was Chambeau Reed [here confuses Archambeau and Reed]. He and his party came in. He had his first trading post at White Rocks—Chambeau Reed. He traded calico, beads, knives and stuff like that to the Indians, and buckskins and furs.

In 1925, Mary Reed Harris, daughter of Jimmie Reed, Sr., and several other Indians, accompanied Mrs. Peter Dillman to the site of Reed's old post, and later, in 1948, when Mrs. Harris was 88 years of age, she accompanied others to the site. According to Mrs. Harris, the old fireplaces stood in ruins for years alongside of the old road which ran through Whiterocks. Jimmie Reed had told his daughter how they brought their goods on pack mules from the states. Among the trade goods were blankets, black with a white border, which came in a belt. The trader would measure them length for length with tanned buckskin, and then cut them to the size of the buckskin. She also mentioned that they traded butcher knives, coffee beans, and other items. "They tried to cook that coffee," she said. "They thought it ought to boil like beans, until it was soft enough to eat. I've heard Father laugh about that."

The Indians called Julien "Julie" and Archambeau "Sambo" or "Chambeau." Nauhnan, the son of Chief Tabby, who lived in a cabin just a few miles from the old post, in an interview in 1948 (when he was 106!) said, "We knew about the earlier trading post. There was a white man the Indians called 'Sambo' and the other one called 'Julie.'"

On 17 April 1969, my uncle, Alma Leroy "Roy" Boren, gave me the following information:

In 1895 my father (William Coleman Boren) came up from Cannonville, Utah, where I was born (1889) and settled early on the reservation. He was well known to the Utes, having freighted flour from Heber City to the reservation under government contract not many years after the reservation was set aside. He lived on an allotment belonging to old Robert Marimon, the Post Trader, between the Marimon ranch and Big Tom's allotment. Old man (Jimmie) Reed lived on Big Tom's allotment, and he showed me several times where he built his trading post. He claimed he was just a boy when his uncle built the post and he ran it afterwards. There was still ruins of the old post on the right (east) bank of the Whiterocks Creek (Uintah River) a mile or two southeast of Whiterocks. But old man Reed said that was the old Robidoux post. He said his (Reed's) post was on the other (west) side of the creek, and twenty yards away. When we left the reservation in 1905, after it was opened, there was still an old rock chimney standing at the Robidoux post.

William Reed sold his interest in the trading post to Antoine Robidoux in 1831 and shortly thereafter returned to Kentucky where he died. Young Jimmie Reed stayed on with Robidoux for a time, and Jimmie Reed, Jr. stated in an interview that his father and "Rubydoe" took bull teams loaded with beaver clear back to the river. At about the age of sixteen, Jimmie Reed was a partner in the post with Robidoux, a strong indication of his maturity. Shortly thereafter, however, he went to California. Archambeau and Julien remained in the region for some time thereafter.

From the journals of Captain John C. Fremont, under date of 3 June 1844, we discover that Archambeau was still residing at the fort:

...we reached, on the afternoon of the 3d, the Uintah Fort, a trading post belonging to a Mr. A. Roubideau, on the principal fork of the Uintah river...and camped near the fort, which is situated a short distance above the junction of the two branches which make the river...I strengthened my party at the place by the addition of August Archambeaux, an excellent voyageur and hunter, belonging to the class of Carson and Godey.

According to Fremont's calculations, Fort Uintah, or Fort Robidoux, was located on the right bank of the Uintah River at precisely latitude 40 degrees, 27 minutes, 45 seconds north, longitude 109, 56 minutes, 42 seconds west. Here it was that Antoine Robidoux, together with his brother Louis, established a headquarters for the trapping and especially for the trading of the northern regions of what is now Utah and Colorado. Antoine Robidoux was made a Mexican citizen at Sante Fe on 16 July 1823, which entitled him to trade freely in the Mexican territory of which the Uintah Basin was then a part. On 19 September 1831, again at Sante Fe, he obtained a license to operate a fort in the Uintah Basin, at which time he purchased the Reed Trading Post.

Meanwhile, Kit Carson arrived at Taos in October 1833 where he joined Captain Stephen Louis Lee, a partner of Bent and St. Vrain, in bringing trade goods to the Uintah Basin. Says Carson, in his autobiography, "We followed the old Spanish trail to California till we struck White river, took down White river till we struck Green river, crossed Green river to Winty (Uintah), one of its tributaries. There we found Mr. Robidoux. He had a party of some twenty men that were trapping and trading."

In 1842 the Methodist missionary Joseph Williams, on his return trip to the east after preaching among the Indians, stopped at Fort Uintah. He left a record of his visit in his journals which articulates the tone of the place:

> We had to wait there (Fort Uintah) for Mr. Robideau about eighteen days till he and his company and horse-drivers were ready to start with us to the United States. This delay was very disagreeable to me on account of the wickedness of the people and the drunkenness and swearing, and the debauchery of the men among the Indian women. They would buy and sell the squaws to one another. One morning I heard a terrible fuss because two of their women had run away the night before. I tried several times to preach to them, but with little or any effect.

> I was told here of a Frenchman, who lived with an Indian woman, and when one of his children became burdensome, he dug a grave and buried it alive. At another time he took one of his children and tied it to a tree, and called it a target, then shot at it and killed it.

> Robideau had collected several of the Indian women to take to New Mexico and keep for his own use. Some of the Spaniards would buy them for wives. This place is equal to any I ever saw for wickedness and idleness.

> The French and Spaniards are all Roman Catholics, but are as wicked men, I think, as ever lived. No one who has not, like me, witnessed it, can have any idea of their wickedness. Some of these people at the Fork are fat, and dirty, and idle, and greasy.

> A small business is carried on also with the Snakes (Shoshone) and Ute Indians, living in the neighborhood of this establishment. The common articles of dealing are beaver, otter, deer, sheep, and elk skins in barter for ammunition, firearms, knives, tobacco, beads, awls, etc.

John C. Fremont, with Kit Carson as guide, came from the Valley of the Great Salt Lake by way of Fort Uintah and Brown's Hole in June of 1844 on the way to Bent's Fort on the Arkansas plains. Shortly after Fremont's visit in 1844, Fort Uintah was attacked by the Ute Indians in great force because of the bad treatment being afforded them by the occupants; Chief Walker was one of the leaders of the attack. The entire garrison was killed with the single exception of Antoine Robidoux who was not present. The destruction of Fort Uintah stands as a singular event in the history of the fur trade of the Far West as the only completely successful attack by Indians upon a trading post whereby every occupant was slain.

Nauhnan is our source for the information that his uncle, Chief Walker, was a leader of the attack upon Fort Uintah. Walker was chief of the Sanpete Utes, but he was allied with his cousins, the Uintah Utes. Walker had been at the fort earlier in the year, at which time he reported his out-of-body vision to the white traders. Walker had only recently inherited the rank of war chief, following the death of his father Moonch the previous year.

The Uintah Utes point out that the site of Fort Uintah is on Big Tom's allotment, about a mile and a half east of the present Whiterocks post office and the Uintah Boarding School. An old dugout near there is said to be the same where Kit Carson traded with the Indians when he visited the fort in 1833-34. As a boy, staying at my uncle Bill Reed's place nearby, I often played in this old dugout with his foster Indian children. The site was last in the possession of John Harmes, who ran Big Tom's allotment, and Ignacio Tom lived on the site prior to 1935. Jimmie Reed also lived on Big Tom's Allotment, and part of his property was handed down to his grandson, Bill Reed, after his grandfather's death in 1925.

A. Reed Morrill, in an article published in the *Utah Historical Quarterly* in 1941 (vo. IX, Nos. 1-2, p.8), states:

> In 1938, certain civic leaders in the Uintah (sic) Basin, in collaboration with some of the older Indians, while agreeing with the identification of the ruins as being an early fur trappers' post, nevertheless disputed the claim that Robidoux had established it. The later claim was that Fort Robidoux, even if it had been established, was not the first year-round trading-post in the Uinta Basin; but that a part built by James Reed had preceded Fort Robidoux, being established about...1828.

In summary, Jimmie Reed was born in Kentucky in 1815, came West to Sante Fe with his uncle and others in 1826 at age eleven, and by 1828 helped his uncle to establish the Reed Trading Post in the Uintah Basin. In about 1832-33 he went to California, but was back in the Uintah Mountains by the winter of 1837-38, where he served as a hunter with Kit Carson and assisted Uncle Jack Robinson at trading with the Indians at Brown's Hole. Together with Carson, Jimmie Reed served as a hunter at the newly established Fort Davy Crockett, "having to keep twenty men supplied with meat." They could not have been very successful since most of the occupants of the fort that winter were relegated to eating "barking mutton"—and because they ate their dogs and starved a good deal of the time, Fort Crockett was also known as "Fort Misery."

During the early 1840s, Jimmie Reed helped Auguste Archambeau to construct a cabin on the Green River some twenty miles north of the confluence of Henry's Fork with that stream (presently known as Buckboard Bay, on Flaming Gorge Reservoir, in Wyoming), and prospected with Archambeau for gold in the vicinity of South Pass. After gold was discovered in California in 1849, Reed returned there to prospect, after which he returned to Brown's Hole with "Uncle" Sam Bassett, Louis Simmons (Kit Carson's son-in-law), and Juan Jose "Mexican Joe" Herrerra (see *The Antonio de Reinaldo Story*). Prior to 1863 he accompanied Robert Hereford and Louis Simmons to Alder Gulch, Montana, where they are credited with early gold discoveries.

There was good reasons for Jimmie Reed's association with men such as Hereford: they all married Indian women, not *just* Indian women, but wives "from among the numerous sisters and daughters" of Chief Washakie of the Shoshones. Among the men who married into this amazing Indian family were Jimmie Reed, Shade Large, Robert Hereford, George Finch, John Baker, Uncle Jack Robinson, and James Bridger, to name but a few.

The descendants of the Large family, who today reside on the Wind River Reservation in Wyoming, maintain that Jimmie Reed obtained his wife—as did Shade Large—by kidnaping her during a raid on a Shoshone village in the Wind River Valley of Wyoming. Shade Large, in fact, married twice into this family: his first wife was a sister of Washakie; his second wife (whom he kidnaped) was Washakie's daughter. She was, in fact, a sister of Jimmie Reed's wife Maggie.

Moreover, according to her grandson, Julius Orn Murray, Maggie's Shoshone name was Wah-ve-dah, and she was a survivor of the Bear River Massacre of 1863. She had been wounded in the leg during that encounter and limped the rest of her life as a result of the injury. Her immediate family had been killed in the massacre, and Wah-ve-dah was carried away to Salt Lake City where, together with another young Shoshone child, a boy named Su-Pickett, she was adopted by Brigham Young and baptized as "Margaret"—to her family, she was "Maggie."

There is no reason to doubt that both accounts are correct. Inasmuch as Jimmie Reed met and married her in Wyoming, she had apparently returned to her people, and may have been carried off by Reed. The unexplained discrepancy, though not insurmountable, is that Jimmie Reed and Wah-ve-dah were married previous to the year 1860, the year of the birth of their eldest child and daughter,

Mary, and at least three years prior to the Bear River Massacre. In 1860, Jimmie Reed operated a trading post on the Wind River Reservation, where the eldest of his children were born. Inasmuch as they resided with the family of Chief Washakie, there is no reason to doubt Maggie's relationship to this remarkable man. Ascending to the chieftainship of the Shoshones in 1848, Washakie ruled for fifty-two years, dying on 2 February 1900, in the hundredth year of this age.

In 1876, Jimmie Reed, his wife Maggie and their children settled in Brown's Park on the south side of the Green River, at the mouth of Jimmie Reed Creek, named in his honor. Here, at least one of his children died and was buried on Bake Oven Flat, near the old John Jarvie ranch, and not far from the ruins of Fort Davy Crockett, where forty years earlier he had been a hunter with Kit Carson.

In 1879 the White River Utes rebelled and killed Indian Agent Nathan C. Meeker in nearby Colorado. When the Indians massacred the troops of Col. T.T. Thornburgh at Milk Creek, the surrounding country was alarmed and, during the winter of 1879-80, the Reeds "forted up" with many other families at the Titsworth Gap, north of Brown's Park.

In the spring of 1880, Jimmie Reed sold his squatter's claim on Green River to Charles Crouse for $600 and moved, more or less permanently, back to the Uintah-Ouray Reservation, settling only about two miles from the old Reed Trading Post. He was then sixty-five years old.

Reed was accompanied to the reservation from Brown's Park by his old friend Louis "Louie" Simmons, Carson's son-in-law. According the Jimmie Reed, Jr., old Louie became insane during his final illness, "ate dirt," and was cared after by the Reed family. He died in the military hospital at Fort Duchesne at an advanced age.

Jimmie Reed remained in and around Whiterocks for the remainder of his life. His later years were involved almost entirely in prospecting, much of it in conjunction with his two close friends,

Caleb Rhoades and Happy Jack, and his claims can be found often in old deed books and claims records. He died in September of 1925, just one month short of 110 years of age. He is buried in the old school cemetery at Whiterocks.

Chapter Nineteen

Some Indian Accounts of the Mines

VIRTUALLY EVERY ACCOUNT OF THE mines contains the stories of various white men who have hunted for them, found them, lost them, or had some connection with them. Few accounts, however, recount the stories of the Ute Indians, they who obviously know more about the mines than anyone.

It should not be assumed that all Utes were privy to the secret knowledge of the location of the mines, more especially the Sacred Mine and Carre-Shinob. In fact, few of them had such knowledge, the secret lying exclusively with the elders of the tribal council, and even then within a very limited inner circle. At any given time no more than four or five elders and one medicine man ever knew the secret of Carre-Shinob; perhaps twice that many knew the locations of the various other old Spanish mines in the Uintah Mountains. Nevertheless, most of the Utes had access to information unavailable to the white men, and further had access to locations that would bring death to white mens' trespass.

Today the secret of Carre-Shinob no longer rests with the tribal council, which the elders have come to mistrust due to white intervention and political machinations. Instead, a sort of "secret society" developed among the elders, who today alone know the secret location. However, a few of the older generation of Utes are aware of the contents of Carre-Shinob, at least generally, though they speak of it rarely.

Utes also have a wily sense of humor, making it difficult to know when they are being serious or when they are "putting you on." They speak freely only to a few who have earned their trust. For this reason, among others, Ute accounts of the mines are rare. Here follows a few verified accounts from Ute elders and tribal members who had specific connections to and knowledge of the mines.

WASH

Tabuache, or Tab-Wash—best known as "Wash"—son of Nauhnan, grandson of Chief Tabiona (Tabby), and grand-nephew of Chief Walker, was one of the tribal elders privy to the secret of the location of Carre-Shinob. True to his trust, he never revealed that secret to any unauthorized person during his lifetime; which is not to say that he did not mention other things of truthful consequence in relation to the numerous other mines and caches throughout the Uintah Mountains. At least two of the stories Wash told me are worth recounting here.

At the base of Rhoades Canyon, just north of Tabby Mountain, near Hanna, there is a large open sagebrush-covered flat, bisected on the far south end by Rock Creek. Wash had intimated to me on more than one occasion that something historic had occurred there, and that relics of that event could still be seen. After considerable urging, he at last agreed to accompany me there and tell me the story.

We parked near Rock Creek at the far southwestern end of the flat and set out on foot to explore. Wash was then in his eighties, but amazingly agile and rugged, well-conditioned from a lifetime in the mountains. He was of larger stature than the average Native American, the only indication of his age being a wrinkled and character-filled face and slightly stooped shoulders. He used a walking stick that had been carved by his father, and his twin braids of hoary hair bounced against a favorite print shirt as he walked; he almost always wore suspenders.

Against the mountain, on the north side of Rhoades Canyon, a stand of stately pine trees bore numerous Spanish symbols carved into the trunks, and farther north, around a point of the mountain, Wash pointed out two rock kilns, partly caved in at the apex. He explained that in his grandfather's time, the Spaniards had used these kilns to process gold ore into bars for transport to Sante Fe.

As we walked back across the flat towards our vehicle, Wash told me the promised story.

When his grandfather, Tabby, was a young man, Wash explained, and Walker was chief of the Sanpete Utes, the O'uatz, or Mexicans, camped in the mountains one summer to mine gold near the headwaters of Rock Creek, and to process the ore into bars for transport by mule train out of the mountains. The year was about "two snows" before the Mormons came., i.e. about 1845.

This was the year of the destruction of Fort Uintah, and the Utes were fired up with a desire to drive the infestations of intruders from their lands. The hated Q'uatz had chosen a bad time to steal the Utes' gold. A tremendous battle ensued on the flat and the Mexicans, greatly outnumbered (according to Wash, there were about 15 Mexicans and perhaps 75 Utes), nevertheless fought a valiant fight. They had the advantage of armor and a 12-pound "grapeshot" cannon, but the outcome was a foregone conclusion. The Mexican miners were killed to a man.

The battle took place near the middle of the flat, about a hundred yards north of the creek. The Indians were led by Tabby, who ordered that all traces of the massacre site be obliterated. The gold bars, six in number, were turned over to squaws, who returned the bars to the mountains near the mine from whence the gold had come, and tossed them into a nearby lake. Meanwhile, the Ute braves dug an open pit in the center of the flat, drove the Mexicans' wagon filled with ore over the hole, then removed the wheels and dropped the wagon into the pit. The bodies of the Mexicans were tossed into the hole and the whole thing covered with dirt. Another pit was dug nearby for the cannon. The Utes raced their horses back and forth across the flat to trample the ground, and then for good measure, set the entire flat on fire. At that time, Wash told me, there were trees also on the flat, but these were completely burned by the fire.

The braves then rounded up the Mexican's mules and drove them to the nearby creek where they summarily killed them all, then cut off their hooves, to prevent their spirits from returning to the mines. When the Utes were done, there was little trace of the massacre or any indication of the purpose of the Mexicans' being there.

By the time we reached the car, Wash had finished telling this story, and I asked him if he could point out the place on the flat where the wagonload of ore was buried, together with the cannon and the bodies of the Mexicans. He grinned facetiously, and said: "We walk over top of wagon little time back." I realized then that we had literally walked all over the flat that day, and there was no telling where the wagon could have been; it was equally obvious that Wash was not going to tell me.

Wash had shown me the trees with the Spanish symbols and the kilns, but little else. He did, however, point at the ledges at the crest of the southern side of Rhoades Canyon and said, "You see that place up there, where rock change color? There is a mine, covered up by my people. Not so rich mebbe as higher up, but pretty good, all same."

I returned to the site with my cousin Gale Rhoades a year or two later, but true to a promise made to Wash, I did not mention the mine to him. We did, however, discover several things at the site which verified Wash's story. Near the creek, at a place where the channel had altered its course over the years, washing out a bank, we discovered several mules' hooves, a Spanish bridle bit, and a 12-pound "grapeshot" cannonball. Moreover, near the center of the flat, we literally stumbled upon the muzzle of the buried cannon protruding several inches above the surface of the ground. We had no tools with which to dig, so we left the area, promising ourselves to return with metal detectors to search for the wagon and to retrieve the cannon.

I never returned to the area, but Gale went back a few years later with a metal detector and excavation equipment. He was disappointed to discover that a dam had been proposed for an irrigation project, and the flat was staked off with survey markers and torn up by heavy equipment. He was not permitted to search the area and was compelled to give up the quest.

The story does not end there, however, for Wash told me the sequel. When he was a young man, the fire of adventure burned in his soul. He remembered the story of the massacre, repeated over many a council fire, and he recalled how the squaws had thrown the gold bars into the lake near the mine. He determined to go there and see for himself, and even retrieve them if possible. It was a foolish mission, done in the passion of his youth, for the gold was sacred and forbidden to be touched. Nevertheless he went.

The year had been one of drought, and the glaciers and massive snow banks which fed the lakes had receded, making the deep ends of the lakes accessible for the first time in years. Wash indicated that the lake containing the gold bars was one of the three Brown Duck Lakes, which appear on Caleb Rhoades' "Pine Tree" map, which are within visual distance of the Bullock discovery.

Wash made it clear that the deep end of the lake, where the gold bars were deposited, was accessible only during years of drought, because a glacier covered the end of the lake during a majority of years. He described the lake as being deep at one end, where it abutted some high ledges, and shallow on the other end, where an outlet traversed a meadow.

Because the glacier had receded, Wash was able to wade out a distance in the icy cold water by stepping on large sliderock, until the water was up to his armpits. By stooping and immersing his head under water, he could see the rectangular shapes of several gold bars laying deep in the submerged sliderock.

Wash was a strong swimmer, but he confessed that the water was too murky and cold to make a bare-skin dive. Anyone who has stood in the waters of these alpine lakes will understand his meaning, for within minutes the freezing waters bring on a stingingly painful numbness.

So Wash went on a "fishing" trip. He retrieved a lodgepole about ten feet in length, to the end of which he tied a piece of baling wire, making a sliding loop. He then probed the water, trying to snag a gold bar. It proved a formidable task. He was compelled to stand on a sliderock about the size of a table, and bend over, submerging his head in the water, barely making out the rectangular shapes in the murky water. He would frequently return to shore to warm himself by a campfire before trying again.

At last he looped one of the gold bars, but he was surprised at how heavy it was. It slipped the loop once, but fell to a shelf near his feet, and so he was able to again retrieve it and finally get it on shore.

Wash then told a most unusual story. He said he was about to return to the water for another bar when he heard a strange sound emanating from beneath the ledges at the deepest part of the lake. Looking up, he saw a creature swimming towards him, an aquatic creature that resembled a dinosaur. Wash swore it was a spirit guardian of the sacred gold, and it so frightened him that he packed his camp and hastily departed.

I have often wondered whether Wash's "monster" story was calculated to scare the curious—such as myself—away, but he told the story in all seriousness, without the usual wily smile that accompanied his occasional dry jests.

One thing is certain beyond doubt: Wash had a gold bar in his possession; I have seen it and handled it. It was rectangular in shape, stamped with a Spanish cross, and weighed 84 pounds!

Wash never disposed of this bar and still had it in his possession the last I saw him, when he was in his nineties (I have been told that Wash lived past 100, though I lost track of him in later years). The gold was sacred to the Utes and so he would never give a thought to cashing it in, though he might have been wealthy by so doing.

A little calculation quickly reveals the immense value of the cache. According to Wash there was a total of six bars, all identical in size and weight, and so each weighed 84 pounds; this means that a total of 504 pounds of pure gold was thrown into the lake. A single bar, at today's values, would net over half a million dollars, and all six would be worth more than three million dollars! There is more than one treasure to be found in the high Uintahs.

UNCA SAM

Unca Sam was a walking history book. Depending upon which account one accepts, when he died he was either 112 or 124 years old!

The former appears the more correct but none the less remarkable. Space does not permit a full recounting of Unca Sam's remarkable life (the authors recommend Dr. Floyd O'Neill's book, *The Ute People,* Univ. of Utah Press), but suffice it that his history spanned the gamut from the opening of the reservation by Abraham Lincoln in 1865 to the development of airplanes and automobiles in the 20th century. He knew Chief Walker and he met Teddy Roosevelt, but most of all he was loved by all who ever knew him.

Unca Sam.

Photograph courtesy Utah State Historical Society.

Unca Sam sat on the tribal council, and he was one of the elders who protected the secret of Carre-Shinob. He did his job well. One of my favorite stories concerning Unca Sam and the mines was his first meeting with Samuel Gilson, father of the Gilsonite mining industry in Utah.

Following the formalities of their initial meeting, Gilson could not contain himself long before asking:

"Is it true that you know where the Sacred Mine of the Utes is located?"

"I know," replied Unca Sam without hesitation.

"And is it as rich as the white men claim it is?" Gilson pressed.

"More," said Unca Sam succinctly.

"And will you take me there and show me?" Gilson winked jokingly.

"Sure," said Unca Sam. "I will take you there and show you."

"You will?" Gilson was astounded. Unca Sam sounded completely serious.

"Sure, I will take you. Mabbe we go tomorrow."

Gilson began to envision his wealth. He did not know why, but the old Indian was willing to show him the location of a mine richer than all the Gilsonite in Utah.

"You really mean it?" he beamed, wanting to be sure he was not being fooled.

"Sure. Unca Sam take you there tomorrow."

"Great!" replied Gilson. "I'll put together a few things and meet you in the morning."

"Oh, you will need take nothing with you," said Unca Sam dryly.

"Why not?" asked Gilson.

"Because you will not be coming back," replied Unca Sam. "You still wanna go?"

Gilson declined.

CUMPANEES

Cump-an-nees, best known as Cumpanees, was one of the Utes who first welcomed my grandfather, William Coleman Boren, to the reservation, and he remained one of the Boren family's closest friends throughout his life. My father and his brothers spent their growing years in his company, and he taught them the Ute language, to hunt and to fish, how to catch wild horses and break them, and all of the rudiments of the Indian way of life. He was a quiet man, self-assured and proud, and was a silent observer of human behavior and an astute judge of character. Like most of the Indian people, he was a man of few words, but his spoken observations were always poignant and astute.

Cumpanees was also an avid and knowledgeable prospector. Indians in general have shown little interest in geology and mining, having a very reverential respect for the earth and its bounty; but a few of them, like Cumpanees, Happy Jack and Pick Murdock, who had measurable contact with white men, discovered the advantages of knowing the white man's ways. In fact, Cumpanees was a close friend and frequent prospecting companion of Happy Jack and Pick Murdock, and thereby knew Caleb Rhoades very well.

Cumpanees related in later years that whenever Rhoades came over from Price to Whiterocks to bring gold out of the mountains, he stayed with Jimmie Reed. Reed supplied Caleb with pack mules, and both Cumpanees and Happy Jack would accompany Rhoades up Whiterocks Canyon. About a quarter of the way up the canyon, Cumpanees dropped off to guard the back trail against anyone who might have followed them. Farther up the Canyon, at a fork in Whiterocks Creek, Happy Jack camped while Caleb went off up the left fork, towards Yellowstone Creek, and after about two days he would return with the pack mules loaded with rich gold ore.

After each trip, Rhoades would give both Happy Jack and Cumpanees leather pouches filled with almost pure gold. Cumpanees spent little of his gains. He bought a few things from the post trader as needed, but the only luxury he ever indulged in was ordering boxes of fine cigars from back East. It was rumored by those who knew him that he hoarded his gold and buried it somewhere near his home on Big Tom's allotment.

MOUNTAIN SHEEP

"As mean an Indian as ever lived," one newspaper reporter proclaimed, voicing the complaints of several local ranchers around Duchesne who had experienced run-ins with Mountain Sheep. The wily old Indian had a reputation for being mean and unpredictable which was, in retrospect, probably not merited. In point of fact, Mountain Sheep was merely a type of the old school, one of the Ute elders who remembered when his people roamed free from the restraint of the encroaching, greedy white man. The fact that he did not like whites in general was well known, while at the same time he had white friends, not the least of whom was Caleb Rhoades.

Mountain Sheep was a sub-chief of the Uintah Utes, which meant, in essence, that he was a chieftain, a fact which he frequently emphasized to the whites. My father, Edward Boren, told me that "Mountain Sheep and Two Horns (the tribal medicine man) got a kick out of dressing up in their feathers and war paint and doing a war dance in the parade compound at Fort Duchesne, scaring hell out of the tourists who stopped off there on the stagecoach on their way to Vernal."

My late uncle, Roy Boren, confirmed this account, but added, "Mountain Sheep liked to scare people, no doubt about it, but most of it was a bluff; but it didn't pay to cross him, either, because behind the bluff was a real hatred of the whites. Everybody knew he left a lot of bones in the mountains."

Mountain Sheep was one of the Utes who put his mark to the Rhoades-Hathenbruck lease. Rhoades was one of the few white men the wily old Indian trusted. Mountain Sheep constructed a cabin on Towanta Flat at the base of Tabby Mountain where he lived for many years, expressly for the purpose of guarding access to the Rock Creek area. More than one white man who rode across Towanta Flat to ascend the mountain never came down again.

Peter Gurr "Pete" Wall, an early settler of the Vernal area, left the following account among his reminiscences:

> One day I was rounding up strays on the mountain above Dry Fork Canyon, high up on the north fork on the Red Cloud Loop. It was the fall of the year and the time when we brought the cattle down from the high summer range. I was riding along the rim above north fork, where it looks down on Mosby Mountain, when I heard the strangest sound I ever did hear. I rode to where the sound was coming from, up a side canyon beneath the rimrock, and there up high on a ledge was old Mountain Sheep, naked as a jaybird, his whole body painted red with ochre, sitting next to a little fire, pulling smoke towards him with his hands and singing a chant.
>
> I sat there on my horse for a long time, just watching him, because I had lived around the Utes for years and never seen nothing

like that. Now I sat there for maybe fifteen or twenty minutes when all of a sudden old Mountain Sheep stopped singing and looked right at me. I was a couple of hundred yards away and in the timber, so I don't know how he spotted me, but he did, and was he ever mad! He jumped up and down, shook his fist at me, and yelled something I couldn't make out. Then he reached down and picked up a tomahawk and started to run right at me, so I wheeled my horse and got the holy hell out of there.

A lot of things have happened to me in my life, but this episode scared me nearly to death. I could feel the hair stand up on the back of my neck as I rode down the canyon, because I could see old Mountain Sheep's naked red body flashing through the trees alongside of me, trying to cut me off, and he nearly succeeded. I have no doubt in my mind that he would have killed and scalped me if he could have caught up to me, and left my body up there in that canyon where nobody would ever find me. He was past middle age when this took place, but he could run like a deer. In the heavy timber, my horse couldn't make good time, and old Mountain Sheep was gaining on me when at last I broke out into a big clearing at the bottom of the canyon and was able to put some distance between us.

I made it back to Vernal late that night. I was afraid to go back to my camp on Little Brush Creek, because I thought old Mountain Sheep might be waiting there for me. I came back two or three days later with several other men and got my tent and camp equipment.

What I think now is that old Mountain Sheep was performing some ceremony connected to the Ute mines that he guarded, and I must have stumbled on one pretty close for him to behave like he did. For a long time after that I was afraid he recognized me and might come after me, and I slept pretty close to my gun for weeks. One day about two months later I passed old Mountain Sheep coming out of the Marimon post at Whiterocks, and he gave me some dirty looks, like he knew it

was me; but then, he gave dirty looks to most whites, so maybe it was my imagination. I only know there must be one of the Ute mines somewhere up that canyon, or else old Mountain Sheep wouldn't have chased me down the mountain with blood in his eye.

A FEW OTHERS

Not all the Indians knew the secret of Carre-Shinob; in fact, only a minority of the Utes ever became privy to the sacred information. In early times, only the medicine man possessed the secret and only he dared to go there. The site was not only considered sacred, but there was instilled in the Utes a reverent superstitious fear of the place. Unless accompanied by a medicine man, nothing could induce them to go anywhere near Carre-Shinob. They did not need to know exactly where it was located in order to avoid it; they knew the area and that was enough.

But the curiosity of some of the younger braves exceeded their superstition, and having knowledge of the general area, they began a concentrated search. Among these ambitious young men were the Murray boys—Harris Murray, Cump Murray, and Junius Murray. The Murrays were inter-related by marriage with the Reed and Harris families.

The Murray boys spent the better part of their lives hunting for the Sacred Mine. It led them down some strange paths of intrigue and even murder. In the first edition of *Footprints in the Wilderness* we recounted the story of old Tom Rhoades on the reservation, wherein the old man was tortured in an effort to learn the secret of the mines. Such stories are common in connection with the mines.

Today there are a number of young Ute men who have an interest in the mines, but they are certainly in the minority. Most of them adhere to the honor of tradition and hold the gold to be sacred to their people. Let there be no mistake about it, these are a good people, and are deserving of their secret trust.

Chapter Twenty

The Happy Jack Journals

MANY YEARS AGO I CAME INTO possession of the journals and maps of Happy Jack, the Ute Indian friend and long-time companion of Gale Rhoades. The acquisition of these items has been a mixed blessing. I have been hounded unmercifully by some of the parties who knew I had them, and I have been threatened, harassed, spied on, maligned, beaten and shot at in an effort by these unscrupulous ruffians to obtain them. One individual, in particular, has gone to extreme measures to obtain these valuable records, including threats, legal blackmail, and the confiscation of personal possessions in an effort to find them, with no success. In point of fact, these items have never been long in my possession, for over the years I have entrusted them to the care of the Indian family on the reservation from whom I initially obtained them.

The journals contain various accounts of Happy Jack's prospecting ventures, beginning in the early 1870s and continuing for the next fifty years. There are notations, in Happy Jack's peculiar script, with frequent bland Indian humor, of events unrelated to the mines and prospecting, including interesting historical sidelights on the Ute culture and traditions, the opening of the reservation lands, his relations with whites, gunfights, bear attacks, and much more. There are accounts of his purchases and expenditures, an account of his visit to Washington, D.C. as part of the Ute delegation concerned with Indian lands, and frequent mention of his friend, Caleb Rhoades.

The journals offer a real challenge, for they are seldom dated except by the year, and seem to have little sense of order, being randomly written, often on loose scraps of paper which had been inserted between bound pages. The information therein, however, is of immense value, because it offers the personal observations of a man intimately acquainted with the sacred Ute gold.

The journals—four in number, being ledger-journals common to the period just before the turn of the century—show considerable use, obviously having been carried along on numerous camping trips (there were even pine needles between some of the pages), and are tied together with rolled buckskin thongs.

In a separate piece of tanned buckskin are a number of letters which Happy Jack received from various persons over the years—friends, Indian agents, merchants, assay companies, and even a commendation letter from Utah's first state governor, Heber M. Wells, thanking him for his participation in the fiftieth anniversary celebration of the arrival of the Mormon pioneers, held in 1897.

Wrapped in the same piece of buckskin are the Happy Jack maps—some of which are reproduced here for the first time—which are of immense value for the information they provide. The maps are numerous; it would appear that nearly every prospect, every claim, every mine that Happy Jack ever found or learned of was mapped by him. There are 78 in all! They are often crude and lacking in exact location, but filled with specific detail, making them valuable tools in searching for the lost veins or mines. In fact, one of the maps—a map that will never be published while in my possession—shows the location of Carre-Shinob, the only such map known to be in existence.

The Boren family has had a long and intimate association with Happy Jack. His journals are replete with mentions of "my friend Will Boren," whom he calls "good friend," "a good man," "my trusted friend," and "friend Will." Through this association, as well as through the journals and some dedicated research, the history of this incredible man has emerged. His history, in fact, is integrally related to the history of my own family.

Happy Jack was born about 1842 on the banks of the Pequi-nary-no-quint (Spanish Fork River), a member of the Pah-gwan-nuance (Lake Shore People) or the Tim-pah-nee (Timpanogos) Utes. His boyhood name is unknown, but his father was Old Elk, a sub-chief of Pahvant's band, and Old Elk was a brother of Chief Ope-carry (called "Stick-in-the-Head").

By the year 1849, Chief Walker had invited Isaac Morley and a colony of Mormon settlers to inhabit the Sanpete Valley. The Utah Valley, farther north, was already occupied, and some of the Ute chiefs, in opposition to Walker, resented the encroachment upon their lands. Led by chieftains Ope-carry and Big Elk (of the Nampa Utes—not to be confused with Old Elk), a party of these Utes launched raids upon the Utah Valley during the winter of 1849-50 until the Mormon settlers had been compelled to move *en masse* into Fort Utah under the leadership of militia Captain Peter W. Conover (a son-in-law of Coleman Boren).

By the early spring of 1850 affairs became so serious that Captain Conover dispatched Miles Weaver with an appeal to Brigham Young and the Territorial Legislature for military relief. Brigham Young called upon Captain Howard Stansbury, who was in the middle of a topographical survey of the Great Salt Lake, to provide a detachment to accompany members of the Mormon militia. Stansbury dispatched Lt. Howland as adjutant with arms and ammunition for the soldiers, Dr. Blake as surgeon, and William W. Potter (my maternal second great-grandfather) and Elijah Barney Ward as scouts and interpreters. They joined 50 minute men under Captain George D. Grant who started from Salt Lake City on 7 February 1850, followed by 50 others commanded by Major Andrew Lytle. Snow lay over a foot deep in the valleys and hard-crusted, rendering progress difficult.

Captain Grant's cavalry marched all night, arriving at the Provo River on the morning of the 8th, finding the settlers in the fort on the south side of the stream, and the Indians strongly entrenched in the timber and willows along the river bottom a mile or two above. The Indians had the added protection of felled cottonwood trees and a double-log house which had been abandoned by James A. Bean, whose family had fled to the fort.

The battle lasted two days and was constantly ferocious. Artillery was employed against the Indians with little effect, except to kill a squaw, which only infuriated them more. The Indians killed Joseph Higbee and wounded several others. In the afternoon of the second day (9 February) Captain Grant ordered Lt. William Kimball, with fifteen picked men, to charge the house and take it at all costs. The names of the men known to have participated in this action are: Robert T. Burton, Lot Smith, James Ferguson, John R. Murdock, Ephraim K. Hanks, A.J. Pendleton, Orson K. Whitney, William W. Potter, Barney Ward, Henry Johnson and Isham Flyn. The battle raged all of that day, but by evening, under cover of a furious barrage, the Indians withdrew into the darkness, retreating after cutting a supply of horsemeat from the dead cavalry horses nearby.

General Daniel H. Wells arrived next morning (10 February) to discover that the Indians had separated into two groups, the main body having fled southward towards Spanish Fork, while a smaller band, nursing their wounded Chief Big Elk, had retreated up Rock Canyon, a rough gorge northeast of Provo. A small party was sent in pursuit of the Rock Canyon group, and William Potter eventually captured Big Elk (near present-day Sundance Resort) who was summarily executed by firing squad.

General Wells commanded the main body of troops in pursuit of the Utes fleeing southward. Several skirmishes occurred on the late afternoon of the tenth at Spanish Fork and Pe-teet-neet (now Payson), and on 11 February the Indians were overtaken near Table Mountain at the south end of Utah Lake. Most of the fighting took place on the ice, making it extremely difficult for the horses to keep their feet. The Indians were practically annihilated. The total Indian losses were about 40, more than half the number of warriors initially involved. Numerous squaws and Indian children were taken captive, including young Happy Jack, who was only about eight years old.

Happy Jack's mother, one of Old Elk's younger wives, died—either in the battles or in the scourge of starvation and disease that followed. His father, Old Elk, was not killed in the battle at Table Mountain, but died of exposure and measles several weeks after the battle. Bill Hickman, Brigham Young's "Destroying Angel," cut the head off Old Elk's body and wrapped it in a blanket, and subsequently tried to pass it off as the head of Big Elk in order to collect a $100 reward offered by Jim Bridger for Big Elk's head.

Happy Jack was taken to Salt Lake City where he was placed in one of the several homes of Brigham young, together with a young Indian girl also orphaned due to the battle. Brigham Young liked to think of himself as a benefactor to the Indians and adopted a number of them over the years. It is said that Brigham bestowed the name "Happy Jack" on the young boy because of his jovial disposition.

Happy Jack received a good education at the expense of the Church leader, attended church regularly, and was baptized as a full-fledged Mormon. After several years in the Brigham Young home, Happy Jack was adopted by Elisha Jones, a farmer who lived in the Heber and Kamas valleys. Elisha Jones was a brother of my great grandfather, James Naylor Jones (1810-1865). Elisha Jones was born 11 June 1813, at Wayne township, Jefferson County, Ohio, and died 18 August 1880 at Heber City, Utah.

Among the children of Elisha Jones who were raised with Happy Jack was Elizabeth Jones (born 20 May 1844), who married James Philander Knight (1838-1909), brother of mining magnate Jesse Knight.

Happy Jack was raised to manhood with the Jones family and attended school at Kamas, where also lived Thomas Rhoades. Here he met young Caleb Rhoades, only several years older than himself, and the two boys were destined to become life-long friends. During his youth, Happy Jack worked on the Jones ranch at the mouth of what is now Rhoades Canyon.

In the meantime, Elisha Jones acquired a trading post of Heber City and managed to obtain a government contract that allowed him to haul supplies for the soldiers, from Heber to the Whiterocks Agency. Happy Jack began freighting the supplies for his foster father.

In March 1880, William Coleman Boren married Elisha Jones' niece, Lovina Jones, at Heber City, and that same year Elisha Jones died. Happy Jack and Will Boren took over the government contract and began freighting together to the reservation, beginning a friendship which lasted the rest of their lives. My grandfather, born in 1853, was about ten years younger than Happy Jack.

It was their custom to leave Heber early one morning, staying at night with the old Indian Mountain Sheep, whose cabin was located about three miles east of Rock Creek on the edge of Towanta Flat. Leaving early the next morning, they would arrive at Whiterocks within one or two days, making the round trip in a week.

On one of these trips, as they approached Towanta Flat, they saw a man on horseback, leading a pack animal. Upon reaching Mountain Sheep's cabin just before dark, Mountain Sheep informed Happy Jack that the man they had encountered was "...the Rhoades man who takes gold out of these mountains." Happy Jack replied that he was sorry to have missed the man, because he and Caleb Rhoades were old friends.

Happy Jack set out immediately on Caleb's trail, but darkness fell too quickly, so he returned to Mountain Sheep's cabin. The following morning, Happy Jack remained behind while Will Boren proceeded on to Whiterocks alone with the supplies. Happy Jack followed Caleb's trail all of that day, across the upper end of Towanta Flat, down Rock Creek Canyon, then up Rock Creek. He noted that Caleb never stayed on the trail, but paralleled it in the heavy timber. He found where Rhoades had staked his horses to graze in the grass, but thereafter he lost the trail and returned to Mountain Sheep's cabin. When my grandfather picked up Happy Jack a day or two later for the return trip to Heber, they crossed Rhoades' tracks where he had returned to Price.

Sometime later Happy Jack again ran into Caleb Rhoades on Towanta Flat, and they sat in Caleb's tent and talked. Caleb asked him to hand him one of the pack saddles, and Caleb opened it, pulling out one of many small sacks which Happy Jack said looked like "bank money bags," and dumped the contents onto a tarp. "Happy, have you ever seen anything quite like that?" The canvas was covered with large gold nuggets.

Thereafter, whenever Caleb Rhoades made plans for a trip into the mountains, he would write first to Happy Jack, who by that time lived at Whiterocks, and ask him to meet at the "usual place"—the junction of Rock Creek and the Duchesne River. One example of these notes, found among the Happy Jack letters and journals, is as follows:

Happy,

    I will be going out as usual on July 18th, by which time I think the snow will be gone off enough to make the high ridges. I expect the meadows to be wet and the mosquitoes bothersome, so I welcome some company to complain to. Meet me at the usual place on July 20th and expect to be away two weeks or more. I intend to bring my new bamboo fishing rod which arrived by train yesterday from Denver, so we can have a little fun and we won't starve.

Your Friend,

Caleb

P.S. If anybody asks, maybe you can tell them you are going on a fishing trip.

The note contains no date, but fortunately was retained in the original envelope which is postmarked at Price on June 10, 1891. The return address is written as "Caleb B. Rhoades, Price Post Office, Price, Utah," and addressed to "H.J. Jones, Whiterocks Post Office, Whiterocks, Utah."

After meeting, the two men would ride together to a place somewhere on the west side of Rock Creek where Happy Jack would remain behind to guard the back-trail while Caleb went after the gold. When Caleb returned, he always gave Happy Jack a fair amount of gold for his own use, and they would return to their respective homes.

Caleb Rhoades revealed a number of mine locations to Happy Jack, but never the Sacred Mine, upon which he had taken an oath. There is no doubt, however, that Happy Jack learned where it was in time, though he never divulged it. The mine was sacred to the Utes and Happy Jack honored his heritage. The location of this particular mine (Sacred Mine #2) was high on the left side of Rock Creek near the old Farm Creek Pass—the trail Caleb Rhoades followed and which was the old wagon road used by my grandfather and Happy Jack to freight supplies from Heber to Whiterocks. The sacred mine near Farm Creek Pass was best known as the Brigham Young Mine—this being the place first visited by Thomas Rhoades in 1852 to bring out gold for the use of the Church.

There were at least twelve sub-chiefs, generally older and well-established braves, assigned to stand guard over the major sacred gold mines of the Uintah Mountains. Mountain Sheep was one of these, which is why his cabin was strategically placed at Towanta Flat. The cabin stood for many years near Mountain Sheep Pass overlooking Rock Creek. Mountain Sheep was eventually relieved of his duty by the Ute Tribal Council for inciting too much trouble with white settlers around Moab, Utah, and Bridger Jim was selected to take his place at Rock Creek. Others whose names are known were: Chief Tworoose, Dick Wanroads, Unatowinorokant (John Duncan), Sagoosie Jack, Ungastonigets, Kochootch (David Copperfield), Cessapoonch, Black Hawk (not to be confused with the famous Ute Chief of the same name), Tab-Wash (Wash), and Apporah (called Appoh). Of course, these names varied over a period of years as new guards were assigned, and those above represent some of the earliest appointees.

Happy Jack lived to be more than 100 years old; he was still alive when I was born in 1941. In July of 1940, when he was was about 98, Happy Jack offered to go with a man named Larsen, who had settled in that area in 1906 and operated a fish hatchery since 1924, on a one-day search for the Brigham Young Mine. According to Larsen's son, Edwin J. Larsen of Roosevelt, Utah, who accompanied them, they crossed Rock Creek and drove to the summit of Farm Creek Pass, where they parked their car and walked north, searching the small canyons sloping off the east towards Rock

Creek. They returned to the car at dusk, having had no success.

Such a search was academic for Happy Jack; had he wanted, he could have taken Larsen precisely to the site. It was a sort of ritual which the Utes underwent with their white friends, in which they delighted, much as old Wash used to toy with me. After walking all day over extensive areas, Wash would tell me of a rich mine in the area. When I would ask him where it was, he would grin from ear to ear and say, "Oh, we walked right by it, little while ago." He did this on numerous occasions.

My father, Edward Boren, knew Happy Jack well. Prior to his death on 14 April 1975, at the age of 81, my father related the following story about Happy Jack, which offers some insight into this amazing man's character.

> My dad (William C. Boren) lived on the reservation on an allotment belonging to old Robert Marimon, the post trader, between the Marimon ranch on Whiterocks (river) and Big Tom's allotment. Happy Jack lived on Big Tom's allotment, between the old Jimmie Reed place and Pick Murdock's cabin. He was over at our place a lot. I remember him having two long braids of hair and wearing a flat-brimmed hat with a feather in it. He was well educated and could speak good English when he wanted to, but like most Indians, he didn't say much.
>
> One day Happy Jack was sitting on a bench outside of Marimon's store, soaking up some sun and passing the time of day with some of the old tribal elders, when two white men from Salt Lake drove up in a Model A Ford and sauntered up to the door. One of the men stopped and listened to the Indians talking in Ute, while his partner went in the store to buy something. As soon as Happy Jack saw that their conversation was being overheard, he stopped talking. Indians are like that. The white man got offended by that and mumbled something under his breath about "dumb savages."
>
> A minute or two later the other man came out of the store and asked which one of the Indians was named Happy Jack. He explained that they were prospectors and Marimon, the post trader, had told him that

> Happy Jack might be able to help him find a prospect over on Farm Creek. Happy Jack could speak good English when he wanted to, but he played dumb, and told the two men they were wasting their time looking for gold on Farm Creek. "We're wasting our time talking to these dumb Injuns," the one man told his partner. "We would be better off to talk to somebody who knows what they're talking about." Happy Jack spoke up then and said, "Me know a man who can help you. This man know rocks pretty much. Him have a white man's degree from the Colorado School of Mines and Mineralogy. Very smart man. Him a partner with Senator Kearns in big mines at Park City and him consult for Anaconda Company. You want Happy jack introduce you to this smart man?" The two prospectors perked up considerably. "Now you're talking, " said the ignorant one, "that's the kind of man we need to ask for advice, not some dumb savage. Who is this man you mentioned?" *"Me,"* Happy Jack answered, then got up and walked away.

My uncle, Roy Boren, who died in his 90th year of age on 2 October 1979, also knew Happy Jack very well. My late uncle related the following information about Happy Jack.

> ...During this time (1905-06) the Cudahy Meat Packing Company was offering a good price for the wild horses which roamed the reservation and I went into the business of catching them, together with several reservation Indians. The horses, which had originally been Indian ponies, were as numerous as grass on the hills above the reservation and they would completely ruin the crops of the homesteaders who first settled there, for, at that time, there were no fences. Together with these Indians, we must have rounded up thousands of horses in the two years I spent at that trade.
>
> My best friend, during this time, was an old Indian named Cump-an-nees. We spent many days together on the trail of wild horses... I became as much Indian as any of the Utes, for they taught me their language and their ways and completely accepted me as one of their own. Their name for me was "Wob-an-nee," which means "Nighthawk," for that is just what I was in those days—but that's another story.

I knew most of the old Indians who were there at the time—Crazy John (Inepegut, the crazy Ute), Provo John, Little Doctor, Happy Jack, John Cump-an-nees, Pete Sause-in-nick, Pick Murdock , Cump Murray and others—and they told me a lot of stories about the early days before the whitemen came.

I knew Happy Jack well; he had a brother named Two Horns who used to love to scare the white people. Two Horns would don his headgear with two cow horns mounted on it, and he would put on lots of paint and feathers and would scare the hell out of the white settlers. Two Horns was the cause of several homesteaders vacating their cabins shortly after the reservation opened. Happy Jack knew Caleb Rhoades, as did most of the other old Indians on the reservation. They had nothing but good words for him.

Rose Daniels, wife of Aaron Daniels.

Courtesy Uintah County Library, Vernal, Ut.

Elsewhere, we have mentioned the valuable journals of Aaron Daniels, dictated to his daughter, Caroline Amelia Mills, on 26 July 1895, shortly before his death. His wife, Rose Daniels, being Indian, destroyed much of his material soon after his death, including valuable maps and notes, but the journals and several maps were preserved by his daughter and came into my possession some years ago.

Rose Daniels, wife of Aaron Daniels.

Courtesy Uintah County Library, Vernal, Ut.

One of the journal entries clearly indicates that Happy Jack certainly knew the location of Sacred Mine #1—and thus also Carre-Shinob. The account is sufficiently important to quote in full:

I first saw the Sacred Mine in about the year 1889 when I was told by my wife's people (the Indians) that I might see it from up close but only if I didn't know where it was located. In the company of Happy Jack, Sagoosie Jack, Ungastonigets, David Copperfield, Cessapoonch, and some others, I was taken blindfolded to an old Indian trail near the chalk cliffs, just below the old boundary of the Indian reservation. (Note: at one time the reservation boundary ran along the crest of the Uintah Mountains, but by treaty violations of the whites, this area was reduced several times prior to the reservation lottery of 1905. By the "old boundary," Daniels apparently means the original boundary along the crest of the mountains).

I was not allowed to see the route by which we ascended the mountains, but at one point we left the trail and climbed the mountain at a place which was very steep, so much so that I had to cling to the horse's back to prevent falling off.

The Indians then took off my blindfold and showed me many old Spanish signs on the trees. Happy Jack tried to explain the history of the Spanish signs, saying that many years earlier, in his father's time, the Spanish had forced the Utes to work the mines for the Gold Ore.

Happy Jack said that he himself had killed several Spaniards in his youth and knowing him as I came to, I never doubted his statement.

Just down the slope of the hill from the Spanish trees there was a mine tunnel which was which was well hidden and seen only by going up a small draw where the tunnel supports could be seen protruding above the tailings which had been drawn out, in a vein which was dark gray but immediately behind the gray vein were long white cliffs of Caleche Clay.

I was blindfolded again before leaving the Spanish trees, but before I was, I could see in a direction which was to the southwest, the Chalk Cliffs where we apparently had started off the trail earlier. We came down from the mountain and stopped to water our horses, at a place I suspect was probably Indian Springs. These two places I have always felt certain of.

When next they unblinded me I found myself sitting on my horse on a bluff near the edge of a swiftly sloping hill or ridge. To the North of me was a series of three large knolls, two were westwardly, rounded, and close (together) and a third eastward and separated from the other two by a little distance.

The trail wound its way up the Eastern slope of the ridge and stopped where I sat. In front of me, below the hill where I sat, were two long ridges running parallel to each other, with a dissecting cut in the Southernmost of lower ridge.

Happy Jack pointed out to me an area to my right, closer to the knolls, where the vein was exposed in a crumbling gray vein in

yellowish soil. There is seen thousands of small crumbled nuggets of Gold like pieces of corn tossed to chickens on the top of the ground. I have never quite forgotten that sight and I have never seen anything any other place to match the corn Gold.

I jumped down from my horse and picked up several pieces of the metal, but Sagoosie Jack knocked them out of my hand and reprimanded me severely for doing it, saying: "YOU TOUCH NOTHING— JUST LOOK!"

We had to leave the horses on top of the hill and descend down over the first ridge on foot. When we were between the two ridges, my Indian companions became very nervous and at one point, withdrew to themselves and talked in low whispers. They finally came to me and Happy Jack told me that they couldn't take me any closer because TOWATS (the Great Spirit) guarded the Sacred Mine and that he would kill us all if we went there.

I was disappointed and told them so, and finally Happy Jack relented and took me to a place near the bottom of the ridge and said, "TUNNEL IS THERE." I couldn't see anything and asked him to take me closer, but he refused and said, "YOU GO BY SELF, UP THE SLOPE TO HEAVY BRUSH. WHEN YOU GET CLOSE, YOU WILL SEE IT." He told me to uncover the rocks that were there and I would see the tunnel going back into the ridge, but he tried very hard to talk me out of going any closer. I was not about to make such a long trip and not see the famous mine.

I climbed back up the slope to a place where it leveled off at the foot of the ridge, and I could see back in the heavy growth a pile of rocks which I did not look natural to the trained eye of a prospector. I knew this was a cleverly concealed tunnel entrance. I rolled a few of the top rocks away and there was a tunnel entrance as I predicted, easily large enough to stand in.

I continued to roll the rocks away carefully, occasionally glancing back across the bottom of the little valley dividing the ridges to see my Indian friends nervously walking up and down, obviously anxious for me to come away.

I made an entrance large enough for me to crawl through and entered on my hands and knees. It was too dark to see much of the interior, except that it was larger than I had supposed and coursed back into the hillside beyond my sight. My years of prospecting experience told me that this was the same gray vein which I had seen on top of the ridge, and there in the crumbling gray rock I could see a vein of pure yellow Gold ore running up the side of the tunnel and out of sight in the ceiling of the shaft. Near the back I thought I could detect another vein, perhaps even larger, but it was too dark to be sure and I had no light at all.

As I walked around, examining the walls, my foot struck something which made a strange sound and I stooped down and felt about to discover that there was a pile of leather bags or sacks with straps secured to the tops, and they were apparently filled with heavy Gold ore and some which felt much like Gold Bars. I tried to open one but found that the top had been sewed shut with stiff rawhide. I didn't dare tear one open with my pocket knife for I had been warned about bothering anything and I knew that they meant it.

Near the front of the tunnel, which might have been a natural cave at one time, excavated by the Spaniards to expose the vein, I removed more rocks to make my crawling out easier and the light from the entrance fell upon the exposed bones and skull of at least one human skeleton and beneath these there was armor and I suspected that these were some of the Spaniards that Happy Jack told me about. Seeing these, I hastened to get out of there myself, wondering if I might not have gone so far as to provoke my Ute friends into leaving my carcass with the others.

I returned the rocks to the entrance of the tunnel as much as I found them and slid down the slope to the bottom of the ridge to discover that my Indian companions were nowhere to be seen. I suspected the very worst until I heard someone hoot and looked up to see them on top of the second hill, mounted and ready to ride. They motioned me to come up, which I did, and I was again blindfolded and hastened away two times as fast as I had been taken there. Not one of the Indians said a word as we dropped down out of the mountains and I felt that they were very scared as an impression, since an Indian will tell you nothing of their feelings.

In conclusion, I might state that I returned to the Sacred Indian Mine only once some several years later to discover I was being followed and watched and therefore abandoned any opportunity I might have had to ascertain if my directions were correct. I now feel, however, in looking back upon those experiences, that I was correct in every detail of my suspicions as to the location of the tunnel and I would know it again immediately if I were to see it, even at a distance, except that it can only be seen from very close...

One of the many notes written by Aaron Daniels, which accompanied his dictated journal, states:

When you go up Farm Creek, turn to the right at the big ledge where the old dead tree with the mark is on it (either a Spanish symbol or initials CBR) and go up that canyon. I have seen that tunnel many times and have had it pointed out to me by Cale Rhoades, but Happy Jack always warned me not to go near the Farm Creek diggings because they were always watched.

Jimmie Reed drew a map to this mine, showing the same general location, near the top of Buck Ridge where there was a tree marked with the initials CBR (Caleb Baldwin Rhoades).

Roy Boren prospected this area during 1906-07, and reported: "I found a filled-in shaft up on the ridge top between Whiterocks River and Farm Creek, north of the Whiterocks Cave (Buck Ridge); the poles or props were sticking up out of the ground, but I never took the time to dig it out to see what it is."

Near the mouth of Farm Creek have been found five or six Spanish smelters, apparently well-used, one of which is ancient enough to have a pine tree growing from the smelter floor.

There is other strong evidence of mines in this area. Few people knew more about the mines in the region than Jimmie Reed, who filed numerous claims in this area as soon as the reservation opened, many with his son-in-law, Henry E. Harris, the reservation interpreter. Just a few of these claims on file are as follows:

The Farm Creek Mine, located 20 May 1906 "in Farm Creek Canyon" by James B. Reed, H.E. Harris and T.H. Murray: *Red Man Mine*, located 29 May 1906 "in Farm Creek Canyon" by James B. Reed and H.E. Harris; *Happy Jack Mine,* located 29 May 1906 "in Farm Creek Canyon" by James B. Reed; *Golden Rod Mine,* located 1 June 1906 "1 1/4 mile northwesterly of the sink in Farm Creek," by James B. Reed and T.W. Watson; *Sheep Rock Mine,* located 3 June 1906 "2500 feet southerly from Farm Creek" by James B. Reed and T.W. Watson; *Elk Mine #1-4,* located 7 July 1906 "in Farm Creek Canyon about 1/2 mile easterly of Farm Creek" by James B. Reed and H.E. Harris; and the *Blue Bell Mine,* located (undated) "in Farm Creek Canyon" by James B. Reed and H.E. Harris. Incidentally, Tom Watson, frequent partner of Jimmie Reed in mines on Farm Creek, was an old gunfighter friend of none other than Matt Warner.

In May 1905, Caleb Rhoades was ill. He had never fully recuperated from the injuries inflicted on him by the roof of his cabin caving in, but he was determined to make one more trip into the mountains before the reservation lands were opened and a flood of prospectors and settlers poured over the region. He wrote to Happy Jack at Whiterocks, telling him to meet him at the "usual place"—the junction of Rock Creek and the Duchesne River.

Caleb set out from Price on horseback, leading his pack animal, as he had done numerous times over the past fifty years; but now he was nearly seventy years old and infirm, and his pace was slow. Happy Jack arrived there before him. Caleb finally came in late in the night, extremely ill. After tossing and turning in his bedroll all night, Caleb arose the next morning and confessed to Happy Jack that he was too ill to make the trip. They returned to their respective homes.

Less than a week later, Happy Jack received another letter from Caleb, this time urging him to come to Price as soon as possible. Happy Jack set out immediately and arrived in Price two days later, finding "Long Whiskers" (his name for Caleb) on his death bed, attended by a Mormon bishop. Caleb called his wife Sidsie into the room, and Happy Jack nearly retreated, supposing that his dying friend was about to bestow his wife on him as a parting gift, according to Indian custom. Instead, Caleb elicited Happy Jack's promise that after his (Caleb's) death, he would take Sidsie to the mine and let her have the gold to cushion her widowhood.

Several days later, with Caleb no better or worse, Happy Jack returned to Whiterocks. Within a few days he received a letter from Sidsie informing him of Caleb's death at nine o'clock on the morning of 2 June 1905. Caleb, she said, was sitting in front of his fireplace when he turned to her and said, "Here they come;" he fell to the floor and died.

Within several weeks of her husband's death, Sidsie Rhoades appeared at Whiterocks to ask Happy Jack to take her to the mine. James Rhoades of Roosevelt, Utah, a nephew of Caleb, stated: "But when she came (to Whiterocks), she had a man named Dodd (sic Dr. Andrew Dodd) with her, and so Happy Jack wouldn't take her to the mine. After this she came again and brought a fine race horse with her to trade Happy Jack for his knowledge of the old mine. But, as before, Happy Jack refused to take her because she still had Mr. Dodd (Dowd) with her. She searched two summers without Happy Jack's help and she found nothing."

Happy Jack's journal clearly indicates that he did not particularly like "Long Whisker's woman." He felt an obligation to keep his word to his old friend Caleb, but he and Sidsie could never achieve a meeting of the minds. In his journal, Happy Jack wrote: "If Long Whiskers woman had come alone, I would help, but do not like her choice of friends. She is more glad to be rich than sad (that her husband was dead)."

Due to promises made at the time, I obtained the journals. I am unable to reproduce the pertinent portions of those records, especially where they concern sacred mines and information. However, a sampling of other portions of those journals reveal not only the character and nature of their author, but specific clues to other possible gold sources. Here follows several examples, never before published:

> [1889, probably summer] …Two days on road from the agency to Heber to deliver a message from Dodds [Pardon Dodds, Indian Agent] to John Murdock for reservation supplies. $7.0 and costs. Rode with Long Whiskers to Towanta [Towanta Flat] where we parted, him to Rock Creek and me to Heber. Will meet (in) two days same place. All trip damn hot, too long, too little pay. Long Whiskers will bring back gold to pay Murdock for new Baker wagon to haul flour when fall come. Better (to receive) gold from Long Whiskers than paper promise from Dodds.

> [1906] Gone all day from camp at Sinks to Red Man Canyon with Reed (Jimmie Reed) and Harris (Henry Harris) to stake claims. Good copper show on west side (of canyon) and quartz vein 45° east side from halfway to level out top of ridge next gray ledge [i.e. "A quartz vein runs up the east side of the canyon at a 45° angle, starting halfway up the canyon and leveling out at the top of the ridge next to a gray ledge"]. …When supper come at night we rode back to Sinks. Bridger Jim and five more wait there and want to know why I prospect on reservation land with whites and I say, No more reservation land, but open for ever body. They left not happy. After supper I tell Reed and Harris maybe we should sleep (in) three places, maybe so they come back in night.

> (next day)…maybe 10 o'clock we staked last can in rocks on eastside (of the canyons) next (to) gray ledge and look up to see Bridger Jim with Little Doctor, Cessapoonch and maybe two, three more sitting on ridge. They watch us all day. Reed was not worried but Harris said maybe we should go home and come other day. I say, No, we are here first, so stay, or they think they scare us away. We must show them we do not scare and Reed say. I show them how Jimmie Reed no scare. He put down his trousers and stick his ass up (i.e. he "mooned" them!) And they ride away quick…[undated—probably circa 1900] …Utes say Happy Jack is white, whites say

Happy Jack is Ute. Towats gave me Indian blood, but white man gave me school and knowledge of white mans ways. I do not know if Happy Jack is white or Ute, only know that he is a man and whites are men and Utes are men so all same to me…

> [1905—probably May or June]…Long Whiskers is bad sick. Letter say, Come quick. Friend Will (i.e. Will Boren) take care of my place and do the chores till I come back, maybe one week. Go same day…

> [1922, about 17 May]…John Blankenship come by in his new Ford car and say, Happy, come with me and I will learn you how to drive, and I say him, No, I do not want learn to drive damn car, thanks same. Happy Jack is horse man. I tell him Happy Jack does not know how to pitch hay to damn car. Too old to learn. We both laugh and have supper.

We have purposely avoided quoting sections of Happy Jack's journals that deal with the sacred mines, due to an oath contingent upon receiving the journals. Therefore we can but quote those parts that give some indication of this unique man's character. We can, however, repeat one entry that dispels all doubt about Happy Jack's knowledge of Carre-Shinob. It is interesting to note that Happy Jack frequently lapsed into the familiar broken Indian brogue when speaking, and in fact seems to have preferred it; his journals reflect this same unusual trait. His education was good, and he could speak fluent English when he wished. The following quote shows that he could also write it when moved to do so:

> [three pages away from the end of the fourth and last journal; thus shortly before his death]…I am very old. I have seen many strange things, but I am Indian and cannot say much. When I was young I prospected with the whites, but now I am old I see all this was wrong. To my people the mines are sacred. The gold belongs to my people. I know where is gold enough to buy all things in the white mans world. But Happy Jack is Indian and I will not tell it. I am Happy Jack and I am rich, for Towats believes me. Soon I will go to sleep with the Old Ones. Long Whiskers is there now. We will camp

together again and tell the stories that friends tell each other....

I do not think, in all my years of research, I have heard a more poignant statement made, nor more profound words spoken, to summarize a man's life, than that single sentence by a hundred-year-old Indian brave: "I am Happy Jack and I am rich, for Towats believes me."

Happy Jack was well past 100 years of age when he died. He lived out his final days on Big Tom's allotment at Whiterocks, adjoining the old Jimmie Reed place. In his final years he was looked after by his friends, the Reeds, especially by Mary Reed Harris. My uncle, Bill Reed, was Happy Jack's particular friend, and it was through my uncle's auspices that I came into possession of Happy Jack's journals and maps. Some of those maps are appended to the end of this narrative.

Chapter Twenty-One

The Secret of Carre-Shinob

I HAVE TRIED, IN THIS BOOK, TO REVEAL some unknown secrets about the Lost Rhoades Mines. I have revealed stories of men and mines that never were imagined when *Footprints in the Wilderness* was published in 1971, or even when it was re-issued with new information appended in 1980. But I reserved the greatest secret for last.

First, however, some clarification is needed. In virtually every account of the mines over the years, the Sacred Mine has been equated with Carre-Shinob, when in fact they are separate in every respect. Indeed, there are two sacred mines—Sacred Mine #1 and Sacred Mine #2. The latter, situated in the upper Rock Creek drainage, we have already discussed. It was likely associated anciently with another sacred site, most probably an Aztec temple.

But Sacred Mine #1 and Carre-Shinob are not associated with Rock Creek. Without exception Carre-Shinob—"Where the Great Spirit Dwells" —has always been associated by the Indians with a sacred site north of Whiterocks River, in the area of the upper Yellowstone River drainage. Whenever Caleb Rhoades made an excursion to the Sacred Mine #1, he went first to Whiterocks where he borrowed pack mules from Jimmie Reed and picked up Happy Jack to guard his back trail.

Moreover, as mentioned above, the Sacred Mine and Carre-Shinob are not the same; Carre-Shinob was definitely "something else." And what Carre-Shinob was is the basis of the secret we are about to reveal.

Not long after the publication of *Footprints*, I came into possession of the journals of my third great-grandfather, Isaac Morley. The pages came alive with vivid descriptions of his friendship with Chief Walker, and his association with what became known as the Lost Rhoades Mine. The revelations of these journals were astounding: that Chief Walker had first revealed the secret of the

gold to him; that he twice visited Carre-Shinob in person, once in the company of a young Caleb Rhoades; that he had officiated at the burial of Chief Walker at Carre-Shinob; and that he had seen and left a vivid description of the "secret" of Carre-Shinob. What was the secret?…That Carre-Shinob was an Aztec Temple containing the treasure of Montezuma!

More than this, Father Morley's journals contain enough information to provide directions to the site. My initial feelings concerning this discovery can better be imagined than described. Almost simultaneously with the acquisition of the Morley journals, I came into possession of the Happy Jack journals, and with them, a detailed map of Carre-Shinob!

In his final days of life, Happy Jack had been cared after by Mary Reed Harris, daughter of Jimmie Reed and wife of Henry Harris, Indian interpreter, both of whom had been Happy Jack's mining partners in earlier years. Mary Reed Harris acquired Happy Jack's effects upon his death, including his journals, letters and maps, together with her solemn vow that the secret of Carre-Shinob and the Sacred Mine be preserved for the benefit of the Ute people. These items, together with the charge, were passed down to my uncle, Bill Reed, who was the nephew of Mary Reed Harris. Subsequently these items came into my possession (though I never removed them from the reservation; today they are in the care of certain members of the Ute tribe).

Now it is remarkable that I, a "white-eyes" without a traceable drop of Native American blood, should come into possession of one of the greatest secrets ever of the Indian people, but such was the case. Fate is often devoid of reason. Part of the reason is perhaps attributable to my family's long amiable association with the Ute people; part of it due to my relationship to the Reed family; and part due to my descent from Chief Walker's great friend, Isaac Morley. More anciently, my direct ancestor was Iorwerth ap Owain Gwynedd, the brother of Madoc, King of the Aztecs and ancestor of Montezuma. Indeed, I had cause for personal interest in the secret of Carre-Shinob. [see *The Widow's Son,* O'Boran, op.cit.]

I have been to Carre-Shinob! In this chapter I will describe what I saw there, but first there needs to be some clarification. I would like to state emphatically that I did not get there on my own, but obtained permission from the inner circle of the Ute elders, and I went there only once—it was enough. I doubt that the Indians would have granted such latitude had they not known that I had independent confirmation of the site. Ultimately, they realized that it was better to concede controlled access than to risk my attempting to go there on my own. For that cause, they elicited my blood oath that, if they permitted my access, I would remove nothing I found, reveal to no one the exact location, and that I would never return without their knowledge and consent—to all of which I readily agreed. I confess that I was afraid, but I wanted to see the treasure of Carre-Shinob—even as Father Morley saw it—more than life itself.

It has been twenty-five years since I saw the sight which changed my life forever, and I am proud to say I have never broken my oath to those good people. At the same time, if I had done so, I have no doubt that I would not be alive to tell about it now. By revealing the contents of Carre-Shinob, I am not breaking that oath; my promise was to take nothing and never return, and never to tell where it lies, and that oath remains inviolate. I might never have written this book and revealed this much had not life's circumstances dictated the need. Having said that much, it is time to tell the tale.

I am not at liberty to divulge either the route or location, nor can I say who escorted me there, except to say that my escort consisted of five mounted Utes, all sworn to the same oath as myself. It should be pointed out, however, that once within a mile or so of the site, these men would go no closer, having a strong superstitious fear of the place. I continued to the site alone, and this much I will say: the location is remote and in

the highest access reaches of the Uintah Mountains northwest of the Whiterocks. I can say without reservation that without the most specific directions given, the site of Carre-Shinob can never be discovered. The main entrance is so cleverly contrived as to fool and confuse the most astute, and the secondary entrance—a tunnel hidden in a high recess—is so inaccessible as to be reached only by ropes and great agility.

Carre-Shinob is composed of a series of caverns with connecting tunnels. I suspect, from what knowledge I have been able to gain on the subject since, that the entire system was formed anciently as a result of lava tubes, for beneath the Uintah Mountains are a series of active volcanoes. The entire range is being thrust upward at the rate of about an inch a year, but erosion wears it down at an equal rate, and so the elevation remains primarily static. Nevertheless, anyone familiar with the mountains has experienced the occasional rumbling that periodically occurs as the pressure builds beneath the surface.

The fabulous lode of the Uintah Mountains, which makes it indisputably the richest source of gold in the world (Caleb Rhoades claimed there was gold enough in the Sacred Mine alone to pave the streets of New York City, with enough left over to pay off the national debt!), apparently derives from these chambers and lava tubes having been filled wall-to-wall with molten gold! This then was what the Old Ones—the Aztecs of their predecessors—mined from the caverns. As they mined out each room, they left the walls plated with the molten gold, and in its soft precious surface carved their strange hieroglyphics and made it a sacred temple.

Entering from the secondary tunnel (the main entrance is contrived to prevent intruders), one first encounters a precipice dropping abruptly to the bottom of a great chamber, of sufficient size to accommodate a three or four-story house. At the bottom, embracing the north wall of the chamber, a stream of icy water courses until it drops away into a subterranean tube. The floor of the chamber slopes upward, ending at the south wall where half a dozen tunnels channel off in various directions.

In this chamber there are skeletons laid out in rows and others propped against the walls. Some of these were originally wrapped in blankets and cedar bark, remnants of which yet remain. These were apparently Indians of a later generation, chieftains and their families. But here too are a number of skeletons in Spanish armor, in disarray, as though tossed from the tunnel at the precipice above; the story speaks for itself.

According to Father Morley's journal, Chief Walker was entombed in a second, interior chamber. The question before me that day was, which of the several tunnels led to that chamber? One of my reasons for being there was to view the burial place of Chief Walker, a man I had come to admire greatly. I entered two tunnels before finding the correct one. Both tunnels, which were very narrow and not very high, led to interior chambers which appeared to have been man-made. These chambers were small, perhaps 10 x 12 feet and some 7 or 8 feet high, and except for two or three stone boxes or chests against the walls of each, the rooms were empty. The lids on the boxes were too heavy for me to remove.

The third tunnel, considerably larger than the other two, led to a cavernous chamber, which appeared to be a natural cave, and here were the remains of Chief Walker, together with the skeletal remains of some two dozen others. Walker's remains were easily identified by the old first edition of the Book of Mormon clutched in his bony fingers; I suspect Brigham Young's letter was folded between the pages, but I touched nothing, as I had pledged.

Walker's corpse was in a good state of preservation, virtually semi-mummified due to the constant dry temperature of the cave. I was struck by the fact that he had a scarf of some sort tied around his jaw and knotted on top of his head, for what purpose I never learned. His body was leaning against a rock wall in a sitting position, as though asleep. Surrounding him were the skeletal remains of his several wives and the slave children I had read so much about. To one side, piles of bones and skulls of his favorite horses lay heaped, together with accoutrements of his interesting life: a rifle, several pistols, bows and arrows, medicine clubs and pouches, blankets, and more. The abundance of artifacts denoted his wealth and importance.

Nearby were other corpses, similarly posed against the wall, obviously chieftains and predecessors of Walker. One of these skeletons belonged to old Chief Sanpete, but I had no way of knowing which; I had only the statements of Father Morley and Happy Jack that the body of Walker's grandfather had been disinterred from the rock cairn grave on Rock Creek where his Mexican murderers had buried him, and entombed with honor at Carre-Shinob, to sleep among his ancestors. Not every chief of the Utes was entombed at Carre-Shinob, but only those who were "Keepers of the Yellow Metal."

It is difficult to convey my feelings as I stood in this chamber among the ghosts of history. The experience was one of euphoria mixed with a sense of eerie awareness and not just a little fear of the unknown. Being absolutely alone in such a place tends to make one acutely aware of one's own mortality, and there is a very real sense that, though surrounded by the dead, "someone" is watching!

From the Walker chamber (which I chose to call it) several tunnels funneled off in different directions as before, but this time I had no difficulty in choosing the one to explore. Above the entrance to one of the tunnels was an intricately carved portal depicting several rather unidentifiable creatures—similar to the Griffin of Wales—and a large sun symbol.

At the end of this quite lengthy and tortuous tunnel one emerges into a cavernous chamber of immense proportions and startling beauty. For reasons soon to be apparent, I dubbed it the Sun chamber. In fact it was a temple almost beyond description.

In the center of this immense room were nine great stone pillars, too large in circumference for a man to encircle his arms. This entire chamber— walls, ceiling, floor, and pillars—was plated with what appeared to be pure gold! In fact, as I have since thought, it might not have been plated with gold so much as the interior was solid natural gold, from which the center had been excavated, leaving a certain amount of thickness around the exterior walls. If so, the amount of gold once filling this chamber staggers the imagination. On the other hand, the amount of gold still in this chamber surpasses anything ever yet discovered, enhanced by the additional number of gold artifacts stored therein.

On opposing walls, facing each other, were two gigantic solar disks, each taller than a man and several inches thick; they were apparently of pure gold and must have weighed tons each. It boggles the mind to conceive how the ancients moved such massive wheels. The disks represented the sun, with rays emanating from the center outward, and between the rays were intricate carvings of signs and symbols of a peculiar nature. In the very center of each disk was a carved cross, very much like the Celtic cross of Ireland (or Wales), with ivy vines woven around the design.

Between the solar disks, but against the south wall, sat a giant stone chair or throne, intricately carved, but one of the few items in the chamber not made of, or covered with, gold. This throne was elevated on a stone slab or shelf, and in front of it, on floor level, was a stone altar. Because the altar had grooves or troughs on either side, and what appeared to be a groove for the head, the logical conclusion was that it had been utilized for human sacrifice.

But the Sun chamber contained an even greater surprise: golden masks and statuettes, and rows of more stone boxes. And many of the boxes were open and filled with treasure of another kind: gold plates with hieroglyphic writing on them! The boxes were of various sizes and also the contents. The boxes were, on the average, about 3 x 4 feet in dimensions and about 3 feet deep. In the bottom of each box was drilled two or three holes, into which were inserted round sticks about two feet in length. Over these sticks were placed stacks of gold plates, more or less round or oval with holes in the center through which the sticks protruded. The plates were each imprinted—that is to say, inscribed by some stone or metal instrument into the soft gold—with curious hieroglyphic symbols. I had no camera, but I did have pen and paper, and I copied as many of the figures as time allowed. The ingenious method of stacking the plates permitted their removal en toto in one stack, and then the plates can be fanned out and read, then returned as easily. However, the stacks of gold plates proved to be heavy.

There were smaller stone boxes, too, and these contained assortments of precious stones—emeralds, rubies, turquoise, sapphires and, strangely, sea shells—and others contained gold bracelets, circlets, rings, earrings, and other ceremonial jewelry. Together with the masks, disks, statuettes and other artifacts, the caverns were a treasure trove like something out of *A Thousand and One Arabian Nights.*

Most of all, in the midst of fabulous treasure, I was most impressed with the room, with the walls and floors and pillars of solid gold with a myriad of inscriptions everywhere to be seen. What I would have given to be able to read those writings! What revelations might be made as to the origins and history of an unknown ancient people!

There were other rooms and chambers—according to the Utes, there are nine gilded chambers in the complex—but I had neither the time nor the means to explore them. Some of the tunnels angled downwards, toward the interior of the mountain, and there may well be miles of such passages within these mountains. In fact, the region is marked by a number of caves, some of notable significance. Big Brush Creek Cave lies at the foot of one of the "baldy" mountains. A stream of water runs into the mouth of the cave, then disappears underground, to emerge some miles below as a tributary of Big Brush Creek. On Icy Cave Peak there are a series of caverns, and in Dry Fork Canyon there are many more. Sheep Creek Canyon Cave runs for miles underground, and has never been fully explored. A stream which bubbles to the surface at the entrance, was traced to its origin by the U.S. Forest Service using colored dye, indicating that it derived some fifteen miles to the west. I have personally explored some six miles of this particular cave.

My time to explore Carre-Shinob was extremely limited; even so, I spent about six hours in the bowels of the mountain. Six days would not have been sufficient. I saw many things therein that, because of my oath to the Ute people and for sundry other reasons, I shall never speak or write about. Suffice it that it is enough to reveal the secret of Carre-Shinob—that it is the repository of Montezuma's vast treasure, the same for which loss Cortes lamented. There can be no doubt that the sacred relics of the Aztecs—ancestors of the Utes—were returned to the source from which the gold came. There is no more sacred site among the Native American peoples than Carre-Shinob.

There is also little doubt that the written records and perhaps the written language itself derives from the influence of the Welsh Prince Madoc ap Owain Gwynedd, first great King of the Aztecs (prior to whom there were presumably only chieftains). Some of the symbols may derive from an earlier native civilization, all of which corresponds to the origins of certain Mormon beliefs pertaining to the source of the "Nephites" and "Lamanites." In fact, the term "Carre-Shinob" itself seems to have been a blend of both Welsh and Hebrew. The Utes claim the meaning as "Where the Great Spirit Dwells." In Welsh the term "Carre" corresponds with "Carreg" which denotes "stone" or "stone dwelling," while in Hebrew the term "Shinob" corresponds with the Hebrew term "Shin-ob," which signifies "Most High God," "Ob" standing for "Abba" or "Father." The two terms are not dissimilar in their meaning.

There is also recent evidence to indicate that the gold recovered by Cortes and a succession of Spaniards after him originated in the Uintah Mountains. Mel Fisher, treasure hunter extraordinaire and discoverer of the sunken Spanish galleon, The Atocha, which produced millions of dollars worth of gold and Aztecan artifacts, has discovered evidence that some of the gold recovered from the Atocha came from a source in the Uintah Mountains. Mel is understandably reluctant to reveal his find, but he has spent several summers in the Uintah Mountains searching for the source of his discovery.

The question I am most often asked is: "If you know where this treasure is, why don't you make yourself rich?" The answer is a complex one, but basically amounts to a moral and religious obligation. To begin with, the gold and the treasure does not belong to me, but to the Ute people. I have sworn an oath to the Utes to keep the secret of the location of Carre-Shinob inviolate, and that oath means more to me than any gain could ever compensate. My late father, whom I admired above all other men I have ever known, used to say that a man is only as good as his word, and I never

knew him to break his oaths. The greatest honor I can give his memory is to emulate his character.

Let there be no doubt about it, either: mine was a blood oath, and it would be worth my life to violate it. There is no treasure so valuable as to be worth more than life itself. Besides, I have never been interested in the "mines" for their wealth, but for their history instead. Two of my closest friends exhausted their entire fortunes in search of the mines (they never knew the secret of Carre-Shinob), only to die tragic deaths without having discovered or seen the elusive treasure they lived and died for. I, on the other hand, have had the rare privilege of seeing it, ironically because I did not seek to be wealthy from it. I have seen, and I am content; I shall never return.

Neither will I write anything further concerning Carre-Shinob or the Lost Rhoades Mines. My purposes for writing this book, the final chapter in my association with the mines, are my own, and of no consequence to anyone else. I will say only that I felt the need to make such a record, to honor the memory of those long forgotten, and to clarify once and for all time the question of ownership.

To those treasure hunters who read this and find my story incredible, I say this: I hope you do not believe me! I do not wish to encourage you to look for the gold of Carre-Shinob. It does not belong to you. It is the sacred treasure of the Utes, and to them only does it belong.

May it ever be so.

Excerpts from Happy Jack's Journal

NOTE: HAPPY JACK'S "JOURNALS" are hardly that; they are four worn notebooks or ledgers, kept in no apparent order, with numerous loose pages, notes, letters and other items tucked between pages. There were also originally some maps, but these have been removed and are kept by a reservation family. The journals were left by Happy Jack to Mary Reed Harris, who took care of him during his last illness. In turn, Mary Reed Harris gave them to her nephew, Bill Reed, who was my uncle by marriage, who provided them to me. All are dead now, except me. What follows are summaries of Happy Jack's notes wherein he mentions Pick Murdock—whom he calls "Supick"—and is a paraphrase of his actual entries. The dates are given as near as they can be determined, since he was not too careful about them generally. Spelling appears as Happy Jack recorded it.

{1886}

Pardon Dodds (Indian Agent) came back with a delegation of Utes from Washington by railroad. A week earlier, Happy Jack came back with Supick Murdock, Dick Wanrodes and Harris Murray (interpreter). Supick and Wanrodes got drunk and caused some trouble on the train and were jailed two days at Denver. Happy Jack met them at Price, Utah, and drove them back to the reservation by wagon. Happy Jack records a "joke" made by Supick: "When white man drunk, all same; when Indian drunk, he is a poor man without friends."

{1899}

Happy Jack went over to Ft. Duchesne with $55.00 bail for Supick who was in jail for fighting with Oren Curry at the Ouray Trading Post.

{1893}

On Saturday Happy Jack went over to Supick's place "by Marimons" near Whiterocks and they put together a camp on two mules for two weeks up Whiterocks River to Yellowstone Creek. They camped on "South Fork" and went two days up the creek to bring out some ore for samples. Met Harris Murray coming down. He had been up to Whiterocks Lake with Cump (either Cump Murray or Cum-an-nees, also sometimes called Cump). Murray gave them a quarter of elk he had shot "en the rim." Camped with them two days. Cump "went on down" and Murray followed two days later. Good samples. Supick will take them by train to Salt Lake for assay "next week"...Supick back from Salt Lake "all happy." Report good on samples. "3 p. gold 1 p. silver 10 p. copper ore in quartz with rose vein." They want to go back and dig deeper for "good rock" below float in summer before snow.

{1885-86}

Supick has been over in Brown's Hole working for Jesse Ewing. Took ore samples from Ewing's mine to Denver for assay, when he returned with results, found Ewing had been killed by his partner Jim Duncan. The assay report showed rich samples of gold and copper ore. Supick wants to go back and hunt for Ewing's vein, but Happy Jack can't go until next year because he has to freight for the cavalry which is building a fort (Duchesne) on the river.

{1883}

Quite a bit of information about Supick and Louis Dyer locating claims at upper Kane Hollow. Supick goes to Jesse Knight to make a partnership in order to get funds.

Eventually forms partnership with Dyer, Edwin Gates, others.

{1888-89}

Story of Dead Man Mine. Quite lengthy. Happy Jack came up to Whiterocks with a load of freight for Marimon. Ran into Supick, Henry Harris, John Murray and Aaron Daniels on the way up Whiterocks River Canyon to locate the vein left by an old prospector who had died some ten years earlier. A. Daniels had been one of the men who found the body talks about the old prospector having been murdered, but salted a shaft before he died, etc. Too lengthy to copy just now—let me know if you are interested.

{1889-90}

Happy Jack talks about meeting Supick at "Murdock's Store" at Whiterocks. Supick was with David Copperfield and Bridger Jim. The four of them met Kale Rhoads at the "Reed place" and negotiated with Reed for some mules to go prospecting.

(Apparently about the same time-loose page).

Happy Jack, Supick, Copperfield, Bridger Jim and Kale Rhoades go out to Yellowstone headwaters. Tells about their trip. Vague about what is found. Interesting details about the country.

[The following letter does not come from Happy Jack, but is a copy given to me by my late uncle Roy Boren. It is a copy of a letter which Pick Murdock wrote to my grandfather, William Coleman Boren, who freighted flour and trade goods to the reservation from Heber Valley for many years. Thought you would find it of interest]

Will Boren

Heber, Utah

June 2, 1886

I am send this by Mr. Brodhead to you that maby you will bring out these things when you come 1 good hat 2 wool shirt new butcher knife and maby new rope. A M will pay he own me 2 mos. wage when you come go his place. I am camp on Du. River with solds (soldiers?). Be careful Indian not all happy maby fight soon. Better not come alone all same with guns in case things go bad. Maby so bring whiskey.

Murdock

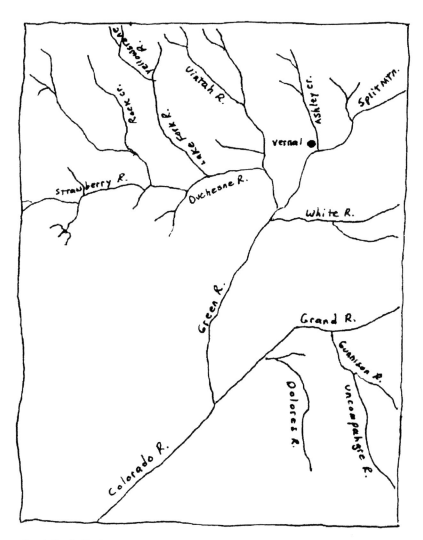

Uintah Basin Drainage

184

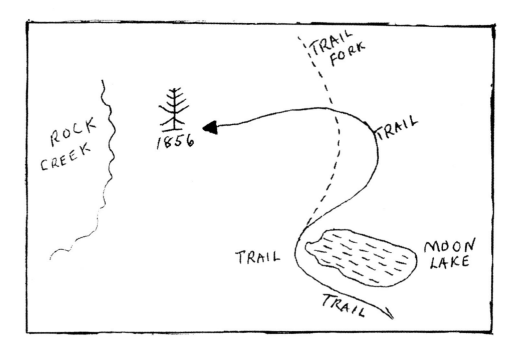

Rhoades Map #1 Version #1

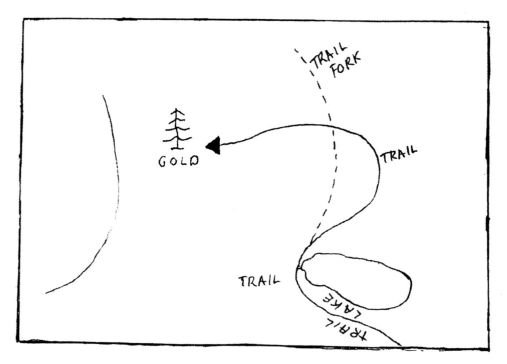

Rhoades Map #2 Version #2

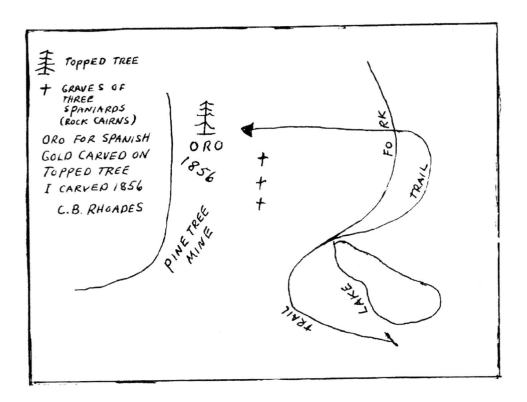

Rhoades Map #1 Original Version

This map was drawn by Caleb Rhoades shortly before his death in 1905. It was burned onto a piece of soft buckskin about 4 by 5 inches in size. This map was given to Happy Jack who in turn gave it to Bill Reed shortly before his death. Near the mine is a tall pine tree which either the Spaniards or Caleb Rhoades "topped" as a marker. On the tree is carved "Oro" by the Spaniards and, as Caleb notes in the symbols of the map, he carved "1856" on the tree—the year he discovered the mine.

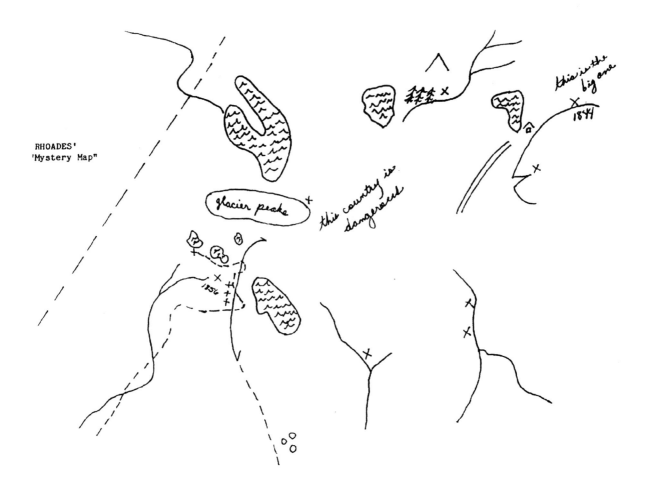

RHOADES'
'Mystery Map"

Caleb Rhoades' 1905 "Mystery Map"

The map was drawn by Caleb Rhoades just days before his death in 1905. The map was drawn on a small piece of paper which appeared to have been ripped from a notebook. The map was given to Happy Jack with instructions to deliver it to Matt Warner. Matt Warner had entered into an agreement with Caleb Rhoades and his partner F.W.C. Hathenbruck on June 23, 1896 which entitled him to one twentieth part of certain mines, apparently those shown on the "Mystery Map" (sometimes referred to as the "Dangerous Country Map"). After the death of Caleb Rhoades, Matt Warner purchased his cabin and ranch properties near Price, Utah, from Caleb's widow, Sidsie. The place marked "This is the big one" is believed to have been the site of the 1920 gunfight. The largest lake indicated on the map is probably Granddaddy Lake. The smaller lake, near the "1856" (Pine Mine) is not Moon Lake, however, as many believe. This map should be compared closely with the Matt Warner version, whereupon Warner both added and deleted landmarks circa 1920. Both maps were left by Matt Warner, upon his death in 1938, to his son Boyo Warner, from whom I obtained them (together with others) in 1971.

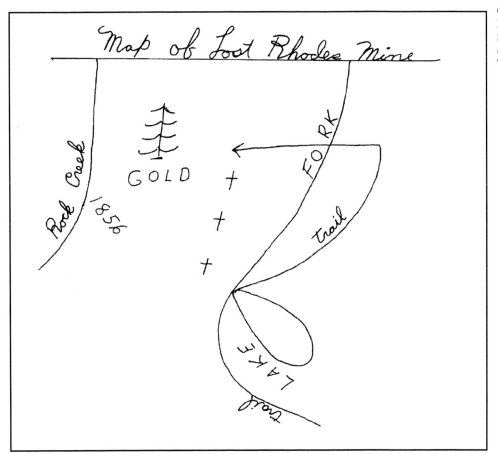

Caleb Rhoades Map to the Sacred Mine #2 (i.e. The Pine Tree Mine)

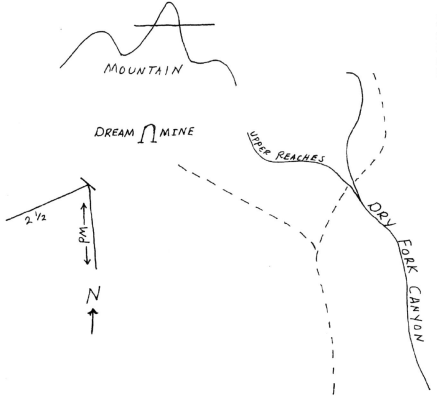

Jessee Knight Map made for William Coleman Boren grandfather of co-author Kerry Ross Boren

188

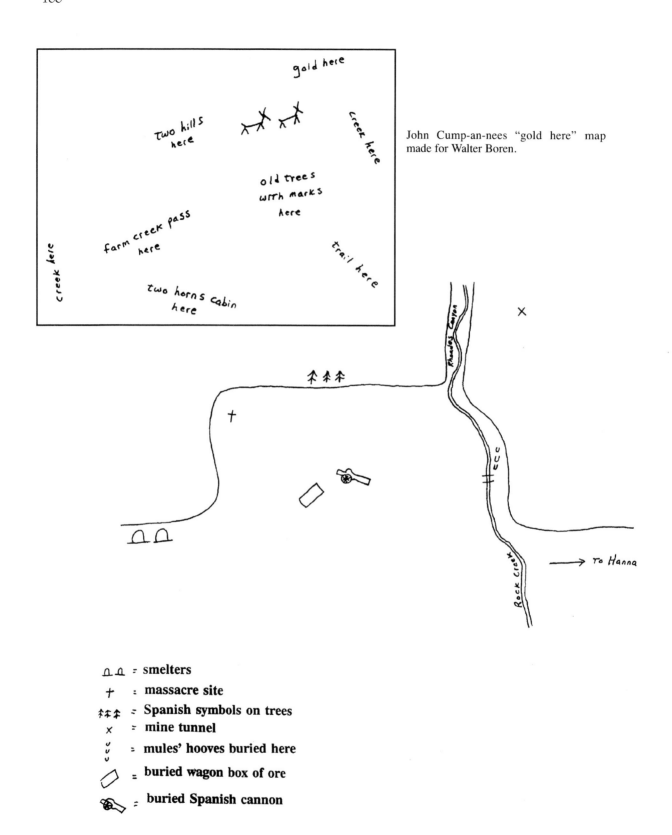

John Cump-an-nees "gold here" map made for Walter Boren.

gold here

two hills here

creek here

old trees with marks here

farm creek pass here

creek here

trail here

two horns cabin here

Phoedos Canyon

Rock Creek

To Hanna

∩ ∩ = smelters

✝ = massacre site

🌲🌲🌲 = Spanish symbols on trees

✕ = mine tunnel

∪∪∪ = mules' hooves buried here

▱ = buried wagon box of ore

⚙ = buried Spanish cannon

Map drawn from Wash's Description of Spanish Massacre Site

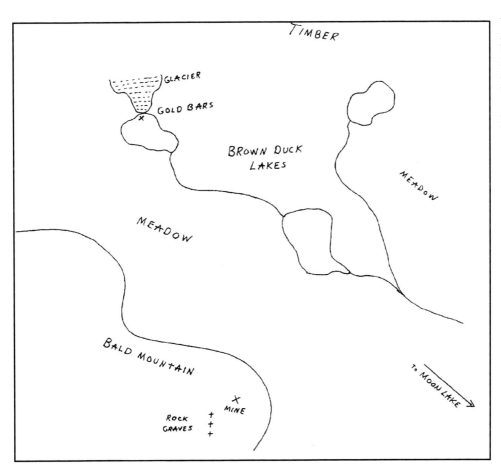

Wash's map to 500 lbs. of gold bars thrown into lake following Spanish massacre.

(authors' rendition of original)

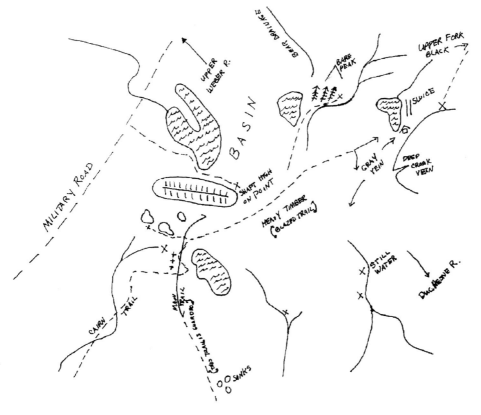

Matt Warner's copy of Caleb Rhoades' 1905 "Mystery Map."

190

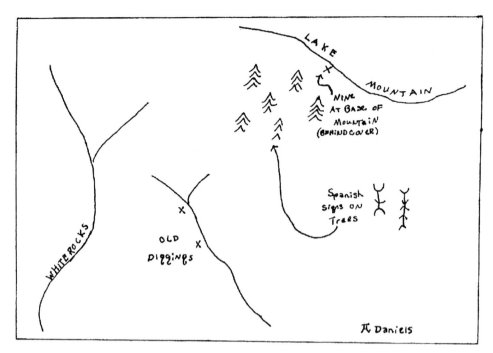

Aaron Daniels Lake Mountain Map (Compare this with "No Pass" map.)

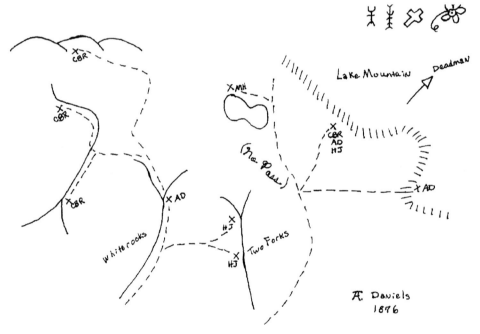

Aaron Daniels "No Pass" Map

Daniels dates this map 1876. It is believed that the names "Whiterocks," "Two Forks," "Lake Mountain," and "Deadman," were added at a later date by a different hand. The initials are believed to represent the following names.

CBR = Caleb Baldwin Rhoades

AD = Aaron Daniels

HJ = Happy Jack

MH = Muse Harris

The meaning of "No Pass" has never been determined. Compare this map with the Daniels "Lake Mountain" map.

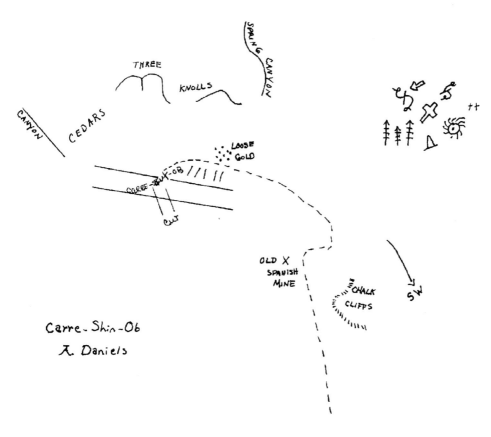

Carre-Shin-Ob
A. Daniels

Aaron Daniels "Carre-Shin-Ob" Map. According to Aaron Daniels, he was taken to the Sacred Mine of the Indians in 1889. This map was drawn from memory by Daniels some five or six years later, not long before his death, for the benefit of his family.

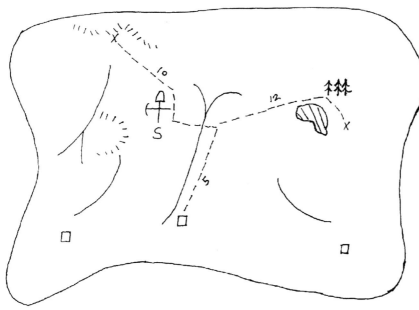

Buckskin Map of Jimmie Reed

It bears a strong similarity to the Aaron Daniels "No Pass" map. The numbers 5, 10, and 12 probably indicate miles. The pick and shovel symbol may have more significance than just a direction indicator. The three squares are believed by some to mark three towns (from left to right) Roosevelt (or Duchesne), Whiterocks, and Vernal. This map is hand-tooled onto a piece of buckskin about 5 x 6 inches in size, and is somewhat worn from handling and folding. The map was drawn by Jimmie Reed for his daughter, Mary Reed Harris, following one of his trips into the mountains at which time he brought back rich gold ore.

192

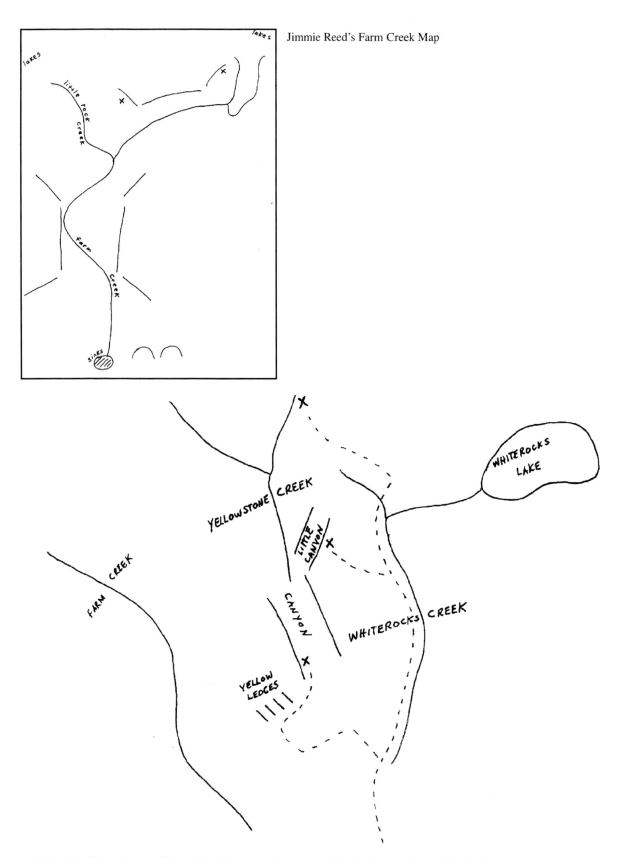

Jimmie Reed's Farm Creek Map

Julius Orn Murray's map of three Spanish mines pointed out to him by his grandfather Jimmie Reed.

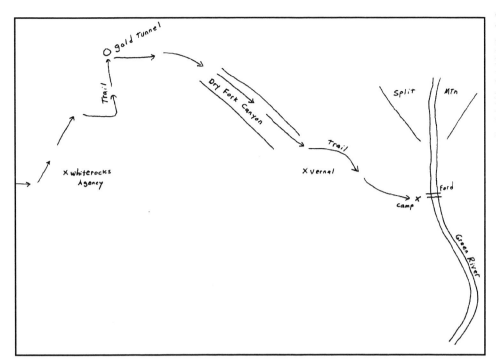

Oren Curry's "High Pass" map; Curry was Indian Agent and Post Trader at Ouray. He married Maud Davis, former wife of the outlaw Elzy Lay.

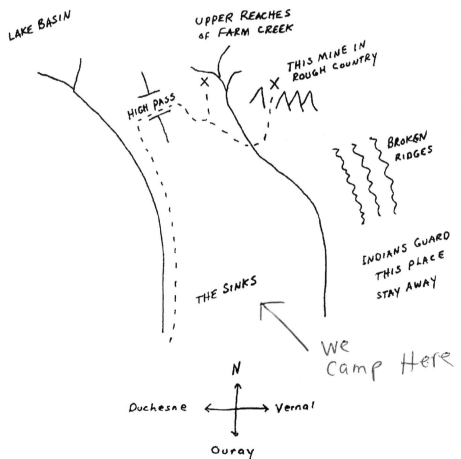

Joe Walker's map of the 1897 Butch Cassidy visit to the gold tunnel. Map drawn by Joseph Sharp from Walker's description.

194

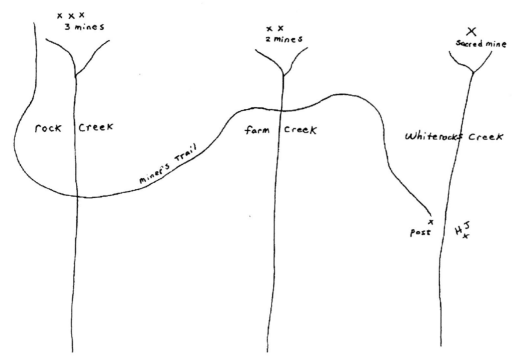

Happy Jack's Miner's Trail Map

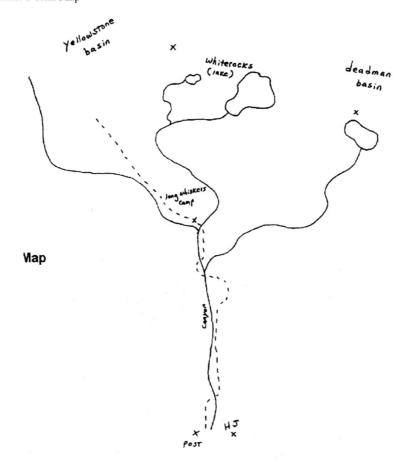

Map

Happy Jack's "Long Whiskers" Map

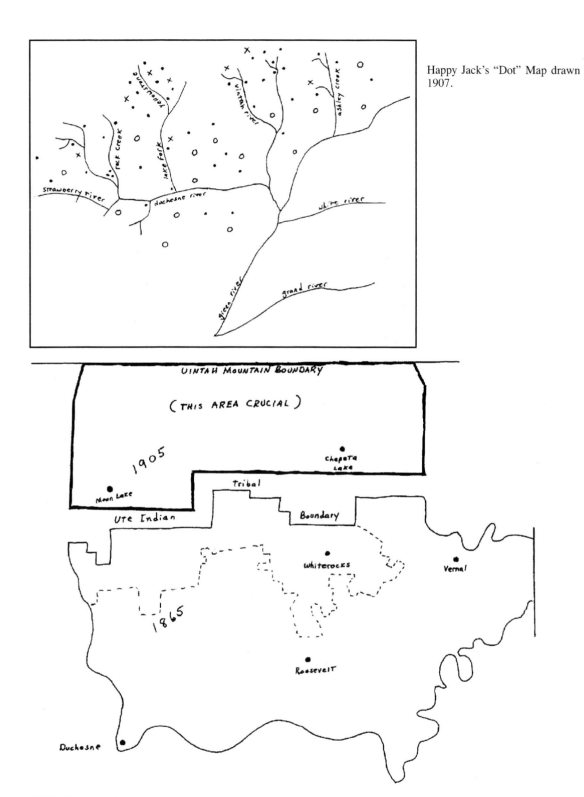

Happy Jack's "Dot" Map drawn 1907.

F.W.C. Hathenbruch Map

This is a facsimile copy of a map discovered in a box of mercantile receipts in the back room of the F.W.C. Hathenbruck store in Provo after his death. The map is apparently the proposed changes to be made to the reservation boundaries in order to gain access to the Rhoades Mines. The mines would presumably be within the area marked "THIS AREA CRUCIAL."

196

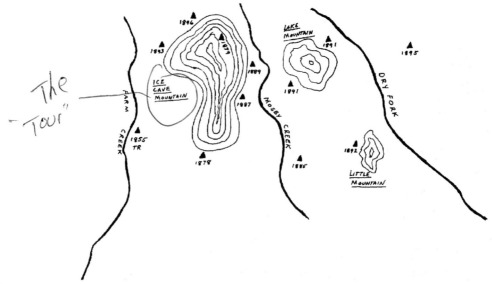

Henry Harris Map

Henry Harris was Indian Interpreter and sometime agent at Whiterocks. He married Mary Reed, daughter of Jimmie Reed. He appears on many mining claims with Reed. All of the landmarks are well known. The site marked 1855 TR might refer to a location made by Thomas Rhoades, but the date would seem to forbid it. The site marked 1895 above Dry Fork might be the mine in dispute between Caleb Rhoades and Jesse Knight, where Matt Warner killed two men in a gunfight.

—Courtesy Bill Reed

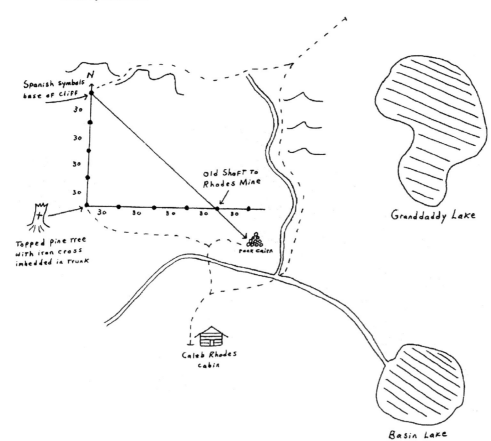

The Macginnis Map

Elzy Lay, alias Bill Macginnis, drew this map for Governor Miguel Otero of New Mexico and for the warden of the New Mexico Penitentiary to secure his release from prison. It apparently denotes the same area shown on the map of Matt Warner, his erstwhile partner. On the bottom of the original, in his own hand, is written: "Come in from Wyoming, the Utah trail is watched by Indians. Macginnis." Basin Lake has not been identified.

—Courtesy Marvel Lay Murdock

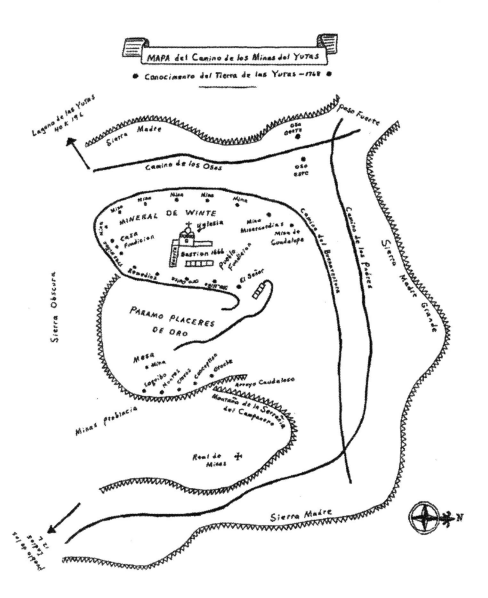

MAPA del Camino de los Minas del Yutas

This map was devised by the Spanish commission on the West Indies and was one of 76 related maps filed in a packet in the *Archivo de Madrid,* originally reposing unexamined in Seville until discovered in the 1960s. That it is a map to gold mines in the Uintahs is evidenced by the map's title and by the mention in the text of "Mineral de Winte;" there is no corresponding word to "winte" in Spanish, and apparently refers to the Ute pronunciation for Uintah.

MAPA del Camino de los Minas del Yutas translates as: "Map of the trail to the Minas of the Utes." *Conocimento del Tierra de las Yutas* translates as: "Recognition of the Land of the Utes." The date 1768 was date of compilation. Interestingly, the map indicates both mines and placer mining. *Real de Minas* translates as: "group of Mines." Most interesting is that the map indicates both a fort and a church (Yglesia) apparently either founded or destroyed in 1666. The indicators to *Laguna del las Yutas* (Utah Lake) and *Pueblo be los Indios* (Indian Village) mention "40 K 19 L" which probably means 40 kilometers *or* 19 Leagues, and 12 L which means Leagues. *Sierra Obscura* translates as "Unknown Mountains." *Paso Fuerte* means "Hard" or Difficult" Pass.

Note that *Camino de los Osos* means "Trail of the Bears," and the map indicates "Bear West" and "Bear East." These probably refer to the two carved bears which the Utes claim in tradition guard the mines.

It is interesting that no lakes or streams are noted on this map, though the region is replete with both. Further, placer mining requires water.